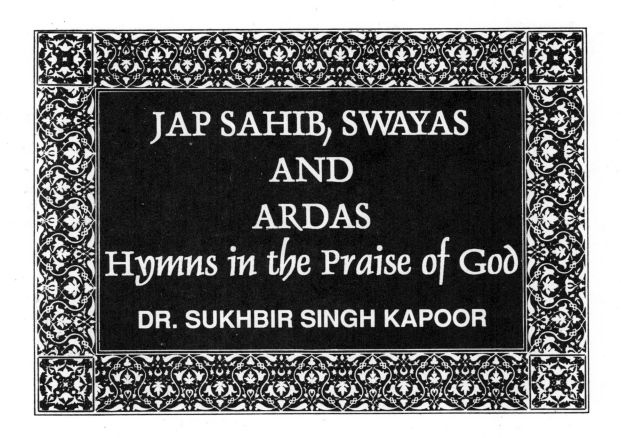

JAP SAHIB, SWAYAS
AND
ARDAS
Hymns in the Praise of God

DR. SUKHBIR SINGH KAPOOR

STERLING PUBLISHERS PRIVATE LIMITED
L-10, Green Park Extension, New Delhi – 110016

Jap Sahib : Swayas and Ardas :
Hymns in the Praise of God
© 1995, Dr. Sukhbir Singh Kapoor

PRINTED IN INDIA

Published by S. K Ghai, Managing Director, Sterling Publishers Pvt. Ltd., L-10 Green Park Extension, New Delhi-110016. Lasertypeset at Fine Impressions, 24 Central Market, Punjabi Bagh (West), New Delhi–110026. Printed at Baba Barkha Nath Printers, New Delhi 110 015.

STERLING PUBLISHERS PRIVATE LIMITED

PREFACE

This book is the third in the present series on 'Nit Nem' - the daily Sikh prayers. The first two books on Japji, Rehras and Sohila have been received with great enthusiasm by the younger generation. In the West, where there has been a recent awakening amongst the Sikh youth, a desire has arisen in their minds to know more about their religion and their identity. These two books have helped them in their quest. The 'Nit Nem' series has been designed to give the readers the theme, the literal meaning and the summary of all the hymns of the daily prayers. In the book of Rehras and Sohila and in the present one Sakhis (the fables) have been included to supplement the text.

Gurbani is a priceless treasure. The translation of the Gurbani into modern world languages is the demand of the day. It is the duty of scholars to deliver the message of Sikh Gurus to the world.

The Jap Sahib, the Swayas and the first section of the Ardas are the compositions of Guru Gobind Singh, the tenth Guru. These are recited by every devout Sikh in the morning along with the Japji of Guru Nanak Dev. As these *banis* are not in Punjabi they are difficult to be understood by the present day readers. I have tried my best to give the readers the meaning of all such words used in these *banis* along with the theme and the summary of the hymns; thus conveying to the readers the literal meaning as well as the essence of the prayer.

I hope that the readers will like my present work and appreciate the efforts and labour which have gone into producing this book.

I am most grateful to my secretary, Mrs. Poonam Kapoor, for helping me in preparing, planning and proofreading this book.

Dr. Sukhbir Singh Kapoor

TO MY DEAREST
CHANDNI-GAZAL-NOORJAHAN
WHO IS MY LOVE, LIFE AND WORSHIP

CONTENTS

PART I : JAP SAHIB

PART II

SWAYAS

PART III

ARDAS

PART I

JAP SAHIB

INTRODUCTION

Jap Sahib is the first 'Bani' recorded in *Dasam Granth,* the second most sacred granth of the Sikhs. There are three old and most well-known compilations of this holy book, viz., Bhai Mani Singh Wali Bir, Patna Sahib Wali Bir and Sangrur Wali Bir. Recently the granth has been published by many authorised publishers. It contains 1,428 pages.

The theme of *Jap Sahib* is the praise of Lord. It is inspired by an ardent faith in the grace of Almighty God. The bani was composed during 1684-1687 while Guru Gobind Singh was staying at Paunta Sahib.

The bani has 199 verses and is composed in ten chhands, viz., Chape, Bhujang Paryat, Chachri, Rasawal, Charpat, Rual, Madhubhar, Bhagwati, Harbolmana and Ek Achri Chhands.

According to Guru Gobind Singh, God has no form, no religion, no caste and no form. He is invisible, immeasurably great, and King of kings. His mystery is impenetrable, His glory indefinable, His holiness unsurpassable and His sovereignty eternal. He is truth, light, love, virtue, power, energy and beauty.

The main language of *Dasam Granth* is Braj, a dialect of Western Hindi. It was the chief dialect for poetry in the sixteenth century. Guru Gobind Singh was born in Bihar where the regional language was Eastern Hindi or Bihari. He might have developed a liking for this language in his young age. Other languages used in *Dasam Granth* are Persian, Arabic, Avadhi, Dingal, Sanskrit, and Punjabi. The language of *Jap Sahib* is a mixture of Sanskrit, Persian and Arabic. It contains the noblest verses in the praise of God.

The bani of Jap is full of devotion, piety and vigour. It has a powerful flow of lyrical poetry and an uncompromising expression of God's beauty. It is one of the greatest hymns ever composed.

ੴ ਸਤਿਗੁਰ ਪ੍ਰਸਾਦਿ ॥

Ik onkar sat(i) gur prasad (i).

ਸ੍ਰੀ ਵਾਹਿਗੁਰੂ ਜੀ ਕੀ ਫਤਹ ॥

Sri Waheguru ji ki fateh

ਸ੍ਰੀ ਮੁਖਵਾਕ ਪਾਤਿਸਾਹੀ ੧੦ ॥

Siri mukhvak patisahi 10 (dasvin).

ਛਪੈ ਛੰਦ ॥ ਤ੍ਵਪ੍ਰਸਾਦਿ ॥

CHHAPAI CHHAND, TAV PRASAD(I).

ਚੱਕ੍ਰ[1] ਚਿਹਨ[2] ਅਰ[3] ਬਰਨ[4] ਜਾਤਿ[5] ਅਰੁ ਪਾਤਿ[6] ਨਹਿਨ[7] ਜਿਹ[8] ॥

Chakr[1] chihan[2] ar (u)[3] baran[4] jat(i)[5] ar(u) pat(i)[6] nahin[7] jeh[8].

ਰੂਪ[9] ਰੰਗ[10] ਅਰੁ ਰੇਖ[11] ਭੇਖ[12] ਕੋਊ[13] ਕਹਿ[14] ਨ[15] ਸਕਤਿ[16] ਕੇਹ[17] ॥

Rup[9] rang[10] ar(u) rekh[11] bhekh[12] kou[13] kah(i)[14] na[15] sakat[16] keh[17].

ਅਚਲ[18] ਮੂਰਤਿ[19] ਅਨਭਉ[20] ਪ੍ਰਕਾਸ[21] ਅਮਿਤੋਜ[22] ਕਹਿਜੈ[23] ॥

Achal[18] murat(i)[19] anbhau[20] prakas[21] amitoj[22] kahijai[23].

ਕੋਟਿ[24] ਇੰਦ੍ਰ[25] ਇੰਦ੍ਰਾਨ[26] ਸਾਹੁ[27] ਸਾਹਾਨਿ[28] ਗਾਵਿਜੈ[29] ॥

Kot(i)[24] indr[25] indran[26] sah(u)[27] sahan[28](i) ganijai[29].

ਤ੍ਰਿਭਵਣ[30] ਮਹੀਪ[31] ਸੁਰ[32] ਨਰ[33] ਅਸੁਰ[34] ਨੇਤਿ[35] ਨੇਤਿ ਬਨ[36] ਤ੍ਰਿਨ[37] ਕਹਤ[38] ॥

Tribhavan[30] mahip[31] sur[32] nar[33] asur[34], net(i)[35] net(i) ban[36] trin[37] kahat[38].

ਤਵ[39] ਸਰਬ[40] ਨਾਮ[41] ਕਥੈ[42] ਕਵਨ[43] ਕਰਮ[44] ਨਾਮ[45] ਬਰਨਤ[46] ਸੁਮਤਿ[47] ॥੧॥

Tav[39] sarab[40] Nam[41] katha[i42] kavan[43] karam[44] Nam[45] barnat[46] sumat(i)[47].-1-

CHHAPAI CHHAND, TAVPRASAD

Notes

[1]the fortune lines of the palm and fingers, distinguishing signs; [2]form, figure; [3]and; [4]colour; [5]caste; [6]clan, lineage; [7-8]does not have; [9]beauty; [10]complexion; [11-12]frame, attire [13]none [14]say; [15]does not; [16]can; [17]describe; [18]unchangeable; [19]form, being; [20]one's feelings, experience; [21]illuminated; [22]omnipotent; [23]is said; [24]million; [25-26]King of heaven; [27-28]King of kings; [29]counted as; [30]the three worlds; [31]ruler; [32]devtas, angels; [33]human beings; [34]demons; [35]unparallel; [36]forests; [37]grass, woods; [38]described as; [39]your; [40]full, complete; [41]name; [42]describe; [43]who; [44]actions; [45]names; [46]description; [47]intelligent, to dedicate, in homage.

COMPOSITION 1

Theme

In His abstract form God cannot be described.

Literal Meaning

i. God has no distinguishing marks, colour or caste and does not belong to a particular clan.

ii. God has no form, colour, complexion, signs and garb, and no one can describe Him.

iii. He is unchangeable; His light can be seen by one's inside feelings. He is omnipotent.

iv. In His court there are millions of Indras and kings. He is the Master of the kings of heaven and all other rulers.

v. All the worlds, angels, humans, demons, other living things, and vegetations bow to Him.

vi. People remember Him with many names and by His actions.

Summary

God must be worshipped in His abstract form. No Sikh is allowed to make any image of God. He is a power beyond human description. No prophet or scripture can narrate His posture, colour, beauty, complexion and lineage. He can only be seen and felt in one's mind and not in a physical form.

ਭੁਜੰਗ ਪ੍ਰਯਾਤ ਛੰਦ ॥

ਨਮਸਤੂੰ[1] ਅਕਾਲੇ[2] ॥ ਨਮਸਤੂੰ ਕ੍ਰਿਪਾਲੇ[3] ॥
ਨਮਸਤੰ ਅਰੂਪੇ[4] ॥ ਨਮਸਤੰ ਅਨੂਪੇ[5] ॥੨॥
ਨਮਸਤੰ ਅਭੇਖੇ[6] ॥ ਨਮਸਤੰ ਅਲੇਖੇ[7] ॥
ਨਮਸਤੰ ਅਕਾਏ[8] ॥ ਨਮਸਤੰ ਅਜਾਏ[9] ॥੩॥
ਨਮਸਤੰ ਅਗੰਜੇ[10] ॥ ਨਮਸਤੰ ਅਭੰਜੇ[11] ॥
ਨਮਸਤੰ ਅਨਾਮੇ[12] ॥ ਨਮਸਤੰ ਅਠਾਮੇ[13] ॥੪॥
ਨਮਸਤੰ ਅਕਰਮੰ[14] ॥ ਨਮਸਤੰ ਅਧਰਮੰ[15] ॥
ਨਮਸਤੰ ਅਨਾਮੰ[16] ॥ ਨਮਸਤੰ ਅਧਾਮੰ[17] ॥੫॥
ਨਮਸਤੰ ਅਜੀਤੇ[18] ॥ ਨਮਸਤੰ ਅਭੀਤੇ[19] ॥
ਨਮਸਤੰ ਅਬਾਹੇ[20] ॥ ਨਮਸਤੰ ਅਧਾਹੇ[21] ॥੬॥
ਨਮਸਤੰ ਅਨੀਲੇ[22] ॥ ਨਮਸਤੰ ਅਨਾਦੇ[23] ॥
ਨਮਸਤੰ ਅਛੇਦੇ[24] ॥ ਨਮਸਤੰ ਅਗਾਧੇ[25] ॥੭॥
ਨਮਸਤੰ ਅਗੰਜੇ[26] ॥ ਨਮਸਤੰ ਅਭੰਜ[27] ॥
ਨਮਸਤੰ ਉਦਾਰੇ[28] ॥ ਨਮਸਤੰ ਅਪਾਰੇ[29] ॥੮॥
ਨਮਸਤੰ ਸੁਏਕੈ[30] ॥ ਨਮਸਤੰ ਅਨੇਕੈ[31] ॥
ਨਮਸਤੰ ਅਭੂਤੇ[32] ॥ ਨਮਸਤੰ ਅਜੂਪੇ[33] ॥੯॥
ਨਮਸਤੰ ਨ੍ਰਿਕਰਮੇ[34] ॥ ਨਮਸਤੰ ਨ੍ਰਿਭਰਮੇ[35] ॥
ਨਮਸਤੰ ਨ੍ਰਿਦੇਸੇ[36] ॥ ਨਮਸਤੰ ਨ੍ਰਿਭੇਸੇ[37] ॥੧੦॥
ਨਮਸਤੰ ਨ੍ਰਿਨਾਮੇ[38] ॥ ਨਮਸਤੰ ਨ੍ਰਿਕਾਮੇ[39] ॥
ਨਮਸਤੰ ਨ੍ਰਿਧਾਤੇ[40] ॥ ਨਮਸਤੰ ਨ੍ਰਿਘਾਤੇ[41] ॥੧੧॥
ਨਮਸਤੰ ਨ੍ਰਿਧੂਤੇ[42] ॥ ਨਮਸਤੰ ਅਭੂਤੇ[43] ॥
ਨਮਸਤੰ ਅਲੋਕੇ[44] ॥ ਨਮਸਤੰ ਅਸੋਕੇ[45] ॥੧੨॥
ਨਮਸਤੰ ਨ੍ਰਿਤਾਪੇ[46] ॥ ਨਮਸਤੰ ਅਥਾਪੇ[47] ॥
ਨਮਸਤੰ ਤ੍ਰਿਮਾਨੇ[48] ॥ ਨਮਸਤੰ ਨਿਧਾਨੇ[49] ॥੧੩॥
ਨਮਸਤੰ ਅਗਾਹੇ[50] ॥ ਨਮਸਤੰ ਅਬਾਹੇ[51] ॥
ਨਮਸਤੰ ਤ੍ਰਿਬਰਗੇ[52] ॥ ਨਮਸਤੰ ਅਸਰਗੇ[53] ॥੧੪॥

BHUJANG PRAYAT CHHAND

Namastang[1] akale[2]. Namastang kripale[3].
Namastang arupe[4]. Namastang anupe[5]. -2-
Namastang abhekhe[6]. Namastang alekhe[7].
Namastang akae[8]. Namastang ajae[9]. -3-
Namastang aganje.[10] Namastang abhanje[11].
Namastang aname[12]. Namastang athame[13]. -4-
Namastang akarmang[14]. Namastang adharmang[15].
Namastang anamang[16]. Namastang adhamang[17]. -5-
Namastang ajite[18]. Namastang abhite[19].
Namastang abahe[20]. Namastang adhahe[21]. -6-
Namastang anile[22]. Namastang anade[23].
Namastang achhede[24]. Namastang agadhe[25]. -7-
Namastang aganje[26]. Namastang abhanj[27].
Namastang udare[28]. Namastang apare[29]. -8-
Namastang su ekai[30]. Namastang anekai[31].
Namastang abhute[32]. Namastang ajupe[33]. -9-
Namastang nrikarme[34]. Namastang nribharme[35].
Namastang nridese[36]. Namastang nribhese[37]. -10-
Namastang nriname[38]. Namastang nrikame[39].
Namastang nridhate[40]. Namastang nrighate[41]. -11-
Namastang nridute[42]. Namastang abhute[43].
Namastang aloke[44]. Namastang asoke[45]. -12-
Namastang nritape[46]. Namastang athape[47].
Namastang trimane[48]. Namastang nidhane[49]. -13-
Namastang agahe[50]. Namastang abahe[51].
Namastang tribarge[52]. Namastang asarge[53]. -14-

BHUJUNG PRYAT CHHAND

Notes

Basic Words

NAMASTANG - Salutation, bow, homage

NAMASTAT - Salutation to you

NAMO - Hail

[1]bow, salutation; [2]Immortal; [3]kind; [4]formless; [5]eulogiless, beyond praises; [6]garbless; [7]stainless, beyond description, beyond a definite image, form [8]bodyless; has no figure; [9]unborn; [10]imperishable; [11]indestructible; [12]nameless; [13]beyond a definite place of residence, lives everywhere; [14]not bound by karmas; [15]not bound by religions; [16]has innumerable names, nameless; [17]many dwellings; [18]invincible; [19]fearless; [20]self-sufficient; [21]one who cannot be defeated, unconquerable; [22]spotless; [23]timeless, beyond time, no beginning; [24]indivisible; [25]unfathomable; [26]imperishable; [27]unbreakable; [28]benevolent, bountiful; [29]boundless, limitless; [30]one, only one;[31]. manifest in all, manifold; [32]beyond birth, beyond human/physical form; [33] free from bondage; [34]beyond the bondage of karmas; [35]devoid of superstition; [36]belongs everywhere and not to a particular nationality; [37]free from cultural bondage; [38]nameless, has no specific name; [39]beyond desires; [40]matterless, no specific physical body; [41]beyond deaths; [42]immoveble, unshakeable; [43]no physical form, unsurpassed; [44]invisible, imperceivable; [45]beyond sorrows; [46]free from infliction; [47]beyond fixation, un-installable; [48]ever-worshipped, everywhere worshipped; [49]Master of all treasures; [50]unfathomable; [51]self-sufficient; [52]deliver of boons (proverbial: three boons); [53]self-illuminated.

COMPOSITION 2

Theme

God is the greatest of all. He is the king of kings, the creator, the sustainer and the destroyer.

Literal Meaning

2. Salutation to God Who is immortal, kind, formless and eulogiless. There is no one equal to Him.

3.. Salutation to God Who is not bound by any uniform, description, form (image) and birth.

4. Salutation to God Who is imperishable, indestructable, and is not bound by any specific name or address.

5. Salutation to God Who is beyond the bondage of karmas, religion, name and place.

6. Salutation to God Who is invincible, fearless, self-sufficient and unconquerable.

7. Salutation to God Who is stainless, beyond time, indivisible and unfathomable.

8. Salutation to God Who is imperishable, unbreakable, benevolent, and boundless.

9. Salutation to God Who is one, manifests in all, is unborn and free from all the bondages.

10. Salutation to God Who is beyond the bondage of karmas, devoid of superstition, omnipresent and is free from cultural linkages.

11. Salutation to God Who is beyond caste, creed and religion, Who is beyond desires, Who has no physical body and Who is beyond death.

12. Salutation to God Who is unshakeable unsurpassed, invisible and beyond sorrows.

13. Salutation to God Who is free from inflictions, is un-installable, is worshipped in all the worlds and is the master of all the treasures.

14. Salutation to God Who is unfathomable, self-sufficient, the Deliverer of boons and self-illuminated.

15. Salutation to God Who is beyond human knowledge. O! Truthful Beauty, I bow to You. Salutation to God Who is vast like an ocean and Who exists without any support.

ਨਮਸਤੰ ਪ੍ਰਭੋਗੇ[54] ॥ ਨਮਸਤੰ ਸੁਜੋਗੇ[55] ॥
ਨਮਸਤੰ ਅਰੰਗੇ[56] ॥ ਨਮਸਤੰ ਅਭੰਗੇ[57] ॥੧੫॥
ਨਮਸਤੰ ਅਗੰਮੇ[58] ॥ ਨਮਸਤੱਸਤੁ[59] ਰੰਮੇ[60] ॥
ਨਮਸਤੰ ਜਲਾਸ੍ਰੇ[61] ॥ ਨਮਸਤੰ ਨਿਰਾਸ੍ਰੇ[62] ॥੧੬॥
ਨਮਸਤੰ ਅਜਾਤੇ[63] ॥ ਨਮਸਤੰ ਅਪਾਤੇ[64] ॥
ਨਮਸਤੰ ਅਮਜਬੇ[65] ॥ਨਮਸਤੱਸਤੁ ਅਜਬੇ[66] ॥੧੭॥
ਅਦੇਸੰ[67] ਅਦੇਸੇ[68] ॥ ਨਮਸਤੰ ਅਭੇਸੇ[69] ॥
ਨਮਸਤੰ ਨ੍ਰਿਧਾਮੇ[70] ॥ ਨਮਸਤੰ ਨ੍ਰਿਬਾਮੇ[71] ॥੧੮॥
ਨਮੋ[72] ਸਰਬ ਕਾਲੇ[73] ॥ ਨਮੋ ਸਰਬ ਦਯਾਲੇ[74] ॥
ਨਮੋ ਸਰਬ ਰੂਪੇ[75] ॥ ਨਮੋ ਸਰਬ ਭੂਪੇ[76] ॥੧੯॥
ਨਮੋ ਸਰਬ ਖਾਪੇ[77] ॥ ਨਮੋ ਸਰਬ ਥਾਪੇ[78] ॥
ਨਮੋ ਸਰਬ ਕਾਲੇ[79] ॥ ਨਮੋ ਸਰਬ ਪਾਲੇ[80] ॥੨੦॥
ਨਮਸਤੱਸਤੁ ਦੇਵੈ[81] ॥ ਨਮਸਤੰ ਅਭੇਵੈ[82] ॥
ਨਮਸਤੰ ਅਜਨਮੇ[83] ॥ ਨਮਸਤੰ ਸੁਬਨਮੇ[84] ॥੨੧॥
ਨਮੋ ਸਰਬ ਗਉਨੇ[85] ॥ ਨਮੋ ਸਰਬ ਭਉਨੇ[86] ॥
ਨਮੋ ਸਰਬ ਰੰਗੇ[87] ॥ ਨਮੋ ਸਰਬ ਭੰਗੇ[88] ॥੨੨॥
ਨਮੋ ਕਾਲ ਕਾਲੇ[89] ॥ ਨਮਸਤੱਸਤੁ ਦਯਾਲੇ[90] ॥
ਨਮਸਤੰ ਅਬਰਨੇ[91] ॥ ਨਮਸਤੰ ਅਮਰਨੇ[92] ॥੨੩॥
ਨਮਸਤੰ ਜਰਾਰੰ[93] ॥ ਨਮਸਤੰ ਕ੍ਰਿਤਾਰੰ[94] ॥
ਨਮੋ ਸਰਬ ਧੰਧੇ[95] ॥ ਨਮੋ ਸਤ ਅਬੰਧੇ[96] ॥੨੪॥
ਨਮਸਤੰ ਨ੍ਰਿਸਾਕੇ[97] ॥ ਨਮਸਤੰ ਨ੍ਰਿਬਾਕੇ[98] ॥
ਨਮਸਤੰ ਰਹੀਮੇ[99] ॥ ਨਮਸਤੰ ਕਰੀਮੇ[100] ॥੨੫॥
ਨਮਸਤੰ ਅਨੰਤੇ[101] ॥ ਨਮਸਤੰ ਮਹੰਤੇ[102] ॥
ਨਮਸਤੱਸਤੁ ਰਾਗੇ[103] ॥ ਨਮਸਤੰ ਸੁਹਾਗੇ[104] ॥੨੬॥
ਨਮੋ ਸਰਬ ਸੋਖੰ[105] ॥ ਨਮੋ ਸਰਬ ਪੋਖੰ[106] ॥
ਨਮੋ ਸਰਬ ਕਰਤਾ[107] ॥ ਨਮੋ ਸਰਬ ਹਰਤਾ[108] ॥੨੭॥
ਨਮੋ ਜੋਗ ਜੋਗੇ[109] ॥ ਨਮੋ ਭੋਗ ਭੋਗੇ[110] ॥
ਨਮੋ ਸਰਬ ਦਯਾਲੇ[111] ॥ ਨਮੋ ਸਰਬ ਪਾਲੇ[112] ॥੨੮॥

Namastang prabhoge[54] . *Namastang sujoge*[55] .
Namastang arange[56] . *Namastang abhange*[57] .-15-
Namastang aganme[58] . *Namastast(u)*[59] *ranme*[60] .
Namastang jalasre[61] . *Namastang nirasre*[62] .-16-
Namastang ajate[63] . *Namastang apate*[64] .
Namastang amajbe[65] . *Namastast(u) ajbe*[66] .-17-
Adesang[67] *adese*[68] . *Namastang abhese*[69] .
Namastang nridhame[70] . *Namastang nribame*[71] .-18-
Namo[72] *sarab kale*[73] . *Namo sarab diale*[74] .
Namo sarab rupe[75] . *Namo sarab bhupe*[76] .-19-
Namo sarab khape[77] ., *Namo sarab thape*[78] .
Namo sarab kale[79] . *Namo sarab pale*[80] .-20-
Namastast(u) devai[81] . *Namastang abhevai*[82] .
Namastang ajanme[83] . *Namastang subanme*[84] .-21-
Namo sarab gaune[85] . *Namo sarab bhaune*[86] .
Namo sarab range[87] . *Namo sarab bhange*[88] .-22-
Namo kal kale[89] . *Namastast(u) diale*[90] .
Namastang abarne[91] . *Namastang amarne*[92] .-23-
Namastang jrarang[93] . *Namastang kritarang*[94] .
Namo sarab dhandhe[95] . *Namo sat abandhe*[96] .-24-
Namastang nrisake[97] . *Namastang nribake*[98] .
Namastang rahime[99] . *Namastang karime*[100] .-25-
Namastang anante[101] . *Namastang mahante*[102] .
Namastast(u) rage[103] . *Namastang suhage*[104] .-26-
Namo sarab sokhang[105] . *Namo sarab pokhang*[106] .
Namo sarab karta[107] . *Namo sarab harta*[108] .-27-
Namo jog joge[109] . *Namo bhog bhoge*[110] .
Namo sarab diale[111] . *Namo sarab pale*[112] . -28-

[54]ever happy; [55]ever perfect; [56]every pure; [57]indestructable; [58]beyond human knowledge; [59]salutation to you; [60]truthful beauty; [61]vast like an ocean; [62]exists without support; [63]has no caste; [64]has no lineage; [65]has no religion; [66]marvellous, sublime; [67]salutation; [68]belongs to all the countries; [69]wears all kind/fashion of clothes; [70]lives everywhere; [71]is on His/Her own, spouseless; [72]salutation; [73]Lord eternal; [74]merciful; [75]extremely beautiful; [76]King of kings; [77]the destroyer; [78]the creator; [79]the great death; [80]the sustainer; [81]the giver; [82]the suspenseful; [83]unborn; [84]self-illuminated; [85]all-invading; [86]all-pervading; [87]manifest in all; [88]destroyer of all; [89]death of all deaths; [90]all merciful; [91]beyond caste and lineage; [92]immortal; [93]beyond age; [94]the creator ; [95]inspirer of all works; [96]limitless truth; [97]has no kith and kin; [98]fearless; [99]merciful; [100]gracious, bountiful; [101]Lord infinite; [102]Lord great; [103]Lord of love and truth; [104]Lord who is ever benevolent; [105]the great consumer; [106]the sustainer; [107]the destroyer; [108]the great yogi; the self-restainer; [109]the great enjoyer; [110]merciful; [111]the sustainer, the father; the mother.

17. Salutation to God who is beyond castes, races and creeds, and Who is great and marvellous.
18. Homage to God who is Omnipresent. Salutation to Him Who wears all sort of clothes, Who lives everywhere and Who is beyond relations.
19. Bow to God Who is Lord Eternal. Salutation to God Who is merciful, beautiful and king of kings.
20. Salutation to God Who is the Destroyer, the Creator, the Great Death and the Sustainer.
21. Homage to God Who is the Giver. Saluation to God Who is a Great Suspense, Who is unborn and self-illuminated.
22. Salutation to God Who is All-Invading, All-Pervading, All-Manifest and All-Destroyer.
23. Salutation to God Who is the Death of all deaths, the Mercy of all mercies, the Description of all descriptions and the Life of all lives.
24. Salutation to God Who hath no age, is the Creator of all, is the Inspirer of all the works and is the Truth of all the truths.
25. Salutation to God Who is beyond kith and kins, Who is fearless, merciful and bountiful.
26. Salutations to God Who is infinite, great, absolute and glorious.
27. Salutation to God Who is the Consumer, the Sustainer, the Creator and the Destroyer.
28. Salutation to God Who is the Great Yogi, Supreme Enjoyer, the Merciful and the Father, Mother, Brother and Sister blended in one.

Summary
Bow and salute to the Greatest Power of all the times – Waheguru to the Sikhs, Parmeshwar to the Hindus, Allah to the Muslims, God to the Christians and Jehovah to the Jews. He is One Reality by whatever name called. He is the Death of deaths, the Lord of the universe, the Creator, the Preserver and the Destroyer. He is the Greatest Donor, the most Lovable Companion, the real Friend in need, the Protector, the Saviour and the Benefactor. He is the Founder of all the religions, the scriptures, the languages, the regions and the lives. He has created different types of worlds in different parts of the universe. He is the King of kings, almighty, invincible, self-illuminated and self-sustained. He is the Creator of the dogma of cause and effect but Himself is beyond its operations. He is the Master of all the treasures, the mines, the vegetation, the fluids, the chemicals and the gases. God is one and is the father of the whole creation.

ਚਾਚਰੀ ਛੰਦ ॥ ਤ੍ਵਪ੍ਰਸਾਦਿ ॥

ਅਰੂਪ[1] ਹੈਂ ॥ ਅਨੂਪ[2] ਹੈਂ ॥ ਅਜੂ[3] ਹੈਂ ॥ ਅਭੂ[4] ਹੈਂ ॥੨੯॥
ਅਲੇਖ[5] ਹੈਂ ॥ ਅਭੇਖ[6] ਹੈਂ ॥ ਅਨਾਮ[7] ਹੈਂ ॥ ਅਕਾਮ[8] ਹੈਂ ॥੩੦॥
ਅਧੇਜ[9] ਹੈਂ ॥ ਅਭੇਜ[10] ਹੈਂ ॥ ਅਜੀਤ[11] ਹੈਂ ॥ ਅਭੀਤ[12] ਹੈਂ ॥੩੧॥
ਤ੍ਰਿਮਾਨ[13] ਹੈਂ ॥ ਨਿਧਾਨ[14] ਹੈਂ ॥ ਤ੍ਰਿਬਰਗ[15] ਹੈਂ ॥ ਅਸਰਗ[16] ਹੈਂ ॥੩੨॥
ਅਨੀਲ[17] ਹੈਂ ॥ ਅਨਾਦਿ[18] ਹੈਂ ॥ ਅਜੇ[19] ਹੈਂ ॥ ਅਜਾਦਿ[20] ਹੈਂ ॥੩੩॥
ਅਜਨਮ[21] ਹੈਂ ॥ ਅਬਰਨ[22] ਹੈਂ ॥ ਅਭੂਤ[23] ਹੈਂ ॥ ਅਭਰਨ[24] ਹੈਂ ॥੩੪॥
ਅਗੰਜ[25] ਹੈਂ ॥ ਅਭੰਜ[26] ਹੈਂ ॥ ਅਝੂਝ[27] ਹੈਂ ॥ ਅਝੰਝ[28] ਹੈਂ ॥੩੫॥
ਅਮੀਕ[29] ਹੈਂ ॥ ਰਫੀਕ[30] ਹੈਂ ॥ ਅਧੰਧ[31] ਹੈਂ ॥ ਅਬੰਧ[32] ਹੈਂ ॥੩੬॥
ਨ੍ਰਿਬੂਝ[33] ਹੈਂ ॥ ਅਸੂਝ[34] ਹੈਂ ॥ ਅਕਾਲ[35] ਹੈਂ ॥ ਅਜਾਲ[36] ਹੈਂ ॥੩੭॥

CHACHRI CHHAND, TAV PRASAD (I)

*Arup[1] hain. Anup[2] hain. Aju[3] hain. Abhu[4] hain. -29-
Alekh[5] hain. Abhekh[6] hain. Anam[7] hain. Akam[8] hain.-30-
Adhe[9] hain. Abhe[10] hain. Ajit[11] hain. Abhit[12] hain. -31-
Triman[13] hain. Nidhan[14] hain. Tribarg[15] hain. Asarg[16] hain. -32-
Anil[17] hain. Anad(i)[18] hain. Aje[19] hain. Ajad(i)[20] hain. -33-
Ajanam[21] hain. Abarn[22] hain. Abhut[23] hain. Abharn[24] hain. -34-
Aganj[25] hain. Abhanj[26] hain. Ajhujh[27] hain. Ajhanjh[28] hain. -35-
Amik[29] hain. Rafik[30] hain. Adhandh[31] hain. Abandh[32] hain. -36-
Nribujh[33] hain. Asujh[34] hain. Akal[35] hain. Ajal[36] hain. -37-*

CHACHRI CHHAND
BY THE GRACE OF GOD

Notes

[1]no form; [2]no worldly status; [3]cannot be moved; [4]beyond birth; [5]beyond description; [6]no specific uniform; [7]no name; [8]no worldly desire; [9]not conceivable; [10]full of suspense; [11]invincible; [12]no fear; [13]worshipped in three zones of the earth, viz., the earth, worlds beneath the earth and worlds above the earth; [14]full of bounties; [15]the giver; [16]self-illuminated; [17]spotless; [18]no beginning; [19]invincible; [20]free from bondage; [21]not born; [22]beyond description; [23]no physical body; [24]unadorned; [25]immortal; [26]indestructible; [27]invincible; [28]not attached, detached; [29]limitless, vast, unfathomable; [30]friend, benefactor; [31]free from bondage; [32]free from entanglement; [33]beyond knowledge; [34]not comprehensible; [35]beyond death; [36]beyond worldly commitments.

COMPOSITION 3

Theme

God does not belong to any specific religion, region, group of people, form or uniform. He is the God of all. He is self-illuminated.

Literal Meaning

29 God has no physical form, is above worldly honours, is firm in decisions and is not born.

30. God is beyond description, wears no specific uniform, has no specific name and is above worldly desires.

31. God cannot be realised by mere thoughts or study, His secrets cannot be found by humans, He is invincible and is beyond all the fears.

32. God is worshipped in all the three known zones of this world, viz., earth, sky and netherland, He is the Master of all the treasures, He is the Cause of the threefold creation Viz., truth, attachments and passion and He Himself is self-illuminated.

33. God is beyond stains, has no beginning, is invincible, and is free from bondage.

34. God is not conceived in a mother's womb, cannot be described by scholars, is not matter, i.e., is not made up of air, water, ether, fire and earth and is not dependent on any one self.

35. God is beyond death, is not subject to destruction, cannot be defeated and is above worldly involvements.

36. God is everywhere, He is the Benefactor, He is above worldly quarrels and is free from social entanglements.

37. God cannot be known by reading only scriptures, or only by performing meditation, or by studying history and by making relations with Him.

38. God is the Supreme Lord, He is not bound by any territories, boundaries or honours.

39. God is beyond beginning and end, is above hatred, needs no wordly assistance and is not subject to cause and effect.

40. God is both abstract and manifest, is not involved in the cycle of birth and deaths, is not a product of synthesis of water, air, fire, earth and ether, and is beyond human eye and touch.

ਅਲਾਹ[37] ਹੈ ॥ ਅਜਾਹ[38] ਹੈ ॥ ਅਨੰਤ[39] ਹੈ ॥ ਮਹੰਤ[40] ਹੈ ॥੧੮॥
ਅਲੀਕ[41] ਹੈ ॥ ਨ੍ਰਿਸ੍ਰੀਕ[42] ਹੈ ॥ ਨਿਲੰਭ[43] ਹੈ ॥ ਅਸੰਭ[44] ਹੈ ॥੧੯॥
ਅਗੰਮ[45] ਹੈ ॥ ਅਜੰਮ[46] ਹੈ ॥ ਅਭੂਤ[47] ਹੈ ॥ ਅਛੂਤ[48] ਹੈ ॥੪੦॥
ਅਲੋਕ[49] ਹੈ ॥ ਅਸੋਕ[50] ਹੈ ॥ ਅਕਰਮ[51] ਹੈ ॥ ਅਬਰਮ[52] ਹੈ ॥੪੧॥
ਅਜੀਤ[53] ਹੈ ॥ ਅਭੀਤ[54] ਹੈ ॥ ਅਬਾਹ[55] ਹੈ ॥ ਅਗਾਹ[56] ਹੈ ॥੪੨॥
ਅਮਾਨ[57] ਹੈ ॥ ਨਿਧਾਨ[58] ਹੈ ॥ ਅਨੇਕ[59] ਹੈ ॥ ਵਿਰਿ[60] ਏਕ ਹੈ ॥੪੩॥

Alah[37] hain. Ajah[38] hain. Anant[39] hain. Mahant[40] hain. -38-
Alik[41] hain. Nrisrik[42] hain. Nrilanbh[43] hain. Asanbh[44] hain. -39-
Aganm[45] hain. Ajanm[46] hain. Abhut[47] hain. Achhut[48] hain. -40-
Alok[49] hain. Asok[50] hain. Akarm[51] hain. Abharm[52] hain. -41-
Ajit[53] hain. Abhit[54] jain. Abah[55] hain. Agah[56] hain. -42-
Aman[57] hain. Nidhan[58] hain. Anek[59] hain. Phir(i)[60] ek hain. -43-

[37]Supreme God; [38]do not belong to one place or region; [39]beyond limits; [40]great; [41]limitless; [42]beyond rivalry; [43]self-sustained; [44]self-created; [45]unfathomable; [46]beyond births; [47]beyond matter; [48]intangible; [49]invisible; [50]beyond sorrows; [51]beyond karma; [52]beyond delusions; [53]invincible; [54]fearless; [55]unshakeable [56]unfathomable; [57]immeasurable; [58]full of treasures; [59]innumerable; [60]one.

41. God cannot be viewed by naked eyes, He can only be seen by the eyes of your heart, emotions and mind. He is beyond known sorrows. He is not subject to human karma theory and cannot be realised by futile rituals and abortive delusions.

42. God is beyond worldly concepts of rise and fall, fear and safety, movement and stagnation, and depth and heights.

43. God incorporates all measures, bounties and forms but is still one, father and master of all of us.

Summary

God, the almighty power pervades everywhere, regulates all the worlds, controls all the movements and causes all the births and deaths. He is the only Reality and Truth. He is self-illuminated and self-supported. He is beyond time, description and count. There is no one other equal to Him. He loves His creation and manifests in all of them. He is beyond worldly theories of comfort and sorrows, success and defeat, profit and loss, and love and hatred.

ਭੁਜੰਗ ਪ੍ਰਯਾਤ ਛੰਦ ॥

ਨਮੋ[1] ਸਰਬ[2] ਮਾਨੇ[3] ॥ ਸਮਸਤੀ[4] ਨਿਧਾਨੇ[5] ॥

ਨਮੋ[6] ਦੇਵ[7] ਦੇਵੇ[8] ॥ ਅਭੇਖੀ[9] ਅਭੇਵੇ[10] ॥੪੪॥

ਨਮੋ ਕਾਲ[11] ਕਾਲੇ[12] ॥ ਨਮੋ ਸਰਬ[13] ਪਾਲੇ[14] ॥

ਨਮੋ ਸਰਬ[15] ਗਉਣੇ[16] ॥ ਨਮੋ ਸਰਬ[17] ਭਉਣੇ[18] ॥੪੫॥

ਅਨੰਗੀ[19] ਅਨਾਥੇ[20] ॥ ਨ੍ਰਿਸੰਗੀ[21] ਪ੍ਰਮਾਥੇ[22] ॥

ਨਮੋ ਭਾਨ[23] ਭਾਨੇ[24] ॥ ਨਮੋ ਮਾਨ[25] ਮਾਨੇ[26] ॥੪੬॥

ਨਮੋ ਚੰਦ੍ਰ[27] ਚੰਦ੍ਰੇ[28] ॥ ਨਮੋ ਭਾਨ[29] ਭਾਨੇ[30] ॥

ਨਮੋ ਗੀਤ[31] ਗੀਤੇ[32] ॥ ਨਮੋ ਤਾਨ[33] ਤਾਨੇ[34] ॥੪੭॥

ਨਮੋ ਨ੍ਰਿਤ[35] ਨ੍ਰਿਤੇ[36] ॥ ਨਮੋ ਨਾਦ[37] ਨਾਦੇ[38] ॥

ਨਮੋ ਪਾਨ[39] ਪਾਨੇ[40] ॥ ਨਮੋ ਬਾਦ[41] ਬਾਦੇ[42] ॥੪੮॥

ਅਨੰਗੀ[43] ਅਨਾਮੇ[44] ॥ ਸਮਸਤੀ[45] ਸਰੂਪੇ[46] ॥

ਪ੍ਰਭੰਗੀ[47] ਪ੍ਰਮਾਥੇ[48] ॥ ਸਮਸਤੀ[49] ਬਿਭੂਤੇ[50] ॥੪੯॥

ਕਲੰਕੰ[51] ਬਿਨਾ[52] ਨੇ-ਕਲੰਕੀ[53] ਸਰੂਪੇ[54] ॥

ਨਮੋ ਰਾਜ[55] ਰਾਜੇਸੁਰੰ[56] ਪਰਮ[57] ਰੂਪੇ[58] ॥੫੦॥

ਨਮੋ ਜੋਗ[59] ਜੋਗੇਸੁਰੰ[60] ਪਰਮ[61] ਸਿੱਧੇ[62] ॥

ਨਮੋ ਰਾਜ[63] ਰਾਜੇਸੁਰੰ[64] ਪਰਮ[65] ਬ੍ਰਿਧੇ[66] ॥੫੧॥

ਨਮੋ ਸਸਤ੍ਰ[67] ਪਾਨੇ[68] ॥ ਨਮੋ ਅਸਤ੍ਰ[69] ਮਾਨੇ[70] ॥

ਨਮੋ ਪਰਮ[71] ਗਯਾਤਾ[72] ॥ ਨਮੋ ਲੋਕ[73] ਮਾਤਾ[74] ॥੫੨॥

ਅਭੇਖੀ[75] ਅਭਰਮੀ[76] ਅਭੋਗੀ[77] ਅਭੁਗਤੇ[78] ॥

ਨਮੋ ਜੋਗ[79] ਜੋਗੇਸੁਰੰ[80] ਪਰਮ[81] ਜੁਗਤੇ[82] ॥੫੩॥

ਨਮੋ ਨਿੱਤ[83] ਨਾਰਾਇਨੇ[84] ਕ੍ਰੂਰ[85] ਕਰਮੇ[86] ॥

ਨਮੋ ਪ੍ਰੇਤ[87] ਅਪ੍ਰੇਤ[88] ਦੇਵੇ[89] ਸੁਧਰਮੇ[90-91] ॥੫੪॥

BHUJANG PRAYAT CHHAND

Namo[1] sarab[2] mane[3]. Samasti[4] nidhane[5].

Namo[6] dev[7] deve[8]. Abhekhi[9] abheve[10]. -44-

Namo kal[11] kale[12]. Namo sarab[13] pale[14].

Namo sarab[15] gaune[16]. Namo sarab[17] bhaune[18]. -45-

Anangi[19] anathe[20]. Nrisangi[21] pramathe[22].

Namo bhan[23] bhane[24]. Namo man[25] mane[26]. -46-

Namo chandr[27] chandre[28]. Namo bhan[29] bhane[30].

Namo git[31] gite[32]. Namo tan[33] tane[34]. -47-

Namo nrit[35] nrite[36]. Namo nad[37] nade[38].

Namo pan[39] pane[40]. Namo bad[41] bade[42]. -48-

Anangi[43] aname[44]. Samasti[45] sarupe[46].

Prabhangi[47] pramathe[48]. Samasti[49] bibhute[50]. -49-

Kalankang[51] bina[52] ne-kalanki[53] sarupe[54].

Namo raj[55] raje[56] swarang param[57] rupe[58]. -50-

Namo jog[59] joge[60] swarang param[61] sidhe[62].

Namo raj[63] raje[64] swarang param[65] bridhe[66]. -51-

Namo sastr[67]-pane[68]. Namo astr[69]-mane[70].

Namo param[71] giata[72]. Namo lok[73] mata[74]. -52-

Abhekhi[75] abharmi[76], abhogi[77] abhugte[78].

Namo jog[79] joge[80] swarang param[81] jugte[82]. -53-

Namo nit[83] naraene[84]. Krur[85] karme[86].

Namo pret[87] apret[88], deve[89] sudharme.[90-91] -54-

BHUJANG PRAYAT CHHAND

Notes

[1]hail; [2]all; [3]believe-in; [4]universal; [5]treasure; [6]hail; [7]angels; [8]divine; [9]no uniform; [10]mysterious; [11-12]death of deaths; [13]universal; [14]to sustain; [15-16]reachable to all; [17-18]omnipresent; [19]formless; [20]master of his own; [21]no companions; [22]destroyers; [23-24]sun of suns; [25-26]honoured by honourable; [27-28]coolness of moons; [29-30]energy of suns; [31-32]lyric of songs; [33-34]melody of tunes; [35-36]posture of dances; [37-38]tune of musics; [39-40]sound of drums; [41-42]celestial of music; [43-44]no form, no name; [45-46]universal spirit; [47]destroyer; [48]oppressors; [49-50]source of all prosperity; [51-52]without blame; [53-54]pure/perfect form; [55-56]king of kings; [57]supreme; [58]beautiful; [59-60]great yogi; [61]supreme; [62]powers; [63-64]supreme king; [65-66]supreme commander; [67-68]wielder of arms; [69-70]pride of arms; [71-72]supreme omniscient; [73-74]divine mother; [75]no uniform; [76]beyond superstitions; [77]limitless; [78]treasures; [79-80]supreme yogi; [81-82]omnipresent; [83]eternal; [84]Lord; [85-86]annihilator of bad karmas; [87-88]destroyer of evil spirits; [89-91]protector of angels.

COMPOSITION 4

Theme

Lord Waheguru is the Master of the whole universe. There are not sufficient words in the known vocabulary which can describe Him and explain His main attributes.

Literal Meaning

44. I bow to Him who—
is worshipped by all,
possesses everlasting treasures for all of us,
is the Master and Light of angels,
does not stick to a specific uniform, and
whose creation is full of mysteries.

45. I bow to Him Who—
is Lord of death,
is Controller of birth,
pervades in all, and
is present in all.

46. I bow to Him Who—
has no specific form and is not born of parents,
has no spouse, and Who is the Destroyer of evils;
gives energy to the suns, and Who is the focus of worship by scholars.

47. I bow to Him Who gives—
coolness to moons,
energy and heat to suns,
lyric to songs and melody to tunes.

48. I bow to Him who gives —
postures to dances,
tune to musics,
shapes to creation,
sound and celestial echoes to drums.

49. I bow to Him Who—
has no form or name,
is manifest in all,
is the Destroyer of all, and is the Source of all life.

ਨਮੋ ਰੋਗ[92] ਹਰਤਾ[93] ਨਮੋ ਰਾਗ[94] ਰੂਪੇ[95] ॥
ਨਮੋ ਸਾਹ[96] ਸਾਹੰ[97] ਨਮੋ ਭੂਪ[98] ਭੂਪੇ[99] ॥੫੫॥
ਨਮੋ ਦਾਨ[100] ਦਾਨੇ[101] ਨਮੋ ਮਾਨ[102] ਮਾਨੇ[103] ॥
ਨਮੋ ਰੋਗ[104] ਰੋਗੇ[105] ਨਮਸਤੰ ਸਨਾਨੇ[106] ॥੫੬॥
ਨਮੋ ਮੰਤ੍ਰ[107] ਮੰਤ੍ਰੰ[108] ਨਮੋ ਜੰਤ੍ਰ[109] ਜੰਤ੍ਰੰ[110] ॥
ਨਮੋ ਇਸ਼ਟ[111] ਇਸ਼ਟੇ[112] ਨਮੋ[113] ਤੰਤ੍ਰ[114] ਤੰਤ੍ਰੰ[115] ॥੫੭॥
ਸਦਾ[116] ਸੱਚਿਦਾਨੰਦ[117] ਸਰਬੰ[118] ਪ੍ਰਨਾਸੀ[119] ॥
ਅਨੂਪੇ[120] ਅਰੂਪੇ[121] ਸਮਸਤੁਲਿ[122] ਨਿਵਾਸੀ[123] ॥੫੮॥
ਸਦਾ[124] ਸਿੱਧਦਾ[125] ਬੁੱਧਦਾ[126] ਬ੍ਰਿੱਧ[127] ਕਰਤਾ[128] ॥
ਅਧੋ[129] ਊਰਧ[130] ਅਰਧੰ[131] ਅੱਘੰ[132] ਓਘ[133] ਹਰਤਾ[134] ॥੫੯॥
ਪਰਮ[135] ਪਰਮ[136] ਪਰਮੇਸ਼ੁਰੰ[137] ਪ੍ਰੋਛ[138] ਪਾਲੰ[139] ॥
ਸਦਾ ਸਰਬਦਾ[140] ਸਿੱਧ[141] ਦਾਤਾ[142] ਦਯਾਲੰ[143] ॥੬੦॥
ਅਛੇਦੀ[144] ਅਭੇਦੀ[145] ਅਨਾਮੰ[146] ਅਕਾਮੰ[147] ॥
ਸਮਸਤੇ[148] ਪਰਾਜੀ[149] ਸਮਸਤਸੱਤੁ[150] ਧਾਮੰ[151] ॥੬੧॥

Namo rog[92] harta[93], namo rag[94] rupe[95].
Namo sah[96] sahang[97], namo bhup[98] bhupe[99]. -55-
Namo dan[100] dane[101], namo man[102] mane[103].
Namo rog[104] roge[105], namastang isnane[106]. -56-
Namo mantr[107] mantrang[108], Namo jantr[109] jantrang[110].
Namo ist[111] iste[112], Namo[113] tantr[114] tantrang[115]. -57-
Sada[116] sach-da-nand[117], sarbang[118] pranasi[119].
Anupe[120] arupe[121], samastul(i)[122] nivasi[123]. -58
Sada[124] sidh-da[125] budh-da[126] bridh[127] karta[128].
Adho[129] urdh[130] ardhang[131] aghang[132] ogh[133] harta[134]. -59-
Param[135] param[136] parmeswarang[137] prochh-palang[138-139].
Sada sarab-da[140] sidh[141] data[142] dialang[143]. -60-
Achhedi[144] abhedi[145], anamang[146] akamang[147].
Samasto[148] paraji[148] samastast(u)[150] dhamang[151]. -61-

[92-93]Healer of diseases; [94-95]embodiment of love; [96-97]King of kings; [98-99]Commander of commanders; [100-101]the Bestower of gifts; [102-103]Honour of honourables; [104-105]the Dispeller of maladies. [106]Symbol of purifications; [107-108]the Divinity of the divine word; [109-110]the Master of the mystic charms; [111-112]the God of gods; [113]hail; [114-115]Master of the occults; [116]eternal; [117]ever truthful; [118-119]the Destroyer; [120]no-form; [121]most beautiful; [122-123]omnipresent; [124]ever; [125]spiritual; [126]intellectual; [127-128]Bestower of powers; [129]sky; [130]earth; [131]atmosphere, space; [132]sins; [133]all of them; [134]destroyer; [135]great; [136]supreme; [137]Lord; [138]invisible; [139]sustainer; [140]ever the master; [141]the treasure of wisdom; [142]bestower; [143]compassionate; [144]impregnable; [145]mysterious; [146]has no name; [147]without desires; [148]all; [149]unconquerable; [150]present everywhere, omnipresent; [151]places.

50. I bow to Him Who — is beyond blemish, is pure and perfect, is the King of kings, is supreme and beautiful.

51. I bow to Him Who — is a great Yogi, Master of all powers, Prince of princes, and a great Scholar.

52. I bow to Him Who — is the Wielder of arms. Power of weapons, Scholar of scholars, and Source of all births.

53. I bow to Him Who — wears no special uniform, is beyond delusions, is beyond worldly desires, is Source of all treasures, is the master of yogis, is omnipresent and is the Director of world affairs.

54. I bow to Him Who — is both Sustainer and Destroyer, is Annihilator of evil spirits and Protector of angels.

55. I bow to Him Who — is Healer of disease, and Bestower of love, is Sovereign of sovereigns, and Commander of commanders.

56. I bow to Him Who —
is Supreme Bestower of gifts and honours,
is the Dispeller of maladies and Symbol of purification.

57. I bow to Him Who — is the Divinity of the divine words, is the Master of mystic charms, is the God of gods and Master of all occult powers.

58. I bow to Him Who — is eternal, ever truthful and God of death, is formless yet all beautiful and pervades in all.

59. I bow to Him Who — is ever spiritual, intellectual and Bestower of all powers, is present in the sky, in the netherland and on the earth, is the Destroyer of all the sins.

60. I bow to Him Who — is the Supreme Lord, is invisible and is the sole Sustainer of this universe, is the great Master and is the Treasure of all the wisdom.

61. I bow to Him who — is impregnable, mysterious, has no name, is beyond karmas, is invincible, and is present at all the places.

Summary

God is the source of all our possessions and belongings. He is both matter and spirit by whatever name called. He lives in heavens but is present in all of us at the same time. He is the Controller of our destinies, shapes, forms and beauty. He is invisible but can be seen by the true devotees. His voice is not audible but can be heard by the real believers. He is the Emperor of emperors, Sovereign of sovereigns, Commander of commanders. There is no one equal to Him.

ਤੇਰਾ ਜੋਰੁ ॥ ਚਾਚਰੀ ਛੰਦ ॥

ਜਲੇ¹ ਹੈਂ ॥ ਥਲੇ² ਹੈਂ ॥ ਅਭੀਤ³ ਹੈਂ ॥ ਅਭੇ⁴ ਹੈਂ ॥੬੨॥
ਪ੍ਰਭੂ⁵ ਹੈਂ ॥ ਅਜੂ⁶ ਹੈਂ ॥ ਅਦੇਸ⁷ ਹੈਂ ॥ ਅਭੇਸ⁸ ਹੈਂ ॥੬੩॥

TERA JOR(U), CHACHRI CHHAND

Jale[1] hain. Thale[2] hain. Abhit[3] hain. Abhe[4] hain. -62-
Prabhu[5] hain. Aju[6] hain. Ades[7] hain. Abhes[8] hain. -63-

TERA JOR CHACHRI CHHAND
THROUGH YOUR POWER

Notes

[1]creator of water; [2] creator of land [3] beyond worldly fears; [4] impossible to apprehend [5] lord; [6] truth, permanent; [7] omnipresent; [8] does not recognise/recommend any specific uniform or dress.

COMPOSITION 5

Theme:

God is great. He is the Creator of all oceans, mountains and lands. He is above all garbs and boundaries.

Literal Meaning

62. He is the Creator of all oceans, seas, rivers and streams;
    He is the Creator of all lands, mountains, deserts and vegetation;
    He is beyond worldly fears and His creation is full with mysteries.

63. He is the great Lord;
    He is the Truth;
    He is Omnipresent;
    He accepts all sort of garbs.

Summary

God, the Lord is the Designer of the whole universe. He has created everything which exists here. He is omnipresent and omnipotent and there is no one equal to Him.

ਭੁਜੰਗ ਪ੍ਰਯਾਤ ਛੰਦ ॥ ਤ੍ਰਿਪਸਾਦਿ ॥

ਅਗਾਧੇ[1] ਅਬਾਧੇ[2] ॥ ਅਨੰਦੀ[3] ਸਰੂਪੇ[4] ॥
ਨਮੋ[5] ਸਰਬ[6] ਮਾਨੇ[7] ॥ ਸਮਸਤੀ[8] ਨਿਧਾਨੇ[9] ॥੬੪॥
ਨਮਸਤ੍ਰੰ[10] ਨ੍ਰਿਨਾਥੇ[11] ॥ ਨਮਸਤ੍ਰੰ ਪ੍ਰਮਾਥੇ[12] ॥
ਨਮਸਤੰ[13] ਅਗੰਜੇ[13] ॥ ਨਮਸਤੰ ਅਭੰਜੇ[14] ॥੬੫॥
ਨਮਸਤੰ[15] ਅਕਾਲੇ[15] ॥ ਨਮਸਤੰ ਅਪਾਲੇ[16] ॥
ਨਮੋ ਸਰਬ[17] ਦੇਸੇ[18] ॥ ਨਮੋ ਸਰਬ ਭੇਸੇ[19] ॥੬੬॥
ਨਮੋ ਰਾਜ[20] ਰਾਜੇ[21] ॥ ਨਮੋ ਸਾਜ[22] ਸਾਜੇ[23] ॥
ਨਮੋ ਸ਼ਾਹ[24] ਸ਼ਾਹੇ[25] ॥ ਨਮੋ ਮਾਹ[26] ਮਾਹੇ[27] ॥੬੭॥
ਨਮੋ ਗੀਤ[28] ਗੀਤੇ[29] ॥ ਨਮੋ ਪ੍ਰੀਤ[30] ਪ੍ਰੀਤੇ[31] ॥
ਨਮੋ ਰੋਖ[32] ਰੋਖੇ[33] ॥ ਨਮੋ ਸੋਖ[34] ਸੋਖੇ[35] ॥੬੮॥
ਨਮੋ ਸਰਬ ਰੋਗੇ[36] ॥ ਨਮੋ ਸਰਬ ਭੋਗੇ[37] ॥
ਨਮੋ ਸਰਬ ਜੀਤੰ[38] ॥ ਨਮੋ ਸਰਬ ਭੀਤੰ[39] ॥੬੯॥
ਨਮੋ ਸਰਬ ਗਿਆਨੰ[40] ॥ ਨਮੇ ਪਰਮ ਤਾਨੰ[41] ॥
ਨਮੋ ਸਰਬ ਮੰਤ੍ਰੰ[42] ॥ ਨਮੋ ਸਰਬ ਜੰਤ੍ਰੰ[43] ॥੭੦॥
ਨਮੋ ਸਰਬ ਦ੍ਰਿਸੰ[44] ॥ ਨਮੋ ਸਰਬ ਕ੍ਰਿਸੰ[45] ॥
ਨਮੋ ਸਰਬ ਰੰਗੇ[46] ॥ ਤ੍ਰਿਭੰਗੀ[47] ਅਨੰਗੇ[48] ॥੭੧॥
ਨਮੋ ਜੀਵ[49] ਜੀਵੰ[50] ॥ ਨਮੋ ਬੀਜ[51] ਬੀਜੇ[52] ॥
ਅਖਿਜੇ[53] ਅਭਿਜੇ[54] ॥ ਸਮਸਤੰ[55] ਪ੍ਰਸਿਜੇ[56] ॥੭੨॥
ਕ੍ਰਿਪਾਲੰ[57] ਸਰੂਪੇ[58] ਕੁਕਰਮੰ[59] ਪ੍ਰਨਾਸੀ[60] ॥
ਸਦਾ[61] ਸਰਬਦਾ[62] ਰਿਧਿ[63] ਸਿੱਧੰ[64] ਨਿਵਾਸੀ[65] ॥੭੩॥

BHUJANG PRAYAT CHHAND

Agadhe[1] abadhe[2]. Anandi[3] sarupe[4].
Namo[5] sarab[6] mane[7]. Samasti[8] nidhane[9]. -64-
Namastang[10] nrinathe[11]. Namastang pramathe[12].
Namastnag aganje[13]. Namastang abhanje[14]. -65-
Namastang akale[15]. Namastang apale[16].
Namo sarab[17] dese[18]. Namo sarab bhese[19]. -66-
Namo raj[20] raje[21]. Namo saj[22] saje[23].
Namo shah[24] shahe[25]. Namo mah[26] mahe[27]. -67-
Namo git[28] gite[29]. Namo prit[30] prite[31].
Namo rokh[32] rokhe[33]. Namo sokh[34] sokhe[35]. -68-
Namo sarab roge[36]. Namo sarab bhoge[37].
Namo sarab jitang[38]. Namo sarab bhitang[39]. -69-
Namo sarab gianang[40]. Namo param tanang[41].
Namo sarab mantrang[42]. Namo sarab jantrang[43]. -70-
Namo sarab drisang[44]. Namo sarab krisang[45].
Namo sarab range[46]. Tribhangi[47] anange[48]. -71-
Namo jiv[49] jivang[50]. Namo bij[51] bije[52].
Akhije[53] abhije[54]. Samastang[55] prasije[56]. -72-
Kripalang[57] Sarupe[58], kukarmang[59] pranasi[60].
Sada[61] sarab[62] da ridh(i)[63] sidhang[64] nivasi[65]. -73-

BHUJANG PRAYAT CHHAND

Notes

[1]unfathomable; [2]free from bondage; [3]blissful, happy; [4]form; [5]salutation; [6]all; [7]belief; [8]all; [9]treasures; [10]I salute; [11]master of his own; [12]destroyer of evil; [13]immortal; [14]indestructible; [15]beyond death; [16]self-sustained; [17-18]present everywhere, omnipresent; [19]uniform, garb, wearing; [20-21]king of kings; [22-23]beauty of the nature, splendour of the universe; [24-25]lord of all sovereigns; [26-27]light of all moons; [28-29]lyric of songs; [30-31]throb of love; [32-33]controller of destruction; [34-35]designer of destruction; [36]cure of diseases; [37]pleasure of consumption; [38]joy of victories; [39]the scare of awe; [40]the source of all knowledge; [41]the source of power; [42]the spirituality of hymns; [43-45]the totality of mystic charms; [46]the beauty of colours; [47]the destroyer of the three worlds; [48]formless; [49-50]the life giver; [51-52]the sprout of seeds; [53]. calm; [54]detached; [55]for all; [56]benevolent, kind; [57]compassionate; [58]embodiment; [59]sins; [60]destroyer; [61]always; [62]of all; [63]wealth; [64]spiritual power; [65]the source of.

Theme

I salute to the all Powerful God for His benevolence, compassion, mercy, perfection, generosity and magnanimity.

Literal Meaning

64. God is unfathomable, free of all bondages and is always happy. I bow to Him Who — is the focus of all the worship and the belief, and Who is the source of all treasures and bounties.

65. I bow to Him Who — is the Master of His Own, the Destroyer of evil, immortal and indestructible.

66. I bow to Him Who — is beyond death, self-sustained, omnipresent and accepts all type of dresses.

67. I bow to Him Who — is the King of kings, Beauty of the entire nature, Lord of all the sovereigns, Light of all the moons.

68. I salute to Him Who — is the Lyric of songs, Throb of love, Controller of destruction, and Designer of deaths.

69. I bow to Him Who — is the Dispeller of all the diseases, Pleasure of all the consumption, Joy of all the victories, and Scare of all the awes.

70. I salute to Him Who — is the Source of all the knowledge, Root of all the power, Spirituality of all the hymns, and Totality of all the mystic powers.

71. I salute to Him Who — is the Guardian of all, Mode of attraction of all, Beauty of all the colours and ultimate, Destroyer of all that exists.

72. I bow to Him Who — is formless, the Life-giver, the Sprout of all the seeds, and ever calm, detached and benevolent.

73. He is the Embodiment of compassion, He is the Destroyer of all the sins, and He is the Eternal Source of all the wealth and powers.

Summary

We all must bow and salute to the Great Lord God Who is the Source of all the light and energy. He Himself is the Creator, Sustainer and Destroyer. He has designed all the worlds in this universe. He gives lyric, tune, melody and rhythm to all that exists. He is the Creator of all the arts, skills and knowledge. He is merciful and compassionate. He is the Master of all the treasures and gifts and distributes them to all of us according to our actions. He is the Ultimate Judge of all our deeds.

ਚਰਪਟ ਛੰਦ ॥ ਤ੍ਵ ਪ੍ਰਸਾਦਿ ॥

ਅੰਮ੍ਰਿਤ^1 ਕਰਮੇ^{2} ॥ ਅੰਬ੍ਰਿਤ^3 ਧਰਮੇ^{4} ॥
ਅਖੱਲ^5 ਜੋਗੇ^{6} ॥ ਅਚੱਲ^7 ਭੋਗੇ^{8} ॥੭੪॥
ਅਚੱਲ ਰਾਜੇ^{9} ॥ ਅਟੱਲ^{10} ਸਾਜੇ^{11} ॥
ਅਖੱਲ ਧਰਮੇ^{12} ॥ ਅਲਖੑ ਕਰਮੇ^{13} ॥੭੫॥
ਸਰਬੰ^{14} ਦਾਤਾ^{15} ॥ ਸਰਬੰ ਗਾਜਾਤਾ^{16} ॥
ਸਰਬੰ ਭਾਨੇ^{17} ॥ ਸਰਬੰ ਮਾਨੇ^{18} ॥੭੬॥
ਸਰਬੰ ਪ੍ਰਾਣੰ^{19} ॥ ਸਰਬੰ ਤ੍ਰਾਣੰ^{20} ॥
ਸਰਬੰ ਭੁਗਤਾ^{21} ॥ ਸਰਬੰ ਜੁਗਤਾ^{22} ॥੭੭॥
ਸਰਬੰ ਦੇਵੰ^{23} ॥ ਸਰਬੰ ਭੇਵੰ^{24} ॥
ਸਰਬੰ ਕਾਲੇ^{25} ॥ ਸਰਬੰ ਪਾਲੇ^{26} ॥੭੮॥

CHARPAT CHHAND, TAVPRASAD(I)

Amrit^1 karme^2. Anbrit^3 dharme^4. Akhal^5 Joge^6. Achal^7 bhoge^8. -74-
Achal raje^9. Atal^{10} saje^{11}.
Akhal dharmang^{12}. Alakh karmang^{13}. -75-
Sarbang^{14} data^{15}. Sarbang giata^{16}.
Sarbang bhane^{17}. Sarbang mane^{18}. -76-
Sarbang pranang^{19}. Sarbang tranang^{20}.
Sarbang bhugta^{21}. Sarbang jugta^{22}. -77-
Sarbang devang^{23}. Sarbang bhevang^{24}.
Sarbang kale^{25}. Sarbang pale^{26}. -78-

CHARPAT CHHAND
BY YOUR GRACE

Notes

[1]immortal; [2]deeds; [3]immutable; [4]laws; [5]constant; [6]detachment; [7]perennial; [8]bliss; [9]authority, rule; [10]everlasting; [11]creation; [12]laws; [13]deeds; [14]of everyone; [15]giver; [16]omniscient; [17]light; [18]adoration; [19]life; [20]protector, vitality; [21]sustainer, reveller; [22]guide ; [23]lord of angels; [24]mysterious; [25]beyond death; [26]preserver.

COMPOSITION 7

Theme

God's laws are not subject to commentary; they are immortal.

Literal Meaning

74. God's actions are not subject to debates, they are immortal, His laws are immutable, He is ever detached, His bliss is perennial.

75. His kingdom is perpetual, His creation is everlasting, His rules are universal, His actions are indescribable.

76. He is the Giver of all the bounties, He is omniscient, He is the Source of light, He is the focal point of worship.

77. He is the Fountainhead of all the life, He is the Protector of all, He is the King of kings, He is the Friend of all.

78. He is the Lord of all the gods, He is the Creator of all the mysteries of nature, He is the Cause of all the deaths, He is the Spring of all the lives.

Summary

Life and death are the rules of nature. Whosoever is born or created has to die and perish. The Almighty God controls all the movements, happenings, actions, changes, motions and developments in this universe. He is the cause of all the effects. No one is allowed to question or interfere in His laws.

ਰੁਆਲ ਛੰਦ ॥ ਤ੍ਰਪ੍ਰਸਾਦਿ ॥

ਆਦਿ[1] ਰੂਪ[2] ਅਨਾਦਿ[3] ਮੂਰਤਿ[4] ਅਜੋਨਿ[5] ਪੁਰਖ[6] ਅਪਾਰ[7] ॥

ਸਰਬ[8] ਮਾਨ[9] ਤ੍ਰਿਮਾਨ[10] ਦੇਵ[11] ਅਭੇਵ[12] ਆਦਿ[13] ਉਦਾਰ[14] ॥

ਸਰਬ[15] ਪਾਲਕ[16] ਸਰਬ ਘਾਲਕ[17] ਸਰਬ ਕੋ ਪੁਨਿ[18] ਕਾਲ[19] ॥

ਜਤ੍ਰ[20] ਤਤ੍ਰ[21] ਬਿਰਾਜਹੀ[22-23] ਅਵਧੂਤ[24] ਰੂਪ[25] ਰਸਾਲ[26] ॥੭੯॥

ਨਾਮ[27] ਠਾਮ[28] ਨ ਜਾਤ[29] ਜਾਕਰਿ[30] ਰੂਪ[31] ਰੰਗ[32] ਨ ਰੇਖ[33] ॥

ਆਦਿ[34] ਪੁਰਖ[35] ਉਦਾਰ[36] ਮੂਰਤਿ[37] ਅਜੋਨਿ[38] ਆਦਿ[39] ਅਸੇਖ[40] ॥

ਦੇਸ[41] ਅਉਰ[42] ਨ[43] ਭੇਸ[44] ਜਾਕਰਿ[45] ਰੂਪ[46] ਰੇਖ[47] ਨ ਰਾਗ[48] ॥

ਜਤ੍ਰ[49] ਤਤ੍ਰ[50] ਦਿਸਾ[51] ਵਿਸਾ[52] ਹੁਇ[53] ਫੈਲਿਓ[54] ਅਨੁਰਾਗ[55] ॥੮੦॥

ਨਾਮ[56] ਕਾਮ[57] ਬਿਹੀਨ[58] ਪੇਖਤ[59] ਧਾਮ[60] ਨੂੰ[61] ਨਹਿ[62] ਜਾਹਿ[63] ॥

ਸਰਬ[64] ਮਾਨ[65] ਸਰਬਤ੍ਰ[66] ਮਾਨ[67] ਸਦੈਵ[68] ਮਾਨਤ[69] ਤਾਹਿ[70] ॥

ਏਕ[71] ਮੂਰਤਿ[72] ਅਨੇਕ[73] ਦਰਸਨ[74] ਕੀਨ[75] ਰੂਪ[76] ਅਨੇਕ[77] ॥

ਖੇਲ[78] ਖੇਲ[79] ਅਖੇਲ[80] ਖੇਲਨ[81] ਅੰਤ[82] ਕੋ ਫਿਰਿ[83] ਏਕ[84] ॥੮੧॥

ਦੇਵ[85] ਭੇਵ[86] ਨ ਜਾਨਹੀ[87] ਜਿਹ[88] ਬੇਦ[89] ਅਉਰ ਕਤੇਬ[90] ॥

ਰੂਪ[91] ਰੰਗ[92] ਨ ਜਾਤਿ[93] ਪਾਤਿ[94] ਸੁ[95] ਜਾਨਈ[96] ਕਿਹ ਜੇਬ[97] ॥

ਤਾਤ[98] ਮਾਤ[99] ਨ ਜਾਤ[100] ਜਾਕਰਿ ਜਨਮ[101] ਮਰਨ[102] ਬਿਹੀਨ[103] ॥

ਚੱਕ੍ਰ-ਬੱਕ੍ਰ[104-105] ਫਿਰੈ[106] ਚਤੁਰ[107] ਚੱਕ[108] ਮਾਨਹੀ[109] ਪੁਰ[110] ਤੀਨ[111] ॥੮੨॥

ਲੋਕ[112] ਚਉਦਹ[113] ਕੇ ਬਿਖੈ[114] ਜਗ[115] ਜਾਪਹੀ[116] ਜਿਹ[117] ਜਾਪ[118] ॥

ਆਦਿ[119] ਦੇਵ[120] ਅਨਾਦਿ[121] ਮੂਰਤਿ[122] ਥਾਪਿਓ[123] ਸਭੈ[124] ਜਿਹ ਥਾਪਿ[125] ॥

ਪਰਮ[126] ਰੂਪ[127] ਪੁਨੀਤ[128] ਮੂਰਤਿ[129] ਪੂਰਨ[130] ਪੁਰਖ[131] ਅਪਾਰ[132] ॥

ਸਰਬ[133] ਬਿਸ੍ਵ[134] ਰਚਿਓ[135] ਸੁਯੰਭਵ[136] ਗੜਨ[137] ਭੰਜਨਹਾਰ[138-139] ॥੮੩॥

ਕਾਲਹੀਨ[140-141] ਕਲਾ[142] ਸੰਜੁਗਤਿ[143] ਅਕਾਲ[144] ਪੁਰਖ[145] ਅਦੇਸ[146] ॥

RUAL CHHAND, TAV PRASAD(I)

Ad(i)[1] *rup*[2] *anad(i)*[3] *murat(i)*[4], *ajon(i)*[5] *purakh*[6] *apar*[7].

Sarab[8] *man*[9] *triman*[10] *dev,*[11] *abhev*[12] *ad(i)*[13] *udar*[14].

Sarab[15] *palak*[16] *sarab ghalak*[17], *sarab ko pun(i)*[18] *kal*[19].

Jatr[20] *tatr*[21] *biraj-hi*[22-23], *avdhut*[24] *rup*[25] *rasal*[26]. -79-

Nam[27] *tham2*[28] *na jat(i)*[29] *jakar(i)*[30], *rup*[31] *rang*[32] *na rekh*[33].

Ad(i)[34] *purakh*[35] *udar*[36] *murat(i)*[37], *ajon(i)*[38] *ad(i)*[39] *asekh*[40].

Des[41] *aur*[42] *na*[43] *bhes*[44] *jakar(i)*[45], *rup*[46] *rekh*[47] *na rag*[48].

Jatr[49] *tatr*[50] *disa*[51] *visa*[52], *hue*[53] *phaileo*[54] *anurag*[55]. -80-

Nam[56] *kam*[57] *bihin*[58] *pekhat*[59], *dham*[60] *hun*[61] *nah(i)*[62] *jah(i)*[63].

Sarab[64] *man*[65] *sarbatr*[66] *man*[67], *sadaiv*[68] *manat*[69] *tah(i)*[70].

Ek[71] *murat(i)*[72] *anek*[73] *darsan*[74], *kin*[75] *rup*[76] *anek*[77].

Khel[78] *khel*[79] *akhel*[80] *khelan*[81], *ant*[82] *ko phir(i)*[83] *ek*[84]. -81-

Dev[85] *bhev*[86] *na janhi*[87], *jeh*[88] *bed*[89] *aur kateb*[90].

Rup[91] *rang*[92] *na jat(i)*[93], *pat(i)*[94] *su*[95] *janii*[96] *keh jeb*[97].

Tat[98] *mat*[99] *na jat*[100] *jakar(i)*, *janam*[101] *maran*[102] *bihin*[103].

Chakar[104] *bakar*[105] *phirai*[106] *chatur*[107] *chak*[108] *man-hi*[109] *pur*[110] *tin*[111]. -82-

Lok[112] *chaudah*[113] *ke bikhai*[114], *jag*[115] *japahi*[116] *jeh*[117] *jap*[118].

Ad(i)[119] *dev*[120] *anad(i)*[121] *murat(i),*[122] *thapio*[123] *sabai*[124] *jeh thap(i)*[125].

Param[126] *rup*[127] *punit*[128] *murat(i)*[129], *puran*[130] *purakh*[131] *apar*[132].

Sarab[133] *bisv*[134] *rachio*[135] *soyambhav*[136], *garan*[137] *bhanjan har*[138-139]. -83-

Kal[140] *hin*[141] *kala*[142] *sanjugat(i)*[143] *akal*[144] *purakh*[145] *ades*[146].

RUAL CHHAND
BY YOUR GRACE

Notes

[1]first; [2]person, being; [3]without; [4]a beginning; [5]unborn; [6]omnipresent; [7]infinite [8]all; [9]honour; [10]three levels of worlds; [11]gods; [12]mysterious; [13]first; [14]generous; [15]. all; [16]sustainer; [17]destroyer; [18]ultimate; [19]death; [20-21]everywhere; [22-23]reside; [24]detached; [25]form; [26]joy, bliss; [27]name; [28]residence; [29]caste; [30]whose; [31]beauty; [32]colour; [33]lineage; [34]primal, first; [35]omnipresent; [36]generous; [37]form; [38]unborn; [39]first; [40]perfect, complete; [41]area; [42]and; [43] neither; [44]garb; [45]his; [46]beauty; [47]lineage; [48]attachment; [49-50]everywhere; [51]direction; [52]place; [53-54]pervading; [55]embodiment of love; [56]name; [57]deeds; [58]without; [59]to watch; [60-61]is his abode; [62]no; [63]place; [64]all; [65]honour; [66]by all; [67]respect; [68]always; [69]believe-in; [70]you; [71-72]only one; [73]many; [74]audience; [75]manifest; [76]beauty; [77]many; [78]perform; [79]actions; [80]destroys; [81] actions; [82]at the end; [83]again; [84]one; [85]gods; [86]mystery; [87]do not know; [88]nor; [89]*Vedas*; [90]*Koran*; [91]beauty; [92]colour; [93]caste; [94]lineage; [95-96]they do not know; [97]features; [98]father; [99]mother; [100]caste; [101]birth; [102]death; [103]beyond; [104]the movement of time; [105]terrible, fearful; [106]moving; [107]four; [108] directions; [109]all believe in; [110-111]the three worlds, all the regions; [112]worlds; [113]fourteen (according to Hindu scriptures there are 14 worlds, 7 above in the space and 7 under the earth); [114]in them; [115]the people; [116]recite, chant; [117]God's; [118]prayer, invocation; [119]first, primal; [120]God; [121]without beginning; [122]form; [123]has created and sustained; [124]all; [125]sustain; [126]supreme; [127]beauty; [128]holy; [129]form, existence; [130]complete, perfect; [131]omnipresent; [132]infinite; [133]all; [134]universe; [135]created; [136]all himself; [137]to create; [138]to destroy; [139]He does it; [140]death; [141]beyond; [142]skill; [143]perfect; [144]beyond death; [145]omnipresent; [146]beyond regions.

COMPOSITION 8

Theme

God is beyond time. He Himself is the Creator, Sustainer and the Destroyer. He is the Master of all the worlds in the universe. He in His abstract form lives in His own abode and in His manifest form resides in all of us.

Literal Meaning

79.   He is —
      the First Person, without a beginning, unborn, omnipresent and infinite. All worship Him.
      He is —
      God of all the worlds, mysterious, primal and generous. the Sustainer of all, the Destroyer of all, the Ultimate Death of all.
      He is —
      Omnipresent, resides everywhere, detached, and the embodiment of happiness.

80.   He has —
      no name, abode, caste, colour and lineage.
      He is —
      the First Person, generous being, unborn, primal and perfect.
      He has —
      no region, no uniform, no features and no form. He is detached.
      He is manifest everywhere and His spirit and love exists in all the known directions.

81.   He is —
      beyond names and karmas, He himself is invisible but is watching His creation all the time.
      He is —
      admired and honoured by all and worshipped by all.
      He is —
      One Reality, manifest in all and has infinite forms. He performs many games, He destroys many games, But He Himself is one.

82.   He is full of suspense,
      No *Vedas* or *Korans* could unfold His mystery. No one can describe His beauty, colour, caste, lineage and features. He has no father or mother. He is beyond births and deaths. The speed of time moves in its own preset velocity, and He is worshipped in all the regions and worlds.

ਧਰਮ[147] ਧਾਮ[148] ਸੁ ਭਰਮ[149] ਰਹਿਤ[150] ਅਭੂਤ[151] ਅਲਖ[152] ਅਭੇਸ[153] ॥

ਅੰਗ[154] ਰਾਗ[155] ਨ ਰੰਗ[156] ਜਾਕਹਿ[157] ਜਾਤਿ[158] ਪਾਤਿ[159] ਨ ਨਾਮ[160] ॥

ਗਰਬ[161] ਗੰਜਨ[162] ਦੁਸਟ[163] ਭੰਜਨ[164] ਮੁਕਤਿ[165] ਦਾਇਕ[166] ਕਾਮ[167] ॥੮੪॥

ਆਪ[168] ਰੂਪ[169] ਅਮੀਕ[170] ਅਨਉਸਤਤਿ[171] ਏਕਪੁਰਖ[172] ਅਵਧੂਤ[173] ॥

ਗਰਬ[174] ਗੰਜਨ[175] ਸਰਬ[176] ਭੰਜਨ[177] ਆਦਿ[178] ਰੂਪ[179] ਅਸੂਤ[180] ॥

ਅੰਗ[181] ਹੀਨ[182] ਅਭੰਗ[183] ਅਨਾਤਮ[184] ਏਕ[185] ਪੁਰਖ[186] ਅਪਾਰ[187] ॥

ਸਰਬ[188] ਲਾਇਕ[189] ਸਰਬ ਘਾਇਕ[190] ਸਰਬ ਕੋ ਪ੍ਰਤਿਪਾਰ[191] ॥੮੫॥

ਸਰਬ ਗੀਤਾ[192] ਸਰਬ ਹੰਤਾ[193] ਸਰਬ ਤੇ ਅਨਭੇਖ[194] ॥

ਸਰਬ ਸਾਸਤ੍ਰ[195] ਨ[196] ਜਾਨਹੀ[197] ਜਿਹ[198] ਰੂਪ[199] ਰੰਗ[200] ਅਰੁ ਰੇਖ[201] ॥

ਪਰਮ[202] ਬੇਦ[203] ਪੁਰਾਣ[204] ਜਾਕਹਿ[205] ਨੇਤ[206] ਭਾਖਤ[207] ਨਿਤ[208] ॥

ਕੋਟਿ[209] ਸਿਮ੍ਰਿਤ[210] ਪੁਰਾਨ[211] ਸਾਸਤ੍ਰ[212] ਨ ਆਵਈ[213] ਵਹੁ[214] ਚਿਤ[215] ॥੮੬॥

Dharam[147] dham[148] su bharam[149] rehat[150], abhut[151] alakh[152] abhes[153].
Ang[154] rag[155] na rang[156] jakeh[157], jat(i)[158] pat(i)[159] na nam[160].
Garab[161] ganjan[162] dust[163] bhanjan[164], mukat(i)[165] daik[166] kam[167]. -84-
Ap[168] rup[169] amik[170] an ustat(i)[171], ek purakh[172] avdhut[173].
Garab[174] ganjan[175] sarab[176] bhanjan,[177] ad(i)[178] rup[179] asut[180].
Ang[181] hin[182] abhang[183] anatam[184], ek[185] purakh[186] apar[187].
Sarab[188] laik[189] sarab ghaik[190], sarab ko pratipar[191]. -85-
Sarab ganta[192] sarab hanta[193], sarab te anbhekh[194].
Sarab sastr[195] na[196] janhi[197] jeh[197] rup[198] rang(u)[199] ar(u)[200] rekh[201].
Param[202] bed[203] puran[204] ja keh[205], net[206] bhakhat[207] nit[208].
Kot(i)[209] simirat[210] puran[211] sastr,[212] na avii[213] voh[214] chit[215]. -86-

147-148the abode of law; 149which is; 150superstitions; 151incorporeal; 152invisible; 157whose; 158caste; 159lineage; 160name; 161pride; 162destroyer; 163evil; 164annihilator; 165 liberation; 166 deliverer; 167actions; 168-169self-illuminated; 170great, beyond praise; 171glorification; 172one reality; 173detached; 174pride; 175destroyer; 176all; 177annihilator; 178. prime; 179beauty; 180unborn; 181part of the body; 182without; 183beyond destruction; 184without soul; 185-186one reality; 187infinite; 188all; 189wise; 190killer; 191sustainer; 192one who reaches all; 193one who destroys all; 194one who is different from others; 195scriptures; 196-197knows not; 198his; 199beauty; 200colour; 201lineage; 202supreme; 203*Vedas;* 204*Puranas;* 205say about God; 206infinite; 207call Him; 208everyday; 209countless; 210scriptures; 211*Puranas;* 212scriptures; 213does not come; 214-215in the thoughts.

83. In the known fourteen worlds His prayers are being chanted,
He is —
the God of gods, the First Person and the Creator of the universe.
He has —
supreme form, holy existence. He is perfect, omnipresent and infinite. He resides everywhere, He Himself is the Creator and He Himself is the Destroyer.

84. He is —
beyond death, all perfect, beyond time, and omnipresent. His abode is religious and without superstitious structures, He is incorporeal, invisble and un-uniformed. His body is unattached, He Himself is beyond colours, castes, names and lineages. He is the Destroyer of pride, the Annihilator of evil and is the Deliverer of liberation.

85. He is —
self-existent the most honoured, full of wisdom and all pervading.
He is —
Killer of pride, the Destroyer of all, and the First Person and unborn.
He is —
incorporeal, imperishable, the spirit of all, and all pervading.
He is —
Omnipotent, the only Utimate Destroyer and the only Ultimate Sustainer.

86. He —
reaches everywhere, destroys all evil, is incomparable.
None of the religious scriptures know about His beauty, colour and lineage. The great *Vedas* and *Puranas* call Him infinite and eternal. Countless scriptures of Hindus and Muslims (the *Smritis* and *Koran*) affirm His existence and cannot describe Him.

Summary

The mystery around God exists since time immemorial. He created this world and many other worlds in this universe. He has made both life and death and is the sole Controller of these functions. Every world is created with a preset timetable. It will exist and be destroyed according to this schedule. He creates and destroys according to His designs and plans. The rules of the time, the life and the death, as we the humans know, apply only to us. The Almighty, Omnipresent and Omnipotent God is beyond these rules. He is the Maker of the rules and is not subject to them. The castes and the lineage, the names and the divisions are all man-made and God is beyond them. He is most merciful and kind. He is the Controller of all the divine rules and laws.

ਮਧੁਭਾਰ ਛੰਦ, ਤੂ ਪ੍ਰਸਾਦਿ ॥

ਗੁਨ[1] ਗਨ[2] ਉਦਾਰ[3] ॥ਮਹਿਮਾ[4] ਅਪਾਰ[5] ॥

ਆਸਨ[6] ਅਭੰਗ[7] ॥ਉਪਮਾ[8] ਅਨੰਗ[9] ॥੮੭॥

ਅਨਭਉ[10] ਪ੍ਰਕਾਸ[11] ॥ਨਿਸਦਿਨ[12-13] ਅਨਾਸ[14] ॥

ਆਜਾਨ[15] ਬਾਹੁ[16] ॥ਸਾਹਾਨ[17] ਸਾਹੁ[18] ॥੮੮॥

ਰਾਜਾਨ[19] ਰਾਜ[20] ॥ਭਾਨਾਨ[21] ਭਾਨ[22] ॥

ਦੇਵਾਨ[23] ਦੇਵ[24] ॥ਉਪਮਾ[25] ਮਹਾਨ[26] ॥੮੯॥

ਇਦ੍ਰਾਨ[27] ਇੰਦ੍ਰ[28] ॥ਬਾਲਾਨ[29] ਬਾਲ[30] ॥

ਰੰਕਾਨ[31] ਰੰਕ[32] ॥ਕਾਲਾਨ[33] ਕਾਲ[34] ॥੯੦॥

ਅਨਭੂਤ[35] ਅੰਗ[36] ॥ਆਭਾ[37] ਅਭੰਗ[38] ॥

ਗਤਿ[39] ਮਿਤਿ[40] ਅਪਾਰ[41] ॥ ਗੁਨ[42] ਗਨ[43] ਉਦਾਰ[44] ॥੯੧॥

ਮੁਨਿ[45] ਗਨ[46] ਪ੍ਰਨਾਮ[47] ॥ਨਿਰਭੈ[48] ਨਿਕਾਮ[49] ॥

ਅਤਿ[50] ਦੁਤਿ[51] ਪ੍ਰਚੰਡ[52] ॥ਮਿਤਿ[53] ਗਤਿ[54] ਅਖੰਡ[55] ॥੯੨॥

ਆਲਿਸਯ[56] ਕਰਮ[57] ॥ਆਦ੍ਰਿਸਯ[58] ਧਰਮ[59] ॥

ਸਰਬਾ[60] ਭਰਨਾਧਯ[61] ॥ਅਨਡੰਡ[62] ਬਾਧਯ[63] ॥੯੩॥

MADHUBHAR CHHAND, TAVPRASAD(I)

Gun[1] gan[2] udar[3]. Mehma[4] apar[5].

Asan[6] abhang[7]. Upma[8] anang[9]. -87-

Anbhau[10] prakas[11]. Nisdin[12-13] anas[14].

Ajan[15] bah(u)[16]. Sahan[17] sah(u)[18]. -88-

Rajan[19] raj[20]. Bhanan[21] bhan[22].

Devan[23] dev[24]. Upma[25] mahan[26]. -89-

Indran[27] indr[28]. Balan[29] bal[30].

Rankan[31] rank[32]. Kalan[33] kal[34]. -90-

Anbhut[35] ang[36]. Abha[37] abhang[38].

Gat(i)[39] mit(i)[40] apar[41]. Gun[42] gan[43] udar[44]. -91-

Mun(i)[45] gan[46] pranam[47]. Nirbhai[48] nikam[49].

At(i)[50] dut(i)[51] prachand[52]. Mit(i)[53] gat(i)[54] akhand[55]. -92-

Alisya[56] karam[57]. Adrisya[58] dharam[59].

Sarba[60] bharnadhya[61]. Andand[62] badhya[63]. -93-

MADHUBAR CHHAND
BY YOUR GRACE

Notes

[1]virtues; [2]pool, fountain; [3]generosity; [4]praises; [5]infinite; [6]throne, seat, existence; [7]unshakeable, irrefutable; [8]grace, greatness, praises; [9]incomparable, beyond words; [10]self-resplendent, self-illuminated; [11]light; [12]night; [13]day; [14]imperishable; [15]reproduction systems; [16]vest with God; [17-18]sovereign of sovereigns; [19-20]king of kings; [21-22]sun of suns; [23-24]God of gods; [25]praises; [26]great; [27-28]Indra of Indras; [29-30]highest of the highs; [31-32]poorest of the poor (humblest of the humble); [33-34]death of the deaths; [35]incorporeal; [36]parts of the body; [37]light, glory; [38]beyond destruction; [39]condition; [40]measurement; [41]infinite; [42]virtues; [43]pool, fountain; [44]generosity; [45]learned; [46]skilful; [47]salute; [48]without fear; [49]beyond worldly desires; [50]too much; [51]light; [52]resplendent; [53-54]beyond measurement and conditions; [55]indivisible; [56]special effort; [57]action; [58]invisible; [59]divine law; [60]all; [61]full, up to to the brim; [62]beyond punishment; [63]definite, unbound.

COMPOSITION 9

Theme

God is great; so are His virtues and bounties. He is self-illuminated and is the Master of the whole universe. He is revered by all the saints, kings and sovereigns.

Literal Meaning

87.   He is the Fountain of virtues and is most generous. His praises are beyond description. His throne is indestructable. His glory is incomparable.

88.   He is illuminated from his own light. His play of days merging with nights and nights dissolving in days is everlasting. He has devised innumerable methods of reproduction. He is the Sovereign of all the sovereigns.

89.   He showers supremacy to the kings. He gives energy to the suns. He provides holiness to the sages. His glory is great.

90.   He established the kingdom of Indra in the heavens. He gives power and courage to the soldiers. He provides humility to the meek. He determines the time of death of all.

91.   He has created the world lives with various elements but He Himself is beyond them. His glow is evershining. He is beyond measures and conditions. He is the Fountain of virtues and generosity.

92.   All sages salute Him. He performs His action without fear and reservations. His light is ever illuminated. His power and estate cannot be counted.

93.   He is not hesitant to perform His work. His rules are beyond questioning. He is ever merciful.

Summary

God is the Creater, Sustainer and Destroyer of all that exists in the universe. He creates when He so pleases and destroys when He so wishes. All world glories, powers and energies emanate from Him. He is the greatest of all and is lower to none. He creates and elevates and then destroys when the stipulated time comes. He is self-made and self-illuminated. He is a Power beyond description and analysis. His rules and laws are universal. He is most generous and merciful.

ਚਾਚਰੀ ਛੰਦ, ਤ੍ਵ ਪ੍ਰਸਾਦਿ॥

ਗੁਬਿੰਦੇ[1] ॥ ਮੁਕੰਦੇ[2] ॥ ਉਦਾਰੇ[3] ॥ ਅਪਾਰੇ[4] ॥੯੪॥

ਹਰੀਅੰ[6] ॥ ਕਰੀਅੰ[7] ॥ ਨ੍ਰਿਨਾਮੇ[8] ॥ ਅਕਾਮੇ[9] ॥੯੫॥

CHACHRI CHHAND, TAVPRASAD(I)

Gubinde[1]. *Mukande*[2]. *Udare*[3]. *Apare*[4]. -94-

Hariang[5]. *Kariang*[6]. *Nirname*[7]. *Akame*[8]. -95-

CHACHRI CHHAND
BY YOUR GRACE

Notes

[1]Lord of the universe, the caretaker of the creation; [2]the liberator; [3]the generous; [4]the infinite; [5]destroyer; [6]creator; [7]beyond names; [8]beyond passions, [9]beyond desires.

Theme

God of all people is the Sustainer and the Liberator.

Literal Meaning

94. God is —

the Omniscient, the Liberator, generous, and limitless.

95. God is —

the Destroyer, the Creator, He belongs to all people, and is beyond desires and passions.

Summary

God knows everyone's inner-thoughts. He is the only Master who grants *mukti*. He is the only Lord who controls both creation and destruction. He Himself is beyond all passions and desires. He is absolutely detached.

ਭੁਜੰਗ ਪ੍ਰਯਾਤ ਛੰਦ ।।

ਚੱਤ੍ਰੁ[1] ਚੱਕ੍ਰ[2] ਕਰਤਾ[3] ।। ਚੱਤ੍ਰੁ ਚੱਕ੍ਰ ਹਰਤਾ[4] ।।

ਚੱਤ੍ਰੁ ਚੱਕ੍ਰ ਦਾਨੇ[5] ।। ਚੱਤ੍ਰੁ ਚੱਕ੍ਰ ਜਾਨੇ[6] ।।੯੬।।

ਚੱਤ੍ਰੁ ਚੱਕ੍ਰ ਵਰਤੀ[7] ।। ਚੱਤ੍ਰੁ ਚੱਕ੍ਰ ਭਰਤੀ[8] ।।

ਚੱਤ੍ਰੁ ਚੱਕ੍ਰ ਪਾਲੇ[9] ।। ਚੱਤ੍ਰੁ ਚੱਕ੍ਰ ਕਾਲੇ[10] ।।੯੭।।

ਚੱਤ੍ਰੁ ਚੱਕ੍ਰ ਪਾਸੇ[11] ।। ਚੱਤ੍ਰੁ ਚੱਕ੍ਰ ਵਾਸੇ[12] ।।

ਚੱਤ੍ਰੁ ਚੱਕ੍ਰ ਮਾਨਯੈ[13] ।। ਚੱਤ੍ਰੁ ਚੱਕ੍ਰ ਦਾਨਯੈ[14] ।।੯੮।।

BHUJANG PRAYAT CHHAND

Chatr(u)[1] chakr[2] karta[3]. Chatr(u) chakr harta[4].

Chatr(u) chakr dane[5]. Chatr(u) chakr jane[6]. -96-

Chatr(u) chakr varti[7]. Chatr(u) chakr bharti[8].

Chatr(u) chakr pale[9]. Chatr(u) chakr kale[10]. -97-

Chatr(u) chakr pase[11]. Chatr(u) chakr vase[12].

Chatr(u) chakr manyai[13]. Chatr(u) chakr danyai[14]. -98-

BHUJANG PRAYAT CHHAND
BY YOUR GRACE

Notes

[1-2]the four directions; [3]creator; [4]destroyer; [5]the donor; [6]one who knows everyone and everything; [7]reside; [8]sustainer; [9]protector; [10]the cause of deaths; [11]present; [12]to reside; [13]to believe in; [14]bestower of bounties.

COMPOSITION 11

Theme

God is the Designer and Controller of all the activities around the universe.

Literal Meaning

96. He is the —
    Creator of the four corners of the universe,
    Destroyer of the four sides of the universe,
    Bestower of the bounties in all the directions of the universe.
    Knower of all the activities all around the globe.

97. He is —
    Omniexistent
    Omnisustainer
    Omniprotector
    Omnidestroyer

98. He is —
    present everywhere,
    resident everywhere,
    worshipped everywhere, and
    Bestower of His bounties everywhere.

Summary

God has created this universe according to His plans and designs. He is manifest in every atom. He is the Controller and Regulator of all the worlds. He is the cause of births and deaths, happiness and sorrows. He is the greatest of all. He is the Protector, Sustainer and Destroyer. We all must salute to Him.

ਚਾਚਰੀ ਛੰਦ ॥

ਨ[1] ਸਤ੍ਰੈ[2] ॥ ਨ ਮਿਤ੍ਰੈ[3] ॥ ਨ ਭਰਮੰ[4] ॥ ਨ ਭਿਤ੍ਰੈ[5] ॥੯੯॥
ਨ ਕਰਮੰ[6] ॥ ਨ ਕਾਏ[7] ॥ ਅਜਨਮੰ[8] ਅਜਾਏ[9] ॥੧੦੦॥
ਨ ਚਿਤ੍ਰੈ[10] ॥ ਨ ਮਿਤ੍ਰੈ[11] ॥ ਪਰੇ[12] ਹੈਂ[13] ॥ ਪਵਿਤ੍ਰੈ[14] ॥੧੦੧॥
ਪ੍ਰਿਥੀਸੈ[15] ॥ ਅਦੀਸੈ[16] ॥ ਅਦ੍ਰਿਸੈ[17] ॥ ਆਕ੍ਰਿਸੈ[18] ॥੧੦੨॥

CHACHRI CHHAND

Na[1] satrai[2]. Na mitrai[3]. Na bharmang[4]. Na bhitrai[5]. -99-
Na karmang[6]. Na kae[7] Ajanmang Ajae[8]. -100-
Na chitrai[10]. Na mitrai[11]. Pare[12] hain[13] Pavitrai[14]. -101-
Prithisai[15]. Adisai[16]. Adrisai[17]. Akrisai[18]. -102-

CHACHRI CHHAND
BY YOUR GRACE

Notes

[1] no; [2]enemy; [3]friends, relations; [4]delusion; [5]discrimination; [6]worldly actions; [7]body, form, figure; [8]beyond births; [9]beyond conception; [10]image; [11]friends, relations; [12-13]transcendent; [14]perfect, holy; [15]Lord of the universe; [16]primal being

COMPOSITION 12

Theme

God is Lord of the whole universe. He has no image and is not born.

Literal Meaning

99. God is detached from His creation. He has no relations or friends according to worldly definition. His acts are above discrimination and delusion.

100 He performs no karmas and is not judged, for He Himself is the Greatest Judge of all. He has no image, is not conceived or born.

101 He has no definite form, is detached, transcendent and holy.

102. He is the Lord of the universe, is the primal being, is invsible and is all-powerful.

Summary

God has created this world and many other worlds. He has made the rules of conception and birth, has made the law of karma, has put emotions and feeling in our hearts, but He Himself is above all these rules, laws and perceptions. Though He regulates His worlds yet He Himself is detached from the creation.

ਭਗਵਤੀ ਛੰਦ ॥ ਤੁਪ੍ਰਸਾਦਿ ਕਥਤੇ ॥

ਕਿ[1] ਆਭਿੱਜ[2] ਦੇਸੈ[3] ॥ ਕਿ ਆਭਿੱਜ[4] ਭੇਸੈ[5] ॥
ਕਿ ਆਗੰਜ[6] ਕਰਮੈ[7] ॥ ਕਿ ਆਭੰਜ[8] ਭਰਮੈ[9] ॥੧੦੩॥
ਕਿ ਆਭਿੱਜ[10] ਲੋਕੈ[11] ॥ ਕਿ ਆਦਿੱਤ[12] ਸੋਕੈ[13] ॥
ਕਿ ਅਵਧੂਤ[14] ਬਰਨੈ[15] ॥ ਕਿ ਬਿਭੂਤ[16] ਕਰਨੈ[17] ॥੧੦੪॥
ਕਿ ਰਾਜੰ[18] ਪ੍ਰਭਾ[19] ਹੈਂ ॥ ਕਿ ਧਰਮੰ[20] ਧੁਜਾ[21] ਹੈਂ ॥
ਕਿ ਆਸੋਕ[22] ਬਰਨੈ[23] ॥ ਕਿ ਸਰਬਾ[24] ਅਭਰਨੈ[25] ॥੧੦੫॥
ਕਿ ਜਗਤੰ[26] ਕ੍ਰਿਤੀ[27] ਹੈਂ ॥ ਕਿ ਛੱਤ੍ਰੰ[28] ਛੱਤ੍ਰੀ[29] ਹੈਂ ॥
ਕਿ ਬ੍ਰਹਮੰ[30] ਸਰੂਪੈ[31] ॥ ਕਿ ਅਨਭਉ[32] ਅਨੂਪੈ[33] ॥੧੦੬॥
ਕਿ ਆਦਿ[34] ਅਦੇਵ[35] ਹੈਂ ॥ ਕਿ ਆਪਿ[36] ਅਭੇਵ[37] ਹੈਂ ॥
ਕਿ ਚਿੱਤ੍ਰੰ[38] ਬਿਹੀਨੈ[39] ॥ ਕਿ ਏਕੈ[40] ਅਧੀਨੈ[41] ॥੧੦੭॥
ਕਿ ਰੋਜ਼ੀ[42] ਰਜ਼ਾਕੈ[43] ॥ ਰਹੀਮੈ[44] ਰਿਹਾਕੈ[45] ॥
ਕਿ ਪਾਕ[46] ਬਿਐਬ[47-48] ਹੈਂ ॥ ਕਿ ਗੈਬੁਲ[49] ਗੈਬ[50] ਹੈਂ ॥੧੦੮॥
ਕਿ ਅਫ਼ਵੁਲ[51] ਗੁਨਾਹ[52] ਹੈਂ ॥ ਕਿ ਸ਼ਾਹਾਨ[53] ਸ਼ਾਹ[54] ਹੈਂ ॥
ਕਿ ਕਾਰਨ[55] ਕੁਨਿੰਦ[56] ਹੈਂ ॥ ਕਿ ਰੋਜ਼ੀ[57] ਦਿਹੰਦ[58] ਹੈਂ ॥੧੦੯॥
ਕਿ ਰਾਜ਼ਕ[59] ਰਹੀਮ[60] ਹੈਂ ॥ ਕਿ ਕਰਮੰ[61] ਕਰੀਮ[62] ਹੈਂ ॥
ਕਿ ਸਰਬੰ[63] ਕਲੀ[64] ਹੈਂ ॥ ਕਿ ਸਰਬ[65] ਦਲੀ[66] ਹੈਂ ॥੧੧੦॥
ਕਿ ਸਰਬਤ੍ਰ[67] ਮਾਨਯੈ[68] ॥ ਕਿ ਸਰਬਤ੍ਰ ਦਾਨਯੈ[69] ॥
ਕਿ ਸਰਬਤ੍ਰ ਗਉਨੈ[70] ॥ ਕਿ ਸਰਬਤ੍ਰ ਭਉਨੈ[71] ॥੧੧੧॥
ਕਿ ਸਰਬਤ੍ਰ ਦੇਸੈ[72] ॥ ਕਿ ਸਰਬਤ੍ਰ ਭੇਸੈ[73] ॥
ਕਿ ਸਰਬਤ੍ਰ ਰਾਜੈ[74] ॥ ਕਿ ਸਰਬਤ੍ਰ ਸਾਜੈ[75] ॥੧੧੨॥
ਕਿ ਸਰਬਤ੍ਰ ਦੀਨੈ[76] ॥ ਕਿ ਸਰਬਤ੍ਰ ਲੀਨੈ[77] ॥
ਕਿ ਸਰਬਤ੍ਰ ਜਾਹੋ[78] ॥ ਕਿ ਸਰਬਤ੍ਰ ਭਾਹੋ[79] ॥੧੧੩॥

BHAGWATI CHHAND, TAV PRASAD(I) KATHATE

Ke[1] achhij[2] desai[3]. Ke abhij[4] bhesai[5].
Ke aganj[6] karmai[7]. Ke abhanj[8] bharmai[9]. -103-
Ke abhij[10] lokai[11]. Ke adit[12] sokai[13].
Ke avdhut[14] barnai[15]. Ke bibhut[16] karnai[17]. -104-
Ke rajang[18] prabha[19] hain. Ke dharmang[20] dhuja[21] hain.
Ke asok[22] barnai[23]. Ke sarba[24] abharnai[25]. -105-
Ke jagtang[26] kriti[27] hain. Ke chhatrang[28] chhatri[29] hain.
Ke brahamang[30] sarupai[31]. Ke anbhau[32] anupai[33]. -106-
Ke ad(i)[34] adev[35] hain. Ke ap(i)[36] abhev[37] hain.
Ke chitrang[38] bihinai[39]. Ke ekai[0] adhinai[41]. -107-
Ke rozi[42] razakai[43]. Rahimai[44] rihakai[45].
Ke pak[46] be-aib[47-48] hain. Ke ghaibul[49] ghaib[50] hain. -108-
Ke afvul[51] gunah[52] hain. Ke shahan[53] shah[54] hain.
Ke karan[55] kunind[56] hain. Ke rozi[57] dihand[58] hain. -109-
Ke razak[59] rahim[60] hain. Ke karmang[61] karim[62] hain.
Ke sarbang[63] kali[64] hain. Ke sarbang[65] dali[66] hain. -110-
Ke sarbatr[67] maniyai[68]. Ke sarbang daniyai[69].
Ke sarbatr gaunai[70]. Ke sarbatr bhaunai[71]. -111-
Ke sarbatr desai[72]. Ke sarbatr bhesai[73].
Ke sarbatr rajai[74]. Ke sarbatr sajai[75]. -112-
Ke sarbatr dinai[76]. Ke sarbatr linai[77].
Ke sarbatr jaho[78]. Ke sarbhatr bhaho[79]. -113-

BHAGWATI CHHAND
BY YOUR GRACE

Notes

[1]is; [2]cannot be torn; [3]realm, abode; [4]getting damaged by drenching, flooding; [5]garbs; [6]invincible; [7]actions; [8]un-obliterated; [9]superstitions; [10]flooding; [11]inhabitants; [12]the energy generated by the sun; [13]barren; [14]detached; [14]lineage, castes; [15]source; [16]to glorify; [17]to do; [18]kings'; [19]light, power; [20]religion, righteousness; [21]banner; [22]beyond worries; [23]form, existence; [24]all; [25]splendour; [26]universe; [27]creator; [28]strength, courage, power; [29]the fighter, the fighting cast of the Hindus; [30]the Creator; [31]form; [32]self illuminated; [33]. beyond praise; [34]. first; [35]who has no superior over him, supreme; [36]himself; [37]mysterious; [38]image, picture; [39]one who cannot be photographed; [40]himself; [41]governed; [42]livelihood; [43]giver, granter; [44]merciful; [45]liberator; [46]pure; [47-48]without any shortcoming; [49]invisible; [50]mystery; [51]one who can pardon; [52]sins; [53]supreme sovereign; [54]of sovereign; [55]cause; [56]the doer; [57]livelihood; [58]giver; [59]provider; [60]merciful; [61]of karmas, actions; [62]forgiver; [63]of all; [64]full of all powers; [65]of all; [66]the destroyer; [67]all; [68]believe in; [69]granter of the gifts; [70]one who can reach all parts of the world; [71]omnipresent; [72]all spheres; [73]garbs; [74]ruler; [75]decorator; [76]bestower of the gifts; [77]engross; [78]glow; [79]light

COMPOSITION 13

Theme
This world called earth is one of His many creations. He has created earth according to His own plans and designs. Every object He has creatd He has put an automatic processing component in it. The development and destruction of a life or an object is according to the programming of the component. Death for a life is as important as its birth and progression. God is the Greatest Reality on earth. He is beyond a name, caste, creed and colour. He is Father of all of us.

Literal Meaning

103. God's realm is beyond destructon, His garb is beyond damage, His actions are beyond defeat, and His existence is beyond any superstitions and rituals.

104. His realm's inhabitants do not suffer from worldly disasters, e.g., flooding and drought. He is the Source of all the glories.

105. He gives power to the kings, He protects those who assemble under the banner of a true religion, He is the Source of all the happines and light, and He is the Fountain of splendour and beauty.

106. He is the Creator of the universe, He is the Power of the soldiers, He is the Pimal Being, and His power is unparallel and can be measured only by contemplation.

107. He is the Superiormost Authority, His creation is full of mysteries and suspense, His identity cannot be shown by an image, He is self-illuminated.

108. He bestows livelihood upon all of us, He grants liberation of all of us, His identity cannot be shown by an image, He is self-illuminated.

109. He is the Forgiver of our sins, He is the Sovereign of all the rulers, He is the Cause of all the existence, and He is the Sustainer of His creation.

110. He is most merciful and gentle Provider, He is most benevolent and graceful Master, He is most powerful and absolutely complete with skills. He is the Annihilator and the Cause of destruction.

ਕਿ ਸਰਬਤ੍ਰ ਦੇਸੈ[80] ॥ ਕਿ ਸਰਬਤ੍ਰ ਭੇਸੈ[81] ॥
ਕਿ ਸਰਬਤ੍ਰ ਕਾਲੈ[82] ॥ ਕਿ ਸਰਬਤ੍ਰ ਪਾਲੈ[83] ॥੧੧੪॥
ਕਿ ਸਰਬਤ੍ਰ ਹੰਤਾ[84] ॥ ਕਿ ਸਰਬਤ੍ਰ ਗੰਤਾ[85] ॥
ਕਿ ਸਰਬਤ੍ਰ ਭੇਖੀ[86] ॥ ਕਿ ਸਰਬਤ੍ਰ ਪੇਖੀ[87] ॥੧੧੫॥
ਕਿ ਸਰਬਤ੍ਰ ਕਾਜੈ[88] ॥ ਕਿ ਸਰਬਤ੍ਰ ਰਾਜੈ[89] ॥
ਕਿ ਸਰਬਤ੍ਰ ਸੋਖੈ[90] ॥ ਕਿ ਸਰਬਤ੍ਰ ਪੋਖੈ[91] ॥੧੧੬॥
ਕਿ ਸਰਬਤ੍ਰ ਤ੍ਰਾਣੈ[92] ॥ ਕਿ ਸਰਬਤ੍ਰ ਪ੍ਰਾਣੈ[93] ॥
ਕਿ ਸਰਬਤ੍ਰ ਦੇਸੈ[94] ॥ ਕਿ ਸਰਬਤ੍ਰ ਭੇਸੈ[95] ॥੧੧੭॥
ਕਿ ਸਰਬਤ੍ਰ ਮਾਨਿਐ[96] ॥ ਸਦੈਵੰ ਪ੍ਰਧਾਨਿਐ[97] ॥
ਕਿ ਸਰਬਤ੍ਰ ਜਾਪਿਐ[98] ॥ ਕਿ ਸਰਬਤ੍ਰ ਥਾਪਿਐ[99] ॥੧੧੮॥
ਕਿ ਸਰਬਤ੍ਰ ਭਾਨੈ[100] ॥ ਕਿ ਸਰਬਤ੍ਰ ਮਾਨੈ[101] ॥
ਕਿ ਸਰਬਤ੍ਰ ਇੰਦੈ[102] ॥ ਕਿ ਸਰਬਤ੍ਰ ਚੰਦੈ[103] ॥੧੧੯॥
ਕਿ ਸਰਬੇ ਕਲੀਮੈ[104] ॥ ਕਿ ਪਰਮੇ ਫਹੀਮੈ[105] ॥
ਕਿ ਆਕਲ ਅਲਾਮੈ[106] ॥ ਕਿ ਸਾਹਿਬ ਕਲਾਮੈ[107] ॥੧੨੦॥
ਕਿ ਹੁਸਨਲ[108] ਵਜੂ[109] ਹੈਂ ॥ ਤਮਾਮੁਲ[110] ਰੁਜੂ[111] ਹੈਂ ॥
ਹਮੇਸੁਲ[112] ਸਲਾਮੈ[113] ॥ ਸਲੀਖਤ[114] ਮੁਦਾਮੈ[115] ॥੧੨੧॥
ਗਨੀਮੁਲ[116] ਸ਼ਿਕਸਤੇ[117] ॥ ਗਰੀਬੁਲ[118] ਪਰਸਤੇ[119] ॥
ਬਿਲੰਦੁਲ[120] ਮਕਾਨੈ[121] ॥ ਜ਼ਮੀਨੁਲ[122] ਜ਼ਮਾਨੈ[123] ॥੧੨੨॥
ਤਮੀਜ਼ੁਲ[124] ਤਮਾਮੈ[125] ॥ ਰੁਜ਼ੁਅਲ[126] ਨਿਧਾਨੈ[127] ॥
ਹਰੀਫ਼ੁਲ[128] ਅਜ਼ੀਮੈ[129] ॥ ਰਜ਼ਾਇਕ[130] ਯਕੀਨੈ[131] ॥੧੨੩॥
ਅਨੇਕੁਲ[132] ਤਰੰਗ[133] ਹੈਂ ॥ ਅਭੇਦ[134] ਹੈਂ ਅਭੰਗ[135] ਹੈਂ ॥
ਅਜ਼ੀਜ਼ੁਲ[136] ਨਿਵਾਜ਼[137] ਹੈਂ ॥ ਗਨੀਮੁਲ[138] ਖਿਰਾਜ[139] ਹੈਂ ॥੧੨੪॥
ਨਿਰੁਕਤਿ[140] ਸਰੂਪ[141] ਹੈਂ ॥ ਤ੍ਰਿਮੁਕਤਿ[142] ਬਿਭੂਤ[143] ਹੈਂ ॥
ਪ੍ਰਭੁਗਤਿ[144] ਪ੍ਰਭਾ[145] ਹੈਂ ॥ ਸੁਜੁਗਤਿ[146] ਸੁਧਾ[147] ਹੈਂ ॥੧੨੫॥

Ke sarbatr desai[80]. *Ke sarbatr bhesai*[81].
Ke sarbatr kalai[82]. *Ke sarbatr palai*[83]. -114-
Ke sarbatr hanta.[84] *Ke sarbatr ganta*[85].
Ke sarbatr bhekhi[86]. *Ke sarbatr pekhi*[87]. -115-
Ke sarbatr kajai[88]. *Ke sarbatr rajai*[89].
Ke sarbatr sokhai[90]. *Ke sarbatr pokhai*[91]. -116-
Ke sarbatr tranai[92]. *Ke sarbatr pranai*[93].
Ke sarbatr desai[94]. *Ke sarbatr bhesai*[95]. -117-
Ke sarbatr maniyai[96]. *sadaivang pradhaniyai*[97].
Ke sarbatr japiyai[98]. *Ke sarbatr thapiyai*[99]. -118-
Ke sarbatr bhanai[100]. *Ke sarbatr manai*[101].
Ke sarbatr indrai[102]. *Ke sarbatr chandrai*[103]. -119-
Ke sarbatr kalimai[104]. *Ke paramang fahimai*[105].
Ke akal alamai[106]. *Ke sahib kalamai*[107]. -120-
Ke husnal[108] *vaju*[109] *hain. Tamamul*[110] *ruju*[111] *hain.*
Hamesul[112] *slamai*[113]. *Salikhat*[114] *mudamai*[115]. -121-
Ghanimul[116] *shikastai*[117]. *Gharibul*[118] *prastai*[119].
Bilandul[120] *makanai*[121]. *Zaminul*[122] *zamanai*[123]. -122-
Tamizul[124] *tamamai*[125]. *Ruzual*[126] *nidhanai*[127].
Hariful[128] *azimai*[129]. *Razaik*[130] *yakinai*[131]. -123-
Anekul[132] *tarang*[133] *hain. Abhed*[134] *hain abhang*[135] *hain.*
Azizul[136] *nivaz*[137] *hain. Ghanimul*[138] *khiraj*[139] *hain.* -124-
Nirukat(i)[140] *sarup*[141] *hain. Trimukat(i)*[142] *bibhut*[143] *hain.*
Prabhugat(i)[144] *prabha*[145] *hain. Sujugat(i)*[146] *sudha*[147] *hain.* -125-

80regions; 81garbs; 82death; 83sustainer; 84destroyer; 85one who knows everything; 86manifest in all forms; 87onlooker, witness; 88. performer; 89ruler; 90destroyer; 91witness; 92the source of energy; 93the giver of the breath; 94regions; 95garbs; 96belief; 97supremacy; 98worship; 99to fix, to abide; 100sun; light, energy; 101belief; 102king of heaven; 103moon, light of moon, 104orator; 105supreme knowledge; 106wisest of all; 107the supreme orator; 108beauty; 109personified; 110all; 111attention; 112ever; 113salutation; 114process of creation; 115perpetual; 116enemy; 117defeat; 118poor; 119protection; 120high; 121houses; 122on the earth; 123time, all the time; 124etiquette; 125perfect; 126treasures; 127focus of attention; 128friend; 129great; 130provider; 131trustworthy; 132of different types; 133waves; 134mysterious; 135imperishable; 136-139destroyer, annihilator; 140indescribable; 141form; 142transcends three virtues-royalty, truth, meditation; 143glory; 144to consume; 145light; 146perfect setting; 147nectar of God's grace bathes all creatures

111. He is worshipped by all, He is given worldly gifts by all, He is called by all that exists in this world, and He is resident in everyone's mind.

112. All regions are created by Him, all uniforms are recommended by Him, all kingdoms are established by Him, and all decorations are set by Him.

113. He is the Bestower of all the gifts, He is the Spirit pervading in all, He is the Cause of all human glories, and He is the Source of the lightening up of all things.

114. All regions are made by Him, all races are created by Him, He decides the death time of all, and He plans the upbringing of all.

115. Everywhere He is the Ultimate Annihilator. Everything is within His reach and knowledge. Everywhere He is manifest in different forms. Everywhere He is the Sustainer.

116. He is the Ultimate Judge of all the the actions, His kingdom pervades all over the universe, He is the Ultimate Decider of all the destruction, He is the Planner of all the creation and its sustenance.

117. He is the Source of all the energy, He is the Fountainhead of all the life, He is the Creator of all the regions, and He is the Designer of all the forms and shapes.

118. He is adored by all, He is Ever Supreme, He is worshipped by all and His kingdom is established everywhere.

119. He provides energy to the suns, He is acclaimed by all, He appoints all the kings of heavens, and He is the Light of all the moons.

120. He gives the speaking power to all, He bestows knowledge on all, He accords knowledge to all, He is Supreme in wisdom and enlightenment.

121. He is Beauty personified, He is the Centre of all attraction, He is the Pivot of all existence, His creation is enduring.

122. He is the Vanquisher of the tyrants, He is the Protector of the weak, His abode is higher than all the mansions, and He sustains this earth all the times.

123. He is the sum total of all the virtues, He is the Ocean of wisdom, He is the greatest of all the friends, He is the Surest Provider of sustenance.

124. You are like an ocean with countless waves, You are ever mysterious and are imperishable, You are the Defender of Your devotees, You are the Destroyer of evil.

ਸਦੈਵੰ[148] ਸਰੂਪ[149] ਹੌ ॥ ਅਭੇਦੀ[150] ਅਨੂਪ[151] ਹੌ ॥
ਸਮਸਤੋ[152] ਪਰਾਜ[153] ਹੌ ॥ ਸਦਾ[154] ਸਰਬ[155] ਸਾਜ[156] ਹੌ ॥੧੨੬॥
ਸਮਸਤੁਲ[157] ਸਲਾਮ[158] ਹੌ ॥ ਸਦੈਵਲ[159] ਅਕਾਮ[160] ਹੌ ॥
ਨ੍ਰਿਬਾਧ[161] ਸਰੂਪ[162] ਹੌ ॥ ਅਗਾਧ[163] ਹੌ ਅਨੂਪ[164] ਹੌ ॥੧੨੭॥
ਓਅੰ[165] ਆਦਿ[166] ਰੂਪੇ[167] ॥ ਅਨਾਦਿ[168] ਸਰੂਪੈ[169] ॥
ਅਨੰਗੀ[170] ਅਨਾਮੇ[171] ॥ ਤ੍ਰਿਭੰਗੀ[172] ਤ੍ਰਿਕਾਮੇ[173] ॥੧੨੮॥
ਤ੍ਰਿਬਰਗੰ[174] ਤ੍ਰਿਬਾਧੇ[175] ॥ ਅਗੰਜੇ[176] ਅਗਾਧੇ[177] ॥
ਸੁਭੰ[178] ਸਰਬ[179] ਭਾਗੇ[180] ॥ ਸੁਸਰਬਾ[181-182] ਅਨੁਰਾਗੇ[183] ॥੧੨੯॥
ਤ੍ਰਿਭੁਗਤ[184] ਸਰੂਪ[185] ਹੌ ॥ ਅਛਿੱਜ[186] ਹੌ ਅਛੂਤ[187] ਹੌ ॥
ਕਿ ਨਰਕੰ[188] ਪ੍ਰਨਾਸ[189] ਹੌ ॥ ਪ੍ਰਿਥੀਉਲ[190] ਪ੍ਰਵਾਸ[191] ਹੌ ॥੧੩੦॥
ਨਿਰੁਕਤਿ[192] ਪ੍ਰਭਾ[193] ਹੌ ॥ ਸਦੈਵੰ[194] ਸਦਾ[195] ਹੌ ॥
ਬਿਭੁਗਤਿ[196] ਸਰੂਪ[197] ਹੌ ॥ ਪ੍ਰਜੁਗਤਿ[198] ਅਨੂਪ[199] ਹੌ ॥੧੩੧॥
ਨਿਰੁਕਤਿ[200] ਸਦਾ[201] ਹੌ ॥ ਬਿਭੁਗਤਿ[202] ਪ੍ਰਭਾ[203] ਹੌ ॥
ਅਨੁਕਤਿ[204] ਸਰੂਪ[205] ਹੌ ॥ ਪ੍ਰਜੁਗਤਿ[206] ਅਨੂਪ[207] ਹੌ ॥੧੩੨॥

Sadaivang[148] sarup[149] hain. Abhedi[150] anup[151] hain.
Samasto[152] paraj[153] hain. Sada[154] sarab[155] saj[156] hain. -126-
Samastul[157] salam[158] hain. Sadaival[159] akam[160] hain.
Nribadh[161] sarup[162] hain. Agadh[163] hain anup[164] hain. -127-
O'ang[165] ad(i)[166] rupe[167]. Anad(i)[168] sarupai[169].
Anangi[170] aname[171]. Tribhangi[172] trikame[173]. -128-
Tribargang[174] tribadhe[175]. Aganje[176] agadhe[177].
Subhang[178] sarab[179] bhage[180]. Su-sarba[181-182] anurage[183]. -129-
Tribhugat[184] sarup[185] hain. Achhij[186] hain achhut[187] hain.
Ke narkang[188] pranas[189] hain. Prithiul[190] pravas[191] hain. -130-
Nirukat(i)[192] prabha[193] hain. Sadaivang[194] sada[195] hain.
Bibhugat(i)[196] sarup[197] hain. Prajugat(i)[198] anup[199] hain. -131-
Nirukat(i)[200] sada[201] hain. Bibhugat(i)[202] prabha[203] hain.
Anukat(i)[204] sarup[205] hain. Prajugat(i)[206] anup[207] hain. -132-

[148]always, eternal; [149]form; [150]esoteric; [151]unparallel; [152]all ; [153]vanquisher; [154]always; [155]entire; [156]setter, designer; [157]all; [158]bow to God; [159]always; [160]above passions, beyond emotions; [161]un-encounterable; [162]firm; [163]unfathomable; [164]peerless; [165]primal; [166]beginning; [167]from; [168]beyond time; [169]existence; [170]incorporeal; [171]beyond names; [172]three worlds (sky, earth and netherland); [173]the controller of satisfaction of desires; [174]three objects (righteousness, prosperity, and liberation)); [175]the ruler of the three worlds; [176]imperishable; [177]limitless; [178]beautiful; [179]all; [180]a part of the body; [181]he; [182]all; [183]loves; [184]sustainer; [185]form; [186]inviable; [187]intangible; [188]destroyer; [189]evil, hell; [190]earthly; [191]temporary stay, transit; [192]indescribable; [193]light, glory; [194]eternal; [195]eternal, always; [196]blissful; [197]form; [198]union with all; [199]. peerless; [200]. indescribable; [201]. ever; [202]the bestower of happiness; [203]great, light, glory; [204]matchless; [205]form; [206]union with all; [207]unparallel.

125. Your form is indescribable, Your power is transcendent, Your glory is all revel, Your nectar is immanent in all.

126. You have an eternal form, You are mysterious and incomparable, You are the Vanquisher of all, You are the Architect of all creation.

127. You are the Protector of all, You are beyond passions and desires, You are beyond obstructions and tangles, You are unfathomable and wonderful.

128. You are the Beginning of all the creation, You Yourself are beyond any beginning, You are beyond physical form and a name, You are the Destroyer and the Sustainer of the three-tier worlds, i.e, sky, earth and netherland.

129. You are the Ruler of all the worlds and the Controller of the three boons, viz., righteousness, prosperity and liberation. You are indestructible and unfathomable, Your entire creation is beautiful, You are the Fountainhead of love.

130. You are the Sustainer of the three-tier worlds, You are inviolable and intangible, You are the Annihilator of evil and hell, You reside in all corners of the universe.

131. Your glory is indescribable, Your existence is eternal, Your presence is blissful, You sublimely permeate the whole creation.

132. You are ever ineffable, Your splendour transcends the whole universe, Your form is indescribable, You sublimely permeate the whole creation.

ਚਾਚਰੀ ਛੰਦ ॥

ਅਭੰਗ[1] ਹੋ ॥ ਅਨੰਗ[2] ਹੋ ॥ ਅਭੇਖ[3] ਹੋ ॥ ਅਲੇਖ[4] ਹੋ ॥੧੩੩॥

ਅਭਰਮ[5] ਹੋ ॥ ਅਕਰਮ[6] ਹੋ ॥ ਅਨਾਦਿ[7] ਹੋ ॥ ਜੁਗਾਦਿ[8] ਹੋ ॥੧੩੪॥

ਅਜੈ[9] ਹੋ ॥ ਅਬੈ[10] ਹੋ ॥ ਅਭੂਤ[11] ਹੋ ॥ ਅਧੂਤ[12] ਹੋ ॥੧੩੫॥

ਅਨਾਸ[13] ਹੋ ॥ ਉਦਾਸ[14] ਹੋ ॥ ਅਧੰਧ[15] ਹੋ ॥ ਅਬੰਧ[16] ਹੋ ॥੧੩੬॥

ਅਭਗਤ[17] ਹੋ ॥ ਬਿਰਕਤ[18] ਹੋ ॥ ਅਨਾਸ[19] ਹੋ ॥ ਪ੍ਰਕਾਸ[20] ਹੋ ॥੧੩੭॥

ਨਿਚਿੰਤ[21] ਹੋ ॥ ਸੁਨਿੰਤ[22] ਹੋ ॥ ਅਲਿਖ[23] ਹੋ ॥ ਅਦਿਖ[24] ਹੋ ॥੧੩੮॥

ਅਲੇਖ[25] ਹੋ ॥ ਅਭੇਖ[26] ਹੋ ॥ ਅਢਾਹ[27] ਹੋ ॥ ਅਗਾਹ[28] ਹੋ ॥੧੩੯॥

ਅਸੰਭ[29] ਹੋ ॥ ਅਗੰਭ[30] ਹੋ ॥ ਅਨੀਲ[31] ਹੋ ॥ ਅਨਾਦਿ[32] ਹੋ ॥੧੪੦॥

ਅਨਿਤ[33] ਹੋ ॥ ਸੁਨਿਤ[34] ਹੋ ॥ ਅਜਾਤ[35] ਹੋ ॥ ਅਜਾਦ[36] ਹੋ ॥੧੪੧॥

CHACHRI CHHAND

Abhang[1] hain. Anang[2] hain.
Abhekh[3] hain. Alekh[4] hain. -133-

Abharam[5] hain. Akaram[6] hain.
Anad(i)[7] hain. jugad(i)[8] hain. -134-

Ajai[9] hain. Abai[10] hain.
Abhut[11] hain. Adhut[12] hain. -135-

Anas[13] hain. Udas[14] hain.
Adhandh[15] hain. Abandh[16] hain. -136-

Abhagat[17] hain. Birakat[18] hain.
Anas[19] hain. Prakas[20] hain. -137

Nichint[21] hain. Sunint[22] hain.
Alikh[23] hain. Adikh[24] hain. -138-

Alekh[25] hain. Abhekh[26] hain.
Adhah[27] hain. Agah[28] hain. -139-

Asanbh[29] hain. Aganbh[30] hain.
Anil[31] hain. Anad(i)[32] hain. -140-

Anit[33] hain. Sunit[34] hain.
Ajat[35] hain. Ajad[36] hain. -141-

CHACHRI CHHAND

Notes

[1]imperishable; [2]incorporeal; [3]informal, one who is not restricted to any uniform; [4]indescribable; [5]beyond delusion; [6]beyond karmas; [7]beyond beginning; [8]beyond time; [9]invincible; [10]unchangeable, imperishable; [11]uncompoundable, incorporeal, unique; [12]unshakeable; [13]imperishable; [14]detached, [15]free from karmas; [16]free from bondage; [17]you yourself do not worship anyone; [18]you are not attached; [19]imperishable; [20]light; [21]beyond worries; [22]eternal; [23]indescribable; [24]invisible; [25]indescribable; [26]not restricted to any particular dress or uniform or garb; [27]invincible; [28]unfathomable; [29]inconceivable; [30]unreachable; [31]stainless; [32]un-inceptible; [33]extraordinary; [34]eternal, perpetual; [35]unborn; [36]free from bondage.

COMPOSITION 14

Theme

God is the Father of all us. We all worship Him and pray to Him. He is self-illuminated, unborn and beyond all the bondage.

Literal Meaning

133. He is—
     imperishable, incorporeal, garbless and indescribable.

134. He is beyond—
     illusions, karmas, beginning and time.

135. He is—
     invincible, imperishable, un-compoundable and unshakable.

136. He is beyond—
     destruction, attachment, karmas and bondage.

137. He is—
     primal, unattached, imperishable and the Global Light.

138. He is beyond—
     worries, death, description and sight.

139. He is—
     indescribable, garbless, invincible and unfathomable.

140. He is—
     inconceivable, unreachable, stainless and un-inceptible

141. He is—
     most extraordinary, eternal, unborn and without bondage.

Summary

God is the most wonderful and extraordinary Being. He is a Power beyond calculations, measurement and description. All beings in the universe are His children. He is our Father, Mother, Friend, Master and Companion. We all worship Him. But He Himself is not born. He has no father or mother. We were born after conception but He is beyond any process of a birth. He does not worship anyone, He is self-illuminated, imperishable and eternal. He loves us all, but still is detached. He is the Greatest of all.

ਚਰਪਟ ਛੰਦ ॥ ਤ੍ਰਪ੍ਰਸਾਦਿ ॥

ਸਰਬੰ[1] ਹੰਤਾ[2] ॥ ਸਰਬੰ ਗੀਤਾ[3] ॥

ਸਰਬੰ ਖਯਾਤਾ[4] ॥ ਸਰਬੰ ਗਯਾਤਾ[5] ॥੧੪੨॥

ਸਰਬੰ ਹਰਤਾ[6] ॥ ਸਰਬੰ ਕਰਤਾ[7] ॥

ਸਰਬੰ ਪ੍ਰਾਣੰ[8] ॥ ਸਰਬੰ ਤ੍ਰਾਣੰ[9] ॥੧੪੩॥

ਸਰਬੰ ਕਰਮੰ[10] ॥ ਸਰਬੰ ਧਰਮੰ[11] ॥

ਸਰਬੰ ਜੁਗਤਾ[12] ॥ ਸਰਬੰ ਮੁਕਤਾ[13] ॥੧੪੪॥

CHARPAT CHHAND, TAV PRASAD (I)

Sarbang[1] hanta[2] . Sarbang ganta[3] .

Sarbang khiata[4] . Sarbang giata[5] . -142-

Sarbang harta[6] . Sarbang karta[7] .

Sarbang pranang[8] . Sarbang tranang[9] . -143-

Sarbang karmang[10] . Sarbang dharmang[11] .

Sarbang jugta[12] . Sarbang Mukta[13] . -144-

CHARPAT CHHAND
BY YOUR GRACE

Notes

[1]of all; [2]annihilator; [3]witness; [4]glory; [5]knower; [6]planner of death; [7]planner of births; [8]giver of life; [9]emancipation; [10]actions; [11]duties; [12]identity; [13]mukti, liberation.

COMPOSITION 15

Theme

God is the Judge of all our actions. He is both the Life-giver and the Life-taker. He controls our destinies.

Literal Meaning

142. God is the —
     Annihilator of evil,
     Witness of actions,
     Glory of saints, and
     Knower of our thoughts.

143. God is the decider of —
     the Time of death,
     the Time of birth,
     the Number of breaths, and
     the Time of emancipation.

144. God is the Judge of —
     karmas,
     duties,
     identity, and
     liberartion (mukti).

Summary

God controls all the functions of creation, sustenance and destruction. He is the Judge and Planner of our destinies. He is the Greatest Architect and there is no one above Him.

ਰਸਾਵਲ ਛੰਦ ॥ ਤ੍ਵਪ੍ਰਸਾਦਿ ॥

ਨਮੋ^{1} ਨਰਕ^2 ਨਾਸੇ^{3} ॥ ਸਦੈਵੰ^{4} ਪ੍ਰਕਾਸੇ^{5} ॥
ਅਨੰਗੀ^{6} ਸਰੂਪੇ^{7} ॥ ਅਭੰਗੀ^{8} ਬਿਭੂਤੇ^{9} ॥੧੪੫॥
ਪ੍ਰਮਾਥੰ^{10} ਪ੍ਰਮਾਥੇ^{11} ॥ ਸਦਾ^{12} ਸਰਬ^{13} ਸਾਥੇ^{14} ॥
ਅਗਾਧ^{15} ਸਰੂਪੇ^{16} ॥ ਨ੍ਰਿਬਾਧ^{17} ਬਿਭੂਤੇ^{18} ॥੧੪੬॥
ਅਨੰਗੀ^{19} ਅਨਾਮੇ^{20} ॥ ਤ੍ਰਿਭੰਗੀ^{21} ਤ੍ਰਿਕਾਮੇ^{22} ॥
ਨ੍ਰਿਭੰਗੀ^{22} ਸਰੂਪੇ^{24} ॥ ਸ੍ਰਬੰਗੀ^{25} ਅਨੂਪੇ^{26} ॥੧੪੭॥
ਨ ਪੋਤ੍ਰੈ^{27} ਨ ਪੁਤ੍ਰੈ^{28} ॥ ਨ ਸਤ੍ਰੈ^{29} ਨ ਮਿਤ੍ਰੈ^{30} ॥
ਨ ਤਾਤੈ^{31} ਨ ਮਾਤੈ^{32} ॥ ਨ ਜਾਤੈ^{33} ਨ ਪਾਤੈ^{34} ॥੧੪੮॥
ਨ੍ਰਿਸਾਕੰ^{35} ਸਰੀਕ^{36} ਹੈ ॥ ਅਮਿਤੋ^{37} ਅਮੀਕ^{38} ਹੈ ॥
ਸਦੈਵੰ^{39} ਪ੍ਰਭਾ^{40} ਹੈ ॥ ਅਜੈ^{41} ਹੈ ਅਜਾ^{42} ਹੈ ॥੧੪੯॥

RASAVAL CHHAND, TAV PRASAD (I)

Namo^1 narak^2 nase^3 . Sadaivang^4 prakase^5 .
Anangi^6 sarupe^7 . Abhangi^8 bibhute^9 . -145-
Pramathang^{10} pramathe^{11} . Sada^{12} sarab^{13} sathe^{14} .
Agadh^{15} sarupe^{16} . Nribadh^{17} bibhute^{18} . -146-
Anangi^{19} aname^{20} . Tribhangi^{21} trikame^{22} .
Nribhangi^{23} sarupe^{24} . Sarbangi^{25} anupe^{26} . -147-
Na potrai^{27} na putrai^{28} . Na satrai^{29} na mitrai^{30} .
Na tatai^{31} na matai^{32} . Na jatai^{33} na patai^{34} . -148-
Nrisakang^{35} sarik^{36} hain. Amito^{37} Amik^{38} hain.
Sadaivang^{39} prabha^{40} hain. Ajai^{41} hain aja^{42} hain -149-

RASAVAL CHHAND
BY YOUR GRACE

Notes

[1]hail; [2]hell; [3]destroyer; [4]everlasting, eternal, perpetual; [5]light; [6]incorporeal, not made of five elements, without limbs; [7]existence; [8]imperishable, immutable; [9]glory; [10]to destroy; [11]tyrants; [12]all the times; [13]of all; [14]supporter, pal; [15]unfathomable; [16]form; [17]limitless; [18]glory; [19]without limbs; [20]nameless; [21]dissipator/destroyer of the three worlds; [22]bestower of the boons/sustainers of the three worlds; [23]indestructible; [24]form; [25]in all forms; [26]unparallel, supremely beautiful; [27]grandson; [28]son; [29]enemy; [30]friend; [31]father; [32]mother; [33]caste; [34]creed; [35]kinless; [36]rival, one claiming an equal status; [37]immeasurable; [38]limitless; [39]always; [40]splendour; [41]unconquerable; [42]unborn.

COMPOSITION 16

Theme

God is the Protector of the good and of His saints and the Destroyer of the evil aand the tryrants.

Literal Meaning

145. Bow to Almighty God Who is—
     the Destroyer of the Evil,
     the Eternal Source of enlightenment,
     beyond form or image, and Whose glory is imperishable.

146. He is—
     the Destroyer of the tyrants,
     and Sustainer of the good.
     He has—
     Unfathomable existence and limitless glory.

147. He is both formless and nameless, He is the Destroyer and Fulfiller of the desires of the three worlds. In all His forms He is indestructible, and in all His forms He is supremely beautiful.

148. In worldly meaning He has no— grandsons or sons, enemies or friends, father or mother, and caste or creed.

149. In worldly meaning He has no—
     close relations or rivals.
     He is immeasurable and unfathomable.
     He possesses eternal splendour and is invincible and unborn.

Summary

God is the Source of all powers and energies. He destroys evil and tyrants and supports good and just rulers. He is the Creator of the whole world. He has created fathers and sons, friends and relatives; but He Himself is beyond all the worldly relationships. He is detached from all the worldly affairs. Though He is the Source of all the relations but He Himself is above all the physical and emotional kinship.

ਭਗਵਤੀ ਛੰਦ ॥ ਤੂਪ੍ਰਸਾਦਿ ॥

ਕਿ[1] ਜਾਹਰ[2] ਜ਼ਹੂਰ[3] ਹੈਂ ॥ ਕਿ ਹਾਜ਼ਰ[4] ਹਜ਼ੂਰ[5] ਹੈਂ ॥

ਹਮੇਸੁਲ[6] ਸਲਾਮ[7] ਹੈਂ ॥ ਸਮਸਤੁਲ[8] ਕਲਾਮ[9] ਹੈਂ ॥੧੫੦॥

ਕਿ ਸਾਹਿਬ[10] ਦਿਮਾਗ[11] ਹੈਂ ॥ ਕਿ ਹੁਸਨਲ[12] ਚਰਾਗ[13] ਹੈਂ ॥

ਕਿ ਕਾਮਲ[14] ਕਰੀਮ[15] ਹੈਂ ॥ ਕਿ ਹਾਜ਼ਕ[16] ਰਹੀਮ[17] ਹੈਂ ॥੧੫੧॥

ਕਿ ਰੋਜੀ[18] ਦਿਹਿੰਦ[19] ਹੈਂ ॥ ਕਿ ਰਾਜ਼ਕ[20] ਰਹਿੰਦ[21] ਹੈਂ ॥

ਕਰੀਮੁਲ[22] ਕਮਾਲ[23] ਹੈਂ ॥ ਕਿ ਹੁਸਨਲ[24] ਜਮਾਲ[25] ਹੈਂ ॥੧੫੨॥

ਗਨੀਮੁਲ[26] ਖਿਰਾਜ[27] ਹੈਂ ॥ ਗਰੀਬੁਲ[28] ਨਿਵਾਜ[29] ਹੈਂ ॥

ਹਰੀਫ਼ਲ[30] ਸ਼ਿਕੰਨ[31] ਹੈਂ ॥ ਹਿਰਾਸੁਲ[32] ਫ਼ਿਕੰਨ[33] ਹੈਂ ॥੧੫੩॥

ਕਲੰਕੰ[34] ਪ੍ਰਨਾਸ[35] ਹੈਂ ॥ ਸਮਸਤੁਲ[36] ਨਿਵਾਸ[37] ਹੈਂ ॥

ਅਗੰਜੁਲ[38] ਗਾਨੀਮ[39] ਹੈਂ ॥ ਰਜ਼ਾਇਕ[40] ਰਹੀਮ[41] ਹੈਂ ॥੧੫੪॥

ਸਮਸਤੁਲ[42] ਜ਼ੁਬਾ[43] ਹੈਂ ॥ ਕਿ ਸਾਹਿਬ[44] ਕਿਰਾਂ[45] ਹੈਂ ॥

ਕਿ ਨਰਕੰ[46] ਪ੍ਰਨਾਸ[47] ਹੈਂ ॥ ਬਹਿਸ਼ਤੁਲ[48] ਨਿਵਾਸ[49] ਹੈਂ ॥੧੫੫॥

ਕਿ ਸਰਬੁਲ[50] ਗਵੰਨ[51] ਹੈਂ ॥ ਹਮੇਸੁਲ[52] ਰਵੰਨ[53] ਹੈਂ ॥

ਤਮਾਮੁਲ[54] ਤਮੀਜ਼[55] ਹੈਂ ॥ ਸਮਸਤੁਲ[56] ਅਜ਼ੀਜ਼[57] ਹੈਂ ॥੧੫੬॥

ਪਰੰ[58] ਪਰਮ[59] ਈਸ[60] ਹੈਂ ॥ ਸਮਸਤੁਲ[61] ਅਦੀਸ[62] ਹੈਂ ॥

ਅਦੇਸੁਲ[63] ਅਲੇਖ[64] ਹੈਂ ॥ ਹਮੇਸੁਲ[65] ਅਭੇਖ[66] ਹੈਂ ॥੧੫੭॥

ਜ਼ਮੀਨੁਲ[67] ਜ਼ਮਾ[68] ਹੈਂ ॥ ਅਮੀਕੁਲ[69] ਇਮਾ[70] ਹੈਂ ॥

ਕਰੀਮੁਲ[71] ਕਮਾਲ[72] ਹੈਂ ॥ ਕਿ ਜ਼ੁਰਅਤਿ[73] ਜਮਾਲ[74] ਹੈਂ ॥੧੫੮॥

ਕਿ ਅਚਲੰ[75] ਪ੍ਰਕਾਸ[76] ਹੈਂ ॥ ਕਿ ਅਮਿਤੋ[77] ਸੁਬਾਸ[78] ਹੈਂ ॥

ਕਿ ਅਜਬ[79] ਸਰੂਪ[80] ਹੈਂ ॥ ਕਿ ਅਮਿਤੋ[81] ਬਿਭੂਤ[82] ਹੈਂ ॥੧੫੯॥

ਕਿ ਅਮਿਤੋ[83] ਪਾਸਾ[84] ਹੈਂ ॥ ਕਿ ਆਤਮ[85] ਪ੍ਰਭਾ[86] ਹੈਂ ॥

ਕਿ ਅਚਲੰ[87] ਅਨੰਗ[88] ਹੈਂ ॥ ਕਿ ਅਮਿਤੋ[89] ਅਭੰਗ[90] ਹੈਂ ॥੧੬੦॥

BHAGWATI CHHAND, TAVPRASAD(I)

Ke[1] zahar[2] zahur[3] hain . Ke hazar[4] hazur[5] hain.

Hamesul[6] salam[7] hain. Samastul[8] kalam[9] hain. -150

Ke sahib[10] dimagh[11] hain. Ke husnal[12] chiragh[13] hain.

Ke kamal[14] karim[15] hain. Ke razak[16] rahim[17] hain. -151-

Ke rozi[18] dihind[19] hain. Ke razak[20] rahind[21] hain.

Karimul[22] kamal[23] hain. Ke husnal[24] jamal[25] hain. -152-

Ghanimul[26] khiraz[27] hain. Gharibul[28] nivaz[29] hain.

Hariful[30] shikan[31] hain. Hirasul[32] phikan[33] hain. -153-

Kalankang[34] pranas[35] hain. Samastul[36] nivas[37] hain.

Aganjul[38] ganim[39] hain. Razaik[40] rahim[41] hain. -154-

Samastul[42] juban[43] hain. Ke sahib[44] kiran[45] hain.

Ke narkang[46] pranas[47] hain. Bahishtul[48] nivas[49] hain. -155-

Ke sarbul[50] gavann[51] hain. Hamesul[52] ravann[53] hain.

Tamamul[54] tamiz[55] hain. Samastul[56] aziz[57] hain. -156-

Parang[58] param[59] is[60] hain. Samastul[61] adis[62] hain.

Adesul[63] alekh[64] hain. Hamesul[65] abhekh[66] hain. -157-

Zaminul[67] zama[68] hain. Amikul[69] ima[70] hain.

Karimul[71] kamal[72] hain. Ke jur-at(i)[73] jamal[74] hain. -158-

Ke achlang[75] prakas[76] hain. Ke amito[77] subas[78] hain.

Ke ajab[79] sarup[80] hain. Ke amito[81] bibhut[82] hain. -159-

Ke amito[83] pasa[84] hain. Ke atam[85] prabha[86] hain.

Ke Achlang[87] anang[88] hain. Ke amito[89] abhang[90] hain. -160-

BHAGWATI CHHAND
BY YOUR GRACE

Notes

[1]that; [2]manifest; [3]splendour; [4]present; [5]glory; [6]eternal; [7]eternity; [8]of all; [9]voice; [10]supreme; [11]wisdom, knowledge; [12]beauty; [13]lantern, light; [14]perfect; [15]gracious; [16]provider; [17]merciful; [18]livelihood; [19]giver; [20]provider; [21]granter of salvation; [22]benevolent; [23]voice, speech; [24]beauty; [25]glow; splendour; [26]enemy, tyrant; [27]destroyer; [28]humble; [29]protector; [30]tyrant, oppressor; [31]annihilate; [32]terrorist; [33]to shatter; [34]blames; [35]remover; [36]everywhere; [37]reside; [38]unconquerable; [39]enemy; [40]provider; [41]merciful; [42]of all; [43]speech, voice; [44]supreme; [45]close, near; [46]hell; [47]redeemer; [48]heaven; [49]inhabitant; [50]of all; [51]redeemer; [51]manifest; [52]every; [53]blissful; [54]all; [55]culture; etiquettes; [56]of all; [57]adore; [58]supreme; [59]sovereign; [60]Lord; [61]of all; [62]prime being, first person; [63]belonging to no one country; [64]beyond description; [65]ever; [66]unparallel; [67]of earth; [68]all times; [69]deep, unfathomable; [70]faith; [71]merciful; [72]exquisite; [73]valour; [74]grace; [75]steady, eternal; [76]enlightenment; [77]immeasurable; [78]fragrance; [79]wonderful; [80]form; [81]immeasurable; [82]effulgence; [83]immeasurable; [84]vastness; [85]spirit; [86]everywhere; [87]immutable; [88]incorporeal; [89]immeasurable; [90]indestructible.

COMPOSITION 17

Theme

God is the most Beautiful Being, He is the Livelihood Giver to all of us. He is the Protector of the weak and Annihilator of the wicked. He is the Source of all the knowledge, wisdom, beauty and arts.

Literal Meaning

150. He is manifest in all with His splendour, and is present in all with all of His glory. and is the Source of all the scriptures, speech and voice.

151. He is the Great Master of intellect, He is the Fountain of Beauty, He is perfect and gracious, He is merciful and the Provider.

152. He grants livelihood to all, He sanctions salvation to those who deserve it, He is exquisitely benevolent, He is the Effulegence of beauty.

153. He is the Dissipator of tyrant, He is the Protector of the humble, He is the Annihilator of oppressors, He is the Shatterer of the terrorists.

154. He is the Remover of blames, He resides everywhere, He is the Conqueror of the foes, He is merciful and the Provider.

155. He is the Voice of every tongue, He is near and close to every being, He is the Destroyer of hells and Redeemer of the sins.

156. He resides and reaches everywhere. He is Master of etiquettes, He is adored by all.

157. He is Supreme and Geat lord, He is the Pirime Being, He belongs to all the regions and is beyond description He is ever unparallel.

158. He controls the planet earth all the times, He is most religious, He is exquisitely merciful, He is the Hero full with valour and grace.

159. He is Perpetual Light, He is Immesurable Fragrance, He is most wonderful, His effulgence is immeasurable.

160. His vastness is limitless, He is the Brightest Spirit, He is both immutable and incorporeal, He is both limitless and indestructible.

Summary

God is beyond time, births, deaths and age. He is most beautiful, greatful and adorable. He is the Fountain of knowledge, happiness, attraction, beauty and arts. He is the Master of all the scriptures, language, writings and lyrics. He is vast, limitless, immeasurable and unfathomable. He is merciful, benevolent, the Provider, the Sustainer and the Creator.

ਮੁਨਿ[1] ਮਨਿ[2] ਪ੍ਰਨਾਮ[3] ॥ ਗੁਨਿ[4] ਗਨ[5] ਮੁਦਾਮ[6] ॥

ਅਰਿ[7] ਬਰ[8] ਅਗੰਜ[9] ॥ ਹਰਿ[10] ਨਰ[11] ਪ੍ਰਭੰਜ[12] ॥੧੬੧॥

ਅੰਗਨ[13] ਪ੍ਰਨਾਮ[14] ॥ ਮੁਨਿ ਮਨਿ[15] ਸਲਾਮ[16] ॥

ਹਰਿ[17] ਨਰ[18] ਅਖੰਡ[19] ॥ ਬਰ[20] ਨਰ[21] ਅਮੰਡ[22] ॥੧੬੨॥

ਅਨਭਵ[23] ਅਨਾਸ[24] ॥ ਮੁਨਿ[25] ਮਨਿ[26] ਪ੍ਰਕਾਸ[27] ॥

ਗੁਨਿ[28] ਗਾਨ[29] ਪ੍ਰਨਾਮ[30] ॥ ਜਲ[31] ਥਲ[32] ਮੁਦਾਮ[33] ॥੧੬੩॥

ਅਨਛਿਜ[34] ਅੰਗ[35] ॥ ਆਸਨ[36] ਅਭੰਗ[37] ॥

ਉਪਮਾ[38] ਅਪਾਰ[39] ॥ ਗਤਿ[40] ਮਿਤਿ[41] ਉਦਾਰ[42] ॥੧੬੪॥

ਜਲ[43] ਥਲ[44] ਅਮੰਡ[45] ॥ ਦਿਸ[46] ਵਿਸ[47] ਅਭੰਡ[48] ॥

ਜਲ[49] ਥਲ[50] ਮਹੰਤ[51] ॥ ਦਿਸ[52] ਵਿਸ[53] ਬਿਅੰਤ[54] ॥੧੬੫॥

ਅਨਭਵ[55] ਅਨਾਸ[56] ॥ ਪ੍ਰਿਤ[57] ਧਰ[58] ਪ੍ਰਰਾਸ[59] ॥

ਆਜਾਨ[60] ਬਾਹੁ[61] ॥ ਏਕੈ[62] ਸਦਾਹੁ[63] ॥੧੬੬॥

ਓਅੰਕਾਰ[64] ਆਦਿ[65] ॥ ਕਥਨੀ[66] ਅਨਾਦਿ[67] ॥

ਖਲ[68] ਖੰਡ[69] ਖਯਾਲ[70] ॥ ਗੁਰਬਰ[71-72] ਅਕਾਲ[73] ॥੧੬੭॥

ਘਰ[74] ਘਰਿ[75] ਪ੍ਰਨਾਮ[76] ॥ ਚਿਤ[77] ਚਰਨ[78] ਨਾਮ[79] ॥

ਅਨਛਿਜ[80] ਗਾਤ[81] ॥ ਆਜਿਜ[82] ਨ[83] ਬਾਤ[84] ॥੧੬੮॥

ਅਨਛੰਝ[85] ਗਾਤ[86] ॥ ਅਨਰੰਜ[87] ਬਾਤ[88] ॥

ਅਨਟੂਟ[89] ਭੰਡਾਰ[90] ॥ ਅਨਠਠ[91] ਅਪਾਰ[92] ॥੧੬੯॥

ਆਦੀਠ[93] ਧਰਮ[94] ॥ ਅਤਿਦੀਠ[95] ਕਰਮ[96] ॥

ਅਨਬ੍ਰਣ[97] ਅਨੰਤ[98] ॥ ਦਾਤਾ[99] ਮਹੰਤ[100] ॥੧੭੦॥

Mun(i)[1] *man(i)*[2] *pranam*[3]. *Gun(i)*[4] *gan*[5] *mudam*[6].

Ar(i)[7] *bar*[8] *aganj*[9]. *Har(i)*[10] *nar*[11] *prabhanj*[12]. -161-

Angan[13] *pranam*[14]. *Mun(i)man(i)*[15] *salam*[16].

Har(i)[17] *nar*[18] *akhand*[19]. *Bar*[20] *nar*[21] *amand*[22]. -162-

Anbhav[23] *anas*[24]. *Mun(i)*[25] *man(i)*[26] *prakas*[27].

Gun(i)[28] *gan*[29] *pranam*[30]. *Jal*[31] *thal*[32] *mudam*[33]. -163-

Anchhij[34] *Ang*[35]. *Asan*[36] *abhang*[37].

Upma[38] *apar*[39]. *Gat(i)*[40] *mit(i)*[41] *udar*[42]. -164-

Jal[43] *thal*[44] *amand*[45]. *Dis*[46] *vis*[47] *abhand*[48].

Jal[49] *thal*[50] *mahant*[51]. *Dis*[52] *vis*[53] *beant*[54]. -165-

Anbhav[55] *anas*[56]. *Dhrit*[57] *dhar*[58] *dhuras*[59].

Ajan[60] *bah(u)*[61]. *Ekai*[62] *sadah(u)*[63]. -166-

Onkar[64] *ad(i)*[65]. *Kathni*[66] *anad(i)*[67].

Khal[68] *khand*[69] *khial*[70]. *Gurbar*[71] *Akal*[72]. -167-

Ghar[74] *ghar(i)*[75] *pranam*[76]. *Chit*[77] *charan*[78] *nam*[79].

Anchhij[80] *gat*[81]. *Ajij*[82] *na*[83] *bat*[84]. -168-

Anjhanjh[85] *gat*[86]. *Anranj*[87] *bat*[88].

Antut[89] *bhandar*[90]. *Anthat*[91] *apar*[92]. -169-

Adith[93] *dharam*[94]. *At(i)*[95] *dhith karam*[96].

Anbran[97] *anant*[98]. *Data*[99] *mahant*[100]. -170-

MADHUBHAR CHHAND
BY YOUR GRACE

Notes

[1]sages; [2]mind; [3]bow, salute; [4]virtues; [5]treasure; [6]always a source; [7]mightiest; [8]enemies; [9]unconquerable; [10]God; [11]human beings; [12]ultimate annihilator; [13]countless; [14]bow; [15]in the minds of the sages; [16]bow; [17]God; [18]man; [19]unbreakable; [20]supreme; [21]man; [22]self-illuminated; [23]intuitively experienced; [24]imperishable; [25]sages; [26]mind; [27]light; [28]virtues; [29]treasure; [30]bow; [31]water; [32]earth; [33]always a source; [34]inviable; [35]limbs; [36]seat, throne; [37]unassailable; [38]glory; [39]incomparable; [40]condition; [41]measure; [42]vast, generous, mighty; [43]water; [44]earth; [45]self-illuminated; [46]directions; [47]corners; [48]not born to a woman; [49]water; [50]earth; [51]great; [52]directions; [53]corners; [54]limitless; [55]intuitive exerience; [56]imperishable; [57]earth; [58]support; [59]pivot; [60]transmigration; [61]in control; [62]only one, unity; [63]always; [64]the maiden word; [65]first; [66]describe; [67]beginning; [68]tyrant; [69]destruction; [70]in a moment; [71]master; [72]supreme; [73]beyond death; [74-75]in every household; [76]bow, salute; [77]mind; [78]feet; [79]hymn, God's words; [80]unbreakable; [81]existence, power; [82]helplessnesses; [83]not; [84]in You; [85]away from worldly strife; [86]power, existence; [87]without annoyance; [88]conversation; [89]unbreakable; [90]stock; [91]self-installable, self-established; [92]vast; [93]invisible; [94]divine-duties, judgement; [95]unflinching; [96]actions; [97]indescribable; [98]limitless; [99]giver, donor; [100]great.

COMPOSITION 18

Theme
God is worshipped by all the sages, kings and emperors. He is the Supreme Power and is the Source of all the energies.

Literal Meaning

161. All sages salute Him, He is the Source of all the treasures, He Himself is invincible and even the mightiest enemies cannot harm Him, He is the Ultimate Annihilator of evil.

162. Countless people bow to You in reverence and worship. Sages hum Your name with adoration in their minds, You are immortal and imperishable, You are supreme and self-illuminated.

163. You reside in feelings and are beyond death, You generate light in the heart of sages. Multitudes of people of wisdom salute You, You are the Master of both land and sea.

164. O Lord God— Your personality is inviolable. Your throne is unassailable, Your glory is incomparable and Your vasteness is immeasurable.

165. O Lord God— Your power is eternally established on earth and on sea, Your glory extends in all lands and seas, Your spread of potency is in all directions and venues.

166. O Lord God— You ever reside in feelings and heart and are beyond death, You are the Support, Centre and Pivot of the universe, You are the sole controller of the transmigration of souls, You are ever One and only One.

167. You created this world with the sound of 'Ongkar', Your own beginning cannot be described, You annihilate tyrants in a moment's time, Supreme Master, You are immortal.

168. O Lord God— You are worshipped in every household, Your word is recited with contemplation of Your lotus feet, Your power and existence are inviolable and Your Word is a hope for the helpless.

169. O Lord God— You are beyond any involvement in the worldly strife, You are beyond anger and annoyance, Your treasures are inexhaustible, You are self-created and beyond limit.

170. O Lord God— Your rule book is invisible, Your laws are unalterable, You are indescribable and infinite, You are benevolent and great.

SUMMARY:
God, Lord has the mightiest and greatest power. He is worshipped by all the sages, kings and rulers. He is the Source of all the beauty, energy and power. He is the Ultimate Judge. His rule book is unquestionable and unalterable. He is the Hope of all of us. He created this world with the sound of 'Onkar' but no one knows the exact date of its creation. He is beyond time and death. He is self-created and self-illuminated.

ਹਰਿਬੋਲਮਨਾ ਛੰਦ ॥ ਤ੍ਵਪ੍ਰਸਾਦਿ ॥

HAR(I)-BOL-MANA CHHAND, TAVPRASAD(I)

ਕਰੁਣਾਲਯ[1] ਹੈਂ ॥ ਅਰਿ[2] ਘਾਲਯ[3] ਹੈਂ ॥

ਖਲ[4] ਖੰਡਨ[5] ਹੈਂ ॥ ਮਹਿ[6] ਮੰਡਨ[7] ਹੈਂ ॥੧੭੧॥

ਜਗਤੇਸੁਰ[8] ਹੈਂ ॥ ਪਰਮੇਸੁਰ[9] ਹੈਂ ॥

ਕਲਿ[10] ਕਾਰਨ ਹੈਂ ॥ ਸਰਬ[11] ਉਬਾਰਨ ਹੈਂ ॥੧੭੨॥

ਪ੍ਰਿਤ[12] ਕੇ ਪ੍ਰਨ[13] ਹੈਂ ॥ ਜਗ[14] ਕੇ ਕ੍ਰਨ[15] ਹੈਂ ॥

ਮਨ[16] ਮਾਨਿਯ[17] ਹੈਂ ॥ ਜਗ[18] ਜਾਨਿਯ[19] ਹੈਂ ॥੧੭੩॥

ਸਰਬੰ[20] ਭਰ[21] ਹੈਂ ॥ ਸਰਬੰ[22] ਕਰ[23] ਹੈਂ ॥

ਸਰਬ[24] ਪਾਸਿਯ[25] ਹੈਂ ॥ ਸਰਬ[26] ਨਾਸਿਯ[27] ਹੈਂ ॥੧੭੪॥

ਕਰੁਣਾਕਰ[28] ਹੈਂ ॥ ਬਿਸੰਭਰ[29] ਹੈਂ ॥

ਸਰਬੇਸੁਰ[30] ਹੈਂ ॥ ਜਗਤੇਸੁਰ[31] ਹੈਂ ॥੧੭੫॥

ਬ੍ਰਹਮੰਡਸ[32] ਹੈਂ ॥ ਖਲ[33] ਖੰਡਸ[34] ਹੈਂ ॥

ਪਰ[35] ਤੇ ਪਰ[36] ਹੈਂ ॥ ਕਰੁਣਾਕਰ[37] ਹੈਂ ॥੧੭੬॥

ਅਜਪਾ[38] ਜਪ[39] ਹੈਂ ॥ ਅਥਪਾ[40] ਥਪ[41] ਹੈਂ ॥

ਅਕ੍ਰਿਤਾ[42] ਕ੍ਰਿਤ[43] ਹੈਂ ॥ ਅੰਮ੍ਰਿਤਾ[44] ਮ੍ਰਿਤ[45] ਹੈਂ ॥੧੭੭॥

ਅਮ੍ਰਿਤਾ[46] ਮ੍ਰਿਤ[47] ਹੈਂ ॥ ਕਰੁਣਾ[48] ਕ੍ਰਿਤ[49] ਹੈਂ ॥

ਅਕ੍ਰਿਤਾ[50] ਕ੍ਰਿਤ[51] ਹੈਂ ॥ ਧਰਨੀ[52] ਪ੍ਰਿਤ[53] ਹੈਂ ॥੧੭੮॥

ਅਮ੍ਰਿਤੇਸੁਰ[54] ਹੈਂ ॥ ਪਰਮੇਸੁਰ[55] ਹੈਂ ॥

ਅਕ੍ਰਿਤਾ[56] ਕ੍ਰਿਤ[57] ਹੈਂ ॥ ਅੰਮ੍ਰਿਤਾ[58] ਮ੍ਰਿਤ[59] ਹੈਂ ॥੧੭੯॥

ਅਜਬਾ[60] ਕ੍ਰਿਤ[61] ਹੈਂ ॥ ਅਮ੍ਰਿਤਾ[62] ਮ੍ਰਿਤ[63] ਹੈਂ ॥

ਨਰ[64] ਨਾਇਕ[65] ਹੈਂ ॥ ਖਲ[66] ਘਾਇਕ[67] ਹੈਂ ॥੧੮੦॥

Karunalya[1] hain. Ar(i)[2] ghalya[3] hain.

Khal[4] khandan[5] hain. Mah(i)[6] mandan[7] hain. -171-

Jagtesvar[8] hain. Parmesvar[9] hain.

Kal(i)[10] karan hain. sarab[11] ubaran hain. -172-

Dhrit[12] ke Dhrun[13] hain. Jag[14] ke Kran[15] hain.

Man[16] maniya[17] hain. Jag[18] janiya[19] hain. -173-

Sarbang[20] bhar[21] hain. Sarbang[22] kar[23] hain.

Sarab[24] pasiya[25] hain. Sarab[26] nasiya[27] hain. -174-

Karunakar[28] hain. Bisvanbhar[29] hain.

Sarbesvar[30] hain. Jagtesvar[31] hain. -175-

Brahmandas[32] hain. Khal[33] khandas[34] hain.

Par[35] te par[36] hain. Karunakar[37] hain. -176-

Ajapa[38] jap[39] hain. Athapa[40] thap[41] hain.

Akrita[42] krit[43] hain. Amrita[44] mrit[45] hain. -177-

Amrita[46] mrit[47] hain. Karuna[48] krit[49] hain.

Akrita[50] krit[51] hain. Dharni[52] dhrit[53] hain. -178-

Amritesvar[54] hain. Parmesvar[55] hain.

Akrita[56] krit[57] hain. Amrita[58] mrit[59] hain. -179-

Ajba[60] krit[61] hain. Amrita[62] mrit[63] hain.

Nar[64] naik[65] hain. Khal[66] ghaik[67] hain. -180-

HAR BOL MANA CHHAND
BY YOUR GRACE

Notes

[1]house of mercy; [2]you; [3]annihilator of evil; [4]ignorance, evil; [5]dispeller; [6]earth; [7]adoration by grace; [8]Lord of the universe; [9]supreme master; [10]controller of destruction; [11]saviour of all; [12]earth; [13]support; [14]cause of ; [15]creation of the world; [16]heart; [17]worship; [18]world; [19]knows you; [20]all; [21]source of sustenance; [22-23]creator of all; [24-25]supporter of all; [26-27]destroyer of all; [28]fountain of mercy; [29]sustainer; [30]Lord of all; [31]sovereign of universe; [32]commander of spheres; [33]evil; [34]destroyer; [35-36]infinite; [37]source of mercy; [38-39]self-innovated; [40-41]self-installed; [42-43]self created; [44]immortal; [45]immortality; [46]immortal; [47]immortality; [48]mercy; [49]nectar, source, ; [50]un-caused, destruction; [51]creation; [52]support; [53]universe; [54]creation; [55]Supreme Lord; [56]Un-caused; [57]Creation; [58]immortal; [59]immortality; [60]wonderful; [61]creation. [62]immortal; [63]immortality; [64]humanity; [65]guiding spirit; [66]evil; [67]destroyer; [68]sustainer.

COMPOSITION 19

Theme

God is the Fountain of mercy. He showers His blessings on all of us and we all must be ready to receive them. He determines the date of birth and the date of death of each one of us.

Literal Meaning

171. Lord God is — the Abode of mercy, the Annihilator of the evil, the Dispeller of the enemies, and the Decorator of the universe.

172. Lord God is — the Master of the universe, the Supreme Controller, the Destroyer of the strife, and the Saviour of all.

173. Lord God is — the support of the universe, the cause of the creation, the centre of all the worship, and the closest relation of all of us.

174. Lord God is — the Sustainer, the Creator, the Provider, and the Destroyer.

175. Lord God is — the Fountain of mercy, the Nourisher of the universe, the Master of all, and the Sovereign of all.

176. Lord God is — the Commander of the Spheres, the Destroyer of the evil, the Supreme of the nobles, and the Spring of mercy.

177. Lord God's — glory cannot be encompassed by any prayer, throne cannot be installed except by Himself, deeds cannot be done except by Himself, existence provides the nectar of immortality.

178. Lord God's — existence provides the nectar of immortality, actions are full of compassion, deeds cannot be done except by Himself, support sustains the universe.

179. Lord God's — power is immeasurable, supremacy is exalting, creation is un-caused, existence provides the nectar of immortality.

180. Lord God's — creation is wonderful, existence provides the nectar of immortality, spirit is the guiding force of the humanity, power kills the evil.

181. Lord God is — Nourisher of the universe, the Fountain of Mercy, the Supreme Guiding Spirit, and the Protector of all.

182. Lord God — dispels the fears, eliminates enemies, chastises sinners, and inspires true worship.

ਬਿਸ੍ਵੰਭਰ[68] ਹੈਂ ॥ ਕਰੁਣਾਲਯ[69] ਹੈਂ ॥

ਨ੍ਰਿਪ[70] ਨਾਇਕ[71] ਹੈਂ ॥ ਸਰਬ[72] ਪਾਇਕ[73] ਹੈਂ ॥੧੮੧॥

ਭਵ[74] ਭੰਜਨ[75] ਹੈਂ ॥ ਅਰਿ[76] ਗੰਜਨ[77] ਹੈਂ ॥

ਰਿਪੁ[78] ਤਾਪਨ[79] ਹੈਂ ॥ ਜਪੁ[80] ਜਾਪਨ[81] ਹੈਂ ॥੧੮੨॥

ਅਕਲੰ[82] ਕ੍ਰਿਤ[83] ਹੈਂ ॥ ਸਰਬਾ[84] ਕ੍ਰਿਤ[85] ਹੈਂ ॥

ਕਰਤਾ[86] ਕਰ[87] ਹੈਂ ॥ ਹਰਤਾ[88] ਹਰ[89] ਹੈਂ ॥੧੮੩॥

ਪਰਮਾਤਮ[90] ਹੈਂ ॥ ਸਰਬਾਤਮ[91] ਹੈਂ ॥

ਆਤਮ[92] ਬਸ[93] ਹੈਂ ॥ ਜਸ[94] ਕੇ ਜਸ[95] ਹੈਂ ॥੧੮੪॥

Bisvanbhar[68] hain. Karunalya[69] hain.

Nrip[70] naik[71] hain. Sarab[72] paik[73] hain. -181-

Bhav[74] bhanjan[75] hain. Ar(i)[76] ganjan[77] hain.

Rip(u)[78] tapan[79] hain. Jap(u)[80] japan[81] hain. -182-

Aklang[82] krit[83] hain. Sarba[84] krit[85] hain.

Karta[86] kar[87] hain. Harta[88] har[89] hain. -183-

Parmatam[90] hain. Sarbatam[91] hain.

Atam[92] bas[93] hain. Jas[94] ke jas[95] hain. -184-

[69]above mercy; [70]supreme; [71]guiding spirit; [72]all; [73]protector; [74]fear; [75]destroyer; [76]enemies; [77]annihilator; [78]opposition; sinners; [79]chastiser; [84]all; [85]creation; [86]creator; [87]absolute; [88]destroyer; [89]absolute; [90]sovereign spirit; [91]manifest in individual souls; [92]self; [93]control [94]praise, glory; [95]praise, glory.

183. Lord God's— creation is the name of perfection, formation is absolute and complete, deeds are above discussion and criticism, actions annihilate the evil and sins.

184. Lord God is— Supreme Spirit, Absolute Manifestation, Perfect Self-controller, and Symbol of Glory and Praise.

Summary

God has created this world and all the other worlds in this universe according to the plan devised by Him. He is the absolute controller and cause of all deeds and actions. He protects His saints and punishes the wicked. He Himself is the Creator, Sustainer and the Destroyer. He is the Source of all the bounties, treasures and gifts.

ਭੁਜੰਗ ਪ੍ਰਜਾਤ ਛੰਦ ॥

ਨਮੇ ਸੂਰਜ^1 ਸੂਰਜੇ^{2} ਨਮੇ ਚੰਦ੍ਰ^3 ਚੰਦ੍ਰੇ^{4} ॥

ਨਮੇ ਰਾਜ^5 ਰਾਜੇ^{6} ਨਮੇ ਇੰਦ੍ਰ^7 ਇੰਦ੍ਰੇ^{8} ॥

ਨਮੇ ਅੰਧਕਾਰੇ^{9} ਨਮੇ ਤੇਜ^{10} ਤੇਜੇ^{11} ॥

ਨਮੇ ਬ੍ਰਿੰਦ^{12} ਬ੍ਰਿੰਦੇ^{13} ਨਮੇ ਬੀਜ^{14} ਬੀਜੇ^{15} ॥੧੮੫॥

ਨਮੇ ਰਾਜਸੇ^{16} ਤਾਮਸੇ^{17} ਸਾਂਤ^{18} ਰੂਪੇ^{19} ॥

ਨਮੇ ਪਰਮ^{20} ਤੱਤੰ^{21} ਅਤੱਤੰ^{22} ਸਰੂਪੇ^{23} ॥

ਨਮੇ ਜੋਗ^{24} ਜੋਗੇ^{25} ਨਮੇ ਗਯਾਨ^{26} ਗਯਾਨੇ^{27} ॥

ਨਮੇ ਮੰਤ੍ਰ^{28} ਮੰਤ੍ਰੇ^{29} ਨਮੇ ਧਯਾਨ^{30} ਧਯਾਨੇ^{31} ॥੧੮੬॥

ਨਮੇ ਜੁਧ^{32} ਜੁਧੇ^{33} ਨਮੇ ਗਯਾਨ^{34} ਗਯਾਨੇ^{35} ॥

ਨਮੇ ਭੋਜ^{36} ਭੋਜੇ^{37} ਨਮੇ ਪਾਨ^{38} ਪਾਨੇ^{39} ॥

ਨਮੇ ਕਲਹ^{40} ਕਰਤਾ^{41} ਨਮੇ ਸਾਂਤ^{42} ਰੂਪੇ^{43} ॥

ਨਮੇ ਇੰਦ੍ਰ^{44} ਇੰਦ੍ਰੇ^{45} ਆਨਦੰ^{46} ਬਿਭੂਤੇ^{47} ॥੧੮੭॥

ਕਲੰਕਾਰ^{48} ਰੂਪੇ^{49} ਅਲੰਕਾਰ^{50} ਅਲੰਕੇ^{51} ॥

ਨਮੇ ਆਸ^{52} ਆਸੇ^{53} ਨਮੇ ਬਾਂਕ^{54} ਬੰਕੇ^{55} ॥

ਅਭੰਗੀ^{56} ਸਰੂਪੇ^{57} ਅਨੰਗੀ^{58} ਅਨਾਮੇ^{59} ॥

ਤ੍ਰਿਭੰਗੀ^{60} ਤ੍ਰਿਕਾਲੇ^{61} ਅਨੰਗੀ^{62} ਅਕਾਮੇ^{63} ॥੧੮੮॥

BHUJANG PRAYAT CHHAND

Namo suraj[1] surje[2], namo chandr[3] chandre[4].

Namo raj[5] raje,[6] namo Indr[7] Indre[8].

Namo andhkare,[9] namo tej[10] teje[11].

Namo brind[12] brinde[13], namo bij[14] bije[15]. -185-

Namo rajsang[16] tamsang[17] sant[18] rupe[19].

Namo param[20] tatang[21] atatang[22] sarupe[23].

Namo jog[24] joge[25], namo gian[26] giane[27].

Namo mantr[28] mantre[29], namo dhian[30] dhiane[31]. -186-

Namo judh[32] judhe[33], namo gian[34] giane[35].

Namo bhoj[36] bhoje[37], namo pan[38] pane[39].

Namo kalah[40] karta[41], namo sant[42] rupe[43].

Namo Indr[44] Indre[45], anadang[46] bibhute[47]. -187-

Kalankar[48] rupe[49], alankar[50] alanke[51].

Namo as[52] ase,[53] namo bank[54] banke[56].

Abhangi[56] sarupe[57], anangi[58] aname[59].

Tribhangi[60] trikale[61], anangi[62] akame[63]. -188-

BHUJANG PRAYAT CHHAND

Notes

[1]energy; [2]sun; [3]coolness; [4]moon; [5]sovereignty; [6]kings; [7]power; [8]king of heaven; [9]cause of darkness; [10]heat; [11]light; [12]beauty; [13]vastness; [14]suspense; [15]invisibility; [16]king of light; [17]king of darkness; [18]virtuous; [19]form; [20]supreme; [21]spirit; [22]incorporeal; [23]form, existence; [24]tutor; [25]the path to be adopted for the union with God; [26]fountain; [27]knowledge; [28]author of hymns; [29]scriptures; [30]essence, concentration; [31]meditation; [32]spirit, glory; [33]wars; [34]knowledge; [35]learning; [36]sustenance; [37]food; [38]thirst; [39]drinks; [40]strife; [41]creator; [42]peace; [43]embodiment; [44]power ; [45]king of heavens; [46]beyond beginning; [47]gifts; [48]skill, essence; [49]arts, adornments; [50]beauty, charm; [51] beautiful; [52]hope; [53] hopeful; [54]delicacy; [55]elegant; [56]imperishable; [57]form; [58]incorporeal; [59]beyond a specific name; [60]destroyer of the three worlds; [61]beyond time, beyond death; [62]incorporeal; [63]beyond desires.

COMPOSITION 20

Theme
Waheguru is the source of all the energies, powers, beauties, lights and darkness. He is the Controller of all the constructions and destructions.

Literal Meaning

185. Hail the Almighty God, Who is the — Source of the energy of the suns, Coolness of the moons, Sovereignty of kings, Power of Indras, Cause of darkness, Heat of light, Beauty of vastness of the universe and Cause of suspense of invisibility.

186. Hail the Almighty God, Who is the— Lord of light, King of darkness, Supreme virtue in every form, spirit and not matter, Tutor of yogis, Fountain of all the knowledge, Author of all the hymns in the scriptures and Bestower of concentration in meditation.

187. Hail the Almighty God, Who is the — Glory of wars, Fountain of knowledge, Sstainer of food, Creator of all the rivers and oceans, Designer of all the strifes and chaos, Architect of peace and harmony, Power of Indras and Embodiment of all the gifts.

188. Hail the Almighty God, Who is the — Punisher of the sinners, Cause of skills in all the arts and artists, Hope in hopeful, Beauty in the beautiful, Elegance in the charming, Hail the Almighty God Who is — imperishable and spirit, incorporeal and nameless, Cause of death and Himself is beyond death and incorporeal and beyond desires.

Summary
Almighty God is the Creator of all the suns, moons, Indras, lights, darkness, spirits, matters, worlds, stars, vegetations, mountains, rivers, seas, oceans, air, skies, earths, netherlands, ignorance, knowledge, scriptures, peace, chaos, arts, skills, tunes, instruments, beauties, elegance, names, languages and desires. But He Himself is detached from all of them.

ਏਕ ਅਛਰੀ ਛੰਦ ॥

ਅਜੈ[1] ॥ ਅਲੈ[2] ॥ ਅਭੈ[3] ॥ ਅਬੈ[4] ॥੧੮੯॥

ਅਭੂ[5] ॥ ਅਜੂ[6] ॥ ਅਨਾਸ[7] ॥ ਅਕਾਸ[8] ॥੧੯੦॥

ਅਗੰਜ[9] ॥ ਅਭੰਜ[10] ॥ ਅਲੱਖ[11] ॥ ਅਭੱਖ[12] ॥੧੯੧॥

ਅਕਾਲ[13] ॥ ਦਿਆਲ[14] ॥ ਅਲੇਖ[15] ॥ ਅਭੇਖ[16] ॥੧੯੨॥

ਅਨਾਮ[17] ॥ ਅਕਾਮ[18] ॥ ਅਗਾਹ[19] ॥ ਅਢਾਹ[20] ॥੧੯੩॥

ਅਨਾਥੇ[21] ॥ ਪ੍ਰਮਾਥੇ[22] ॥ ਅਜੋਨੀ[23] ॥ ਅਮੋਨੀ[24] ॥੧੯੪॥

ਨ ਰਾਗੇ[25] ॥ ਨ ਰੰਗੇ[26] ॥ ਨ ਰੂਪੇ[27] ॥ ਨ ਰੇਖੇ[28] ॥੧੯੫॥

ਅਕਰਮੰ[29] ॥ ਅਭਰਮੰ[30] ॥ ਅਗੰਜੇ[31] ॥ ਅਲੇਖੇ[32] ॥੧੯੬॥

EK ACHHARI CHHAND

Ajai[1]. *Alai*[2]. *Abhai*[3]. *Abai*[4]. -189-

Abhu[5]. *Aju*[6]. *Anas*[7]. *Akas*[8]. -190-

Aganj[9]. *Abhanj*[10]. *Alakh*[11]. *Abhakh*[12]. -191-

Akal[13]. *Dial*[14]. *Alekh*[15]. *Abhekh*[16]. -192-

Anam[17]. *Akam*[18]. *Agah*[19]. *Adhah*[20]. -193-

Anathe[21]. *Pramathe*[22]. *Ajoni*[23]. *Amoni*[24]. -194-

Na rage[25]. *Na range*[26]. *Na rupe*[27]. *Na rekhe*[28]. -195-

Akarmang[29]. *Abharmang*[30]. *Aganje*[31]. *Alekhe*[32]. -196-

EK ACHHARI CHHAND

Notes

[1]invincible; [2]indestructible; [3]fearless; [4]eternal; [5]unborn; [6]unshakeable; [7]imperishable; [8]all pervading; [9]invincible; [10]imperishable; [11]invisible; [12]needs no sustenance; [13]beyond time; [14]compassionate; [15]beyond karmas; [16]beyond uniform; [17]beyond name; [18]beyond desires; [19]unfathomable; [20]boundless, who cannot be displaced; [21]who is the seniormost; [22]annihilator; [23]beyond birth; [24]God's voice is ever active, is never silent, non-mute; [25]detached; [26]without colour; [27]without form; [28]without shape; [29]beyond the law of karma; [30]beyond delusions; [31]imperishable; [32]beyond the scope of written description.

COMPOSITION 21

Theme

God is the greatest power in the universe. He is master of all and there is no master above him.

Literal Meaning

189.   God is — invincible, imperishable, fearless, beyond deaths.

190.   God is — unborn, unshakeable, imperishable, all pervading.

191.   God is — invincible, imperishable, invisible, beyond the need of any sustenance.

192.   God is — beyond death, all merciful, beyond the doctrine of karmas,
beyond all garbs.

193.   God is — beyond name, beyond desires, unfathomable, un-displaceable.

194.   God is the Master of all, He determines the time of death for all, He is beyond births, His inspiration and voice is ever active.

195.   God is detached, He is beyond colours, He is beyond form, He is beyond shape.

196.   God is beyond — karmas, delusions, destruction, description.

Summary

God's universe was a suspense, is a suspense and will always remain a suspense. He is the Creator and Master of all His creation. He is the Sole Decider of the time of birth and death of the whole creation. He Himself is self-illuminated, self-sustained and self-created. He is most powerful and is greatest of all. He is not born and is beyond deaths. His theories are for His creation and not for Himself. He is beyond all rules and laws.

ਭੁਜੰਗ ਪ੍ਰਯਾਤ ਛੰਦ ॥

ਨਮਸਤੁਲ[1] ਪ੍ਰਨਾਮੇ[2] ਸਮਸਤੁਲ[3] ਪ੍ਰਨਾਸੇ[4] ॥

ਅਗੰਜੁਲ[5] ਅਨਾਮੇ[6] ਸਮਸਤੁਲ[7] ਨਿਵਾਸੇ[8] ॥

ਨ੍ਰਿਕਾਮੇ[9] ਬਿਭੁਤੇ[10] ਸਮਸਤੁਲ[11] ਸਰੂਪੇ[12] ॥

ਕੁਕਰਮੇ[13] ਪ੍ਰਨਾਸੀ[14] ਸੁਧਰਮੇ[15] ਬਿਭੁਤੇ[16] ॥197॥

ਸਦਾ[17] ਸੱਚਿਦਾਨੰਦ[18] ਸਤ੍ਰੰ[19] ਪ੍ਰਨਾਸੀ[20] ॥

ਕਰੀਮੁਲ[21] ਕੁਨਿੰਦਾ[22] ਸਮਸਤੁਲ[23] ਨਿਵਾਸੀ[24] ॥

ਅਜਾਇਬ[25] ਬਿਭੁਤੇ[26] ਗਜਾਇਬ[27] ਗਨੀਮੇ[28] ॥

ਹਰਿਅੰ[29] ਕਰਿਅੰ[30] ਕਰੀਮੁਲ[31] ਰਹੀਮੇ[32] ॥198॥

ਚਤੂੰ[33] ਚਕੂ[34] ਵਰਤੀ[35] ਚਤੂੰ ਚਕੂ ਭੁਗਤੇ[36] ॥

ਸੁਯੰਭਵ[37] ਸੁਭੰ[38] ਸਰਬਦਾ[39] ਸਰਬ[40] ਜੁਗਤੇ[41] ॥

ਦੁਕਾਲੰ[42] ਪ੍ਰਨਾਸੀ[43] ਦਿਆਲੰ[44] ਸਰੂਪੇ[45] ॥

ਸਦਾ[46] ਅੰਗ[47] ਸੰਗੇ[48] ਅਭੰਗੰ[49] ਬਿਭੁਤੇ[50] ॥199॥

BHUJANG PRAYAT CHHAND

Namastul[1] praname[2], samastul[3] pranase[4].

Aganjul[5] aname[6], samastul[7] nivase[8].

Nrikamang[9] bibhute[10], samastul[11] sarupe[12].

Kukarmang[13] pranasi[14], sudharmang[15] bibhute[16]. -197-

Sada[17] sach(i) da-nand[18] satrang[19] pranasi[20].

Karimul[21] kuninda[22], samastul[23] nivasi[24].

Ajaib[25] bibhute[26] gajaib[27] ganime[28].

Hariang[29] kariang[30] karimul[31] rahime[32]. -198-

Chatr[33] chakr[34] varti[35], chatr chakr bhugte[36].

Suyanbhav[37] subhang[38] sarab-da[39] sarab[40] jugte[41].

Dukalang[42] pranasi[43] dialang[44] sarupe[45].

Sada[46] ang[47] sange[48] abhangang[49] bibhute[50]. -199-

BHUJANG PRAYAT CHHAND

Notes

[1]adorable Lord; [2]salutation; [3]universal; [4]judge for destruction; [5]indestructible; [6]beyond name; [7]universal; [8]resident; [9]beyond desire; [10]source of treasure; [11]universal; [12]manifest; [13]sin; [14]destroyer; [15]righteousness; [16]one who glorifies; [17]always; [18]eternal truth; [19]enemies; [20]destroyer; [21]compassionate; [22]creator; [23]universal; [24]resident; [25]wonderful; [26]treasure; [27]terrorist; [28]enemy; [29]destroyer; [30]creator; [31]merciful; [32]benevolent; [33]in the four quarters, everywhere; [34]corners, directions; [35]pervading; [36]king; [37]self-created; [38]glorious; [39]eternal; [40]all; [41]the unifying force; [42]at the time of birth and death, duality of life and death, bad times; [43]destroyer; [44]merciful; [45]embodiment; [46]always; [47-48]companion, close as the limbs of the body; [49]everlasting; [50]glory, power.

COMPOSITION 22

Theme

God Himself is the Creator and Destroyer of the universe. He is Omnipresent, Omnipotent and Omniscient. He is the most Generous and Kind Father.

Literal Meaning

197.   Salutation to most Adorable God, Who is the Destroyer of the evil everywhere, Who is indestructible and beyond specific names, Who is omnipresent, Who is beyond desires and is the Source of all gifts, Who is manifest in all forms; Who is the Destroyer of the sins, Who is Rewardgiver to the righteous,

198.   Who is Eternal Truth, Who is Annihilator of the tyrant, Who is Merciful Creator, Who abides in all, Who is wonderful and glorious, Who is Terror for the villains, Who is both Destroyer and the Creator, Who is merciful and benevolent,

199.   Who pervades in all quarters, Who commands in all the directions, Who is self-created, compassionate and auspicious, Who is Eternal Binding Force, Who is the Destroyer of the pain of life and death, Who is the Eembodiment of Compassion, who is the Companion of all of us, Who has everlasting treasures of power and glory.

Summary

Hail the Great Lord who is our Creator, Sustainer and Destroyer. He is most Kind, Benevolent and Merciful Father. He looks after all of us in both comforts and miseries. He is the Master of all the treasures, bounties and gifts. He resides in everyone's mind and body. He is our Guide and Companion. He is the Controller of all the worlds in the universe. He is the Final Judge of the time of birth and death of all of us. He plans the mode of death for each one of us. He destroys the sinners and tyrant and protects the righteous and noble.

SAKHI 1

Guru Gobind Singh was born in 1666 at Patna, now the capital of the Eastern state of Bihar. In the old Bihar were also born the prophets of both Buddhism and Jainism, Buddha and Mahavir. His childhood name was Gobind Rai. He lived in Patna for about six years and then came to Anandpur to join his father, Guru Tegh Bahadur.

When Guru Gobind Singh was born, a Muslim saint called Bhikhan Shah, a resident of Karnal, saw a divine star in the East and said his prayers facing East rather than West, in the direction of Mecca.

Next day Bhikhan Shah set out for Patna to have an audience with the divine child. The journeys in those days were very hazardous and dangerous and the main modes of travelling were either on foot or on a horse. Patna is about 500 miles from Karnal and it took the saint about nine months to reach Patna.

On reaching Patna he enquired about Guru's residence and went straight to meet the Guru. He took with him two clay cups and a bottle of milk. The Guru at that time had learned to crawl around the house. Saint Bhikhan Shah announced his arrival and told about his mission to Mata Gujri, the mother of Guru Gobind Singh. The saint was welcomed by the household and was offered a seat in the sitting room. He filled the two cups with milk and placed them on the floor in front of him and waited for the Guru's arrival. The Guru entered the room, looked at the people sitting in the room and then crawled towards the milk cups. He sat near them and then to the astonishment of all sitting around him he covered both the cups with his hands. His tiny left and right hands covering the two cups, he looked towards the saint who immediately fell on the ground to bow to the Guru and then raised his hands, looked towards the skies and thanked God for bringing him here all the way from Karnal.

Later the saint explained to his followers and other people present in the room that he wanted to know if the Guru was a Muslim-prophet or a Hindu-prophet. He had thought in his own mind that if the Guru covered the left hand cup then he would be a Muslim prophet and if he had covered the right hand cup then he would be a Hindu prophet. By covering both the cups the God had given the message that prophets belonged to God and not to any religion; the religions are man-made institutions.

SAKHI 2

At Anandpur Sahib, Guru Gobind Singh had a beautiful garden. The gardener was one Bhai Kesra Singh. He was a very devout Sikh. Once a couple named Bhai Mohna and Bibi Sohna came to him and requested him to employ them as his assistants. In real life they were rich and noble people. Once they had refused to offer water, which they were carrying to a temple for use in the prayers, to a dying man. The man, before his death, had cursed them, saying that the Guru should never grant them audience for the sin they had committed. This curse had been haunting both of them and they had come to Anandpur for forgiveness from the Guru but had no courage to face him. They worked very hard and planted beautiful flowers. Once Kesra Singh made a beautiful bouquet of the flowers so grown by Mohna and Sohna and sent them to the Guru. The Guru understood the message but did not send for the couple.

One day, a roaming ascetic called Roda came to see the Guru. On his way to the Guru he saw the garden and the beautiful flowers. He plucked all the flowers and offered them to the Guru as his own offering. The Guru, looking at flowers cried with pain and ran barefooted to the garden to see Mohna and Sohna. The couple, having found that their flowers had gone, had taken poison and were dead before the Guru reached them. The Guru sat on the ground and put their heads in his lap and said that their sin had been pardoned and they could have the audience and meeting with the Guru before they left this mortal world. In front of hundreds of Sikhs, who followed the Guru to the garden, Mohna and Sohna came back to life; they touched the Guru's feet and then went back to everlasting sleep.

SAKHI 3.1

Bhai Nand Lal was an eminent scholar and a great poet. He wrote a large number of poems in the praise of Guru Gobind Singh. He was born in Ghazni in Afghanistan. He left Emperor Aurangzeb's service and came to Anandpur to serve the Guru. When he first came to Anandpur, he did not announce his arrival and virtually hid himself in a small house. In his heart he prayed to the Guru to call him and employ him in his court. The silent message of Bhai Nand Lal's heart reached the Guru's thoughts and he immediatelly sent a messenger to escort Bhai Nand Lal to his court. Bhai Nand Lal was both stunned and amused by this call. He rushed to the Guru and fell at the Guru's feet. The Guru lifted him, embraced him and said, "Dear friend, I have been waiting for you since yesterday." Bhai Nand Lal touched his feet once again.

SAKHI 3.2

Mandi is a small hill station in Himachal. Guru Gobind Singh loved this place. Once Guru Gobind Singh came here to attend a conference of the hill chiefs. The Guru was warmly welcomed and greatly honoured by the local ruler. In front of a large gathering the Guru floated a raw earthen pot in the territorial lake. It got filled with water but did not sink. It also did not dissolve away. Pointing to this unusual happening the Guru said that as his earthen pot ware was saved by Waheguru, so would be the city of Mandi in the horrific times to come. History stands witness that despite the repeated brutal invasions by the foreigners, the city of Mandi was never plundered or destroyed.

SAKHI 3.3

A similar Sakhi is also true regarding the state of Malerkotla situated in Punjab. When the two younger sons of Guru Gobind Singh were being tried in a special court at Sarhind, the Nawab of Malerkotla rose for the defence of the young princes of Guru Gobind Singh. When the news reached the Guru, he blessed the Nawab and the state of Malerkotla. It is a fact of history that despite the gruesome massacre and destruction of 1947 in and around Punjab the state of Malerkotla was not touched by the gangs and the rioters.

SAKHI 4.1

Padma was a daughter of the Chief of Nahan. She was popularly known as Princess Padma. She had an audience with Guru Gobind Singh at Riwalsar where he had gone at the invitation of the hill chiefs to see the floating island in the lake of Riwalsar. Padma was greatly impressed by the spirituality of the Guru and became his disciple. The Guru blessed her and took her in his fold. A few days after the arrival of the Guru at Riwalsar the hill chief held a secret meeting to assassinate the Guru while he was there. Padma overhead this conversation and ran to the Guru to inform him about the evil designs of his hosts. The Guru told her that they would not be successful in their attempt of assassination but a war between the two groups was destined for the evil in the rajas had taken over them. Padma looked deeply distressed and requested the Guru that she would like to leave her worldly body before seeing the killings of her kith and kin and destruction of her father's territory. Guru Gobind Singh reluctantly granted her unusual wish. Though the hill chief failed to harm the Guru on that occasion, later, at the instigatiion of the Raja of Bilaspur they mounted an attack on Anandpur. Padma had died a few days before this bloody war.

SAKHI 4.2

At the end of the seventeenth century there was a great famine in India. There was an acute shortage of water and scarcity of food all over Punjab. At Anandpur the community kitchen of Guru Gobind Singh was also affected. Whereas the number of people eating at the langar increased, the supply of rations and water ran down. On the complaint of the storekeeper of the langar, the Guru's mother, Mata Gujri, ordered a proportionate reduction in the distribution of rations per individual. The frequency of the distribution of the langar was also reduced from twice a day to once a day. When Guru Gobind Singh came to know about this he felt very much distressed. He said to himself that the langar should go on undisturbed. He spoke to God and then hurried to the kitchen stores. He shut himself in the store for a little while. When he came out he looked very calm and relaxed. He went to his mother, talked with her and then summoned for his courtiers. He said that taking into account the drought and misery of the neighbouring villages, the frequency of the distribution of langar should be increased rather than reduced. On enquiry by the courtiers how the increased demand of the rations would be met, he said that God had spoken to him and that He would fill the stores with the required demand. After that the Guru's langar fed all who came there in search of food. The langar ran for 24 hours and miraculously the bins in the stores remained filled all the times.

SAKHI 5.1

Guru Gobind Singh used to go to river Sutlej to take bath. Once he went there with his young friends and started playing a game of splashing water. One team was led by him and the other team was led by a young boy called Gulab Rai. The team of Gulab Rai was defeated. In utter shame and confusion, Gulab Rai ran to the bank of the river and began to put on the Guru's turban, believing it to be his own. One of the Guru's escorts, Bhai Sango, immediately restrained him, for it would be a sacrilege for anyone to put on the Guru's turban. The Guru came to Gulab Rai, held his arm and said that one day he would become a great Sikh and would take charge of the gurdwaras at Anandpur. Many years later, when the Guru left Anandpur and went to Nanded, Gulab Rai took possession of Anandpur gurdwaras and looked after them with zeal and enthusiasm.

SAKHI 5.2

Dilawar Khan was an Afghan general posted in Punjab. He became very jealous of Guru Gobind Singh's fame and success. He sent his son with a strong contingent to plunder Anandpur and to kill the Guru, but Dilawar's son was badly defeated by the Sikhs. To revenge his son's defeat, Dilawar Khan chose one of his brave slaves, Hussain, to march on Anandpur. In 1693, Hussain attacked Anandpur with a two-thousand-strong contingent. He was joined by the combined armies of Raja Bhim Chand and Raja Kirpal. On hearing of the attack, a delegation of the masands residing in Anandpur rushed to the Guru's mother and advised her to come to terms with the mighty Hussain and the hill rajas. They refused to join in with the Guru's forces to repulse the attack by the Hussain's combined forces. The Guru was not surprised to hear about the treachery of the masands; he expelled them from Anandpur. Later, in a meeting with his generals, he prophesied that he could see the death of Hussain and that his army would not be able to touch the outskirts of Anandpur. Hussain was slain by Gulab Rai of Guler, a disciple of the Guru, in a skirmish a few miles away from Anandpur. The hill rajas and Hussain's army retreated and abandoned the idea of attacking Anandpur.

SAKHI 6.1

Diwan Nand Chand was a very trustworthy minister of Guru Gobind Singh. He had accompanied the Guru to a number of battles and fought with great skill and bravery. Once a group of Udasis brought a very beautiful handwritten copy of *Guru Granth Sahib* for Guru Gobind Singh's signatures and attestation. The copy was submitted to Diwan Nand Chand for verification and initial remarks. Looking at the elegance of the *Granth*, Nand Chand asked the Udasis if he could keep the *Granth* for himself. When the Udasis refused to accept Nand Chand's request, he threatened them with dire consequences and severe punishment. The Udasis then complained to the Guru. The Guru, at once, sent a messenger to Diwan Nand Chand and commanded him to return the *Granth* to the Udasis. Diwan Nand Chand refused to obey even the Guru's command and fled to Kiratpur. When the Guru was informed about this he sighed in grief and said that Nand Chand had gone to embrace his death on the outskirts of Kiratpur. When Diwan Nand Chand reached Kiratpur he was shot by Dhirmal's followers and succumbed to his injuries soon after.

SAKHI 6.2

One Duni Chand was a soldier in Guru Gobind Singh's army. In one of the battles with the hill chiefs, he was asked by the Guru to go forward and engage with an intoxicated elephant sent by the enemy. Duni Chand had no confidence in his own strength, and defying Guru's orders, he fled from the battefield en-route to his home in Amritsar. When the Guru was informed about this, he innocently said that he who had run away from the fear of death from the battlefield would find death waiting for him at home. Soon after, Duni Chand reached home and was bitten by a poisonous snake and died almost instantaneously.

SAKHI 7.1

Kahn Singh was a devout Sikh and a mason by profession. Once, when he was plastering a wall in the Guru's court, a drop of cement fell on the Guru. Kahn Singh was very sorry and begged the Guru to punish him for this lapse. On his insistence the Guru ordered that Kahn Singh should be given a mild stroke on his back. The person entrusted to punish Kahn Singh hit him harder than the Guru had meant. As a gesture of reparation the Guru said to the congregation that the best reparation to Kahn Singh would be if one of Guru's Sikhs could offer his daughter in matrimony to the young Kahn Singh. One Ajaib Singh of Khandahar immediately offered his daughter Meera to the Guru. Meera went forward and bowed to the Guru. Soon afterwards Meera and Kahn Singh were married and with the blessings of Guru Gobind Singh had five brave and distinguished sons.

SAKHI 7.2

Once a family of Sikhs came from Peshawar to visit Anandpur and have the blessings of the Guru. The youngest of the family, Joga Singh, chose to remain with the Guru to serve in His army. Joga Singh grew up to be a very devout and obedient Sikh. One day the Guru received a message from Joga Singh's father, requesting the Guru to send Joga Singh back to Peshawar for a short period as he had arranged Joga Singh's marriage with a local girl. Joga Singh was reluctant to go, as he did not want to leave the Guru for a moment. On the persuasion of the Guru, Joga Singh left for Peshawar with a lot of gifts for his bride from the Guru and his friends. On the marriage day, just when three out of four lavans had been completed a note from the Guru was delivered to Joga Singh asking him to return to Anandpur immediately. Joga Singh at once stood up, suspended the marriage ceremony and proceeded to Anandpur. On the way back he felt elated with his action and thus committed the sin of pride. Blinded in his ego he forgot the Guru's teachings and decided to visit a local prostitute to satisfy his unfulfilled passions. Whenever he stopped at the prostitute's door, a watchman warned him away. Then Joga tried to use a rope to climb the rear window of the house, but the rope turned into a snake and Joga Singh rushed back home in utmost confusion and fear. Next day, he reached Anandpur and presented himself to the Guru in shame and contempt. The Guru smiled and said that next time when Joga Singh came back from Peshawar he should avoid the route via Hoshiarpur as the Guru might not be able to warn him, or turn the rope into a snake next time.

SAKHI 8.1

Saiyad Khan was a general in the Imperial army. He had heard a lot about Guru Gobind Singh and had become a great admirer of him. Once, when an army of Mughal soldiers was being commissioned to plunder Anandpur and molest the Guru, Saiyad Khan contrived to be put in command so that he would be able to help the Guru. The Guru did read Saiyad Khan's mind, and when the Mughal army reached the out-skirts of Anandpur, the Guru went forward to meet him and his army with only five Sikhs accompanying him. The Guru spoke to Saiyad Khan about the injustices inflicted upon him by the Mughal Government and the hill chiefs, and the reasons why he had to resort to the sword in his own defence. The Guru also said that he would not attack Saiyad Khan for he was the Guru's admirer and follower. On hearing this Saiyad Khan at once dismounted from his horse and sought the Guru's blessings.

On Saiyad Khan's defection from the Mughal army, one Ramzan Khan took the command in his hands and with all available might made a fierce onslaught on the Guru. Following their own strategic planning, the Guru and his army evacuated Anandpur, to ambush the Mughal army which, ignorant of the Guru's move, entered Anandpur and was immediately surrounded by the Sikh forces. Ramzan Khan was killed and the Mughal army surrendered to the Guru.

SAKHI 8.2

Once, during the siege of Anandpur in its third and last war, the Guru saw the Mughal generals playing 'Chaupar' (Indian draughts) under a tree, about two miles away from the Anandpur fort. The Guru, out of sheer fun, discharged an arrow into their midst. The generals got scared and thought that only by a miracle could the Guru have discharged that arrow to such a great distance and with such accuracy. The Guru then sent a second arrow with a note which read that it was the Guru's archery and not a miracle that the arrow had covered such a large range and with such accuracy.

SAKHI 9.1

Before leaving the city of Anandpur, at the end of its siege in 1704, Guru Gobind Singh went to pray in the Gurdwara of Guru Tegh Bahadur and there entrusted its custody to one of his disciples, Bhai Gurbakhs Singh. The Guru told him that so long as he remained the caretaker of that shrine nothing would harm him, a prophecy which was duly fulfilled.

SAKHI 9.2

After the war at Chamkaur in 1704, Guru Gobind Singh spent a few difficult days in the Machiwara forest. From there, he proceeded north and took shelter in a house of a Sikh called Gulab. The Guru gave Gulab the address of an old lady and asked him to hurry to her and bring from her a piece of blue cloth which she had dyed and knitted for the Guru. On enquiry by Gulab, the Guru told him that the cloth the lady had knitted had been predicted by the Guru in his first worldly body as Guru Nanak and the Guru then narrated to Gulab a hymn from *Asa Di Var-*

> Nir Vastar le kapre pahire, Turk
> Pathani amal kiya . . . . . .

meaning that blue colour clothes were worn and the disguise of a Turk was made. Guru Gobind Singh told Gulab that he had to wear those clothes and disguise himself as a Turk to escape from Machiwara to Damdama. A few days later, Guru Gobind left his hideout in Machiwara disguised as a Muslim saint in the blue garb, with the help of two Pathans known as Nabi Khan and Ghani Khan.

SAKHI 10.1

On his way to Damdama Sahib the Guru stayed at Dina for a few days. There two Sikhs named Param Singh and Dharam Singh came to see him and presented him with a horse and a new dress. The Guru gave these presents to a Sikh named Shamira Singh and said that all the land over which Shamira would ride on this horse, in the next couple of days, would become his. Shamira, greatly delighted by the Guru's grace, hurried back to his home and told about the Guru's generosity to his uncle. The uncle, however, rejected the blessing saying it was a mere hoax. Shamira out of sheer curiosity rode the horse only around his own village. History records that Shamira and his descendent remained owners of that land for generations.

SAKHI 10.2

When the Guru reached Kot-Kapura, a small village in Farid-kot region, he met a nephew of the chief of that area. He complained to the Guru about his uncle's excesses in taking possepssion his estate and property and sought the Guru's advice. The Guru said that he should not, at any cost, engage in a fight with his uncle as the Guru could see his death in the battle, and advised him to settle the dispute through negotiations. The wife of the nephew, however, disagreed with the Guru and incited her husband to attack his uncle. In disregard to the Guru's advice the nephew attacked his uncle and was killed in the very first moments of the battle.

SAKHI 11.1

Two Sikhs, Tilok Singh and Ram Singh were the Guru's comrades during the battle of Chamkaur, fought in 1704. After the battle they arranged the cremation of the Guru's older sons, Ajit Singh and Jughar Singh, who had died in the battle a day before. This was a very courageous and heroic act as the Mughals had strictly forbidden the cremation of the Sikh martyrs. While at Damdama Sahib, the Guru sent for them. Whey they arrived, the Guru embraced them and said that he was very pleased with their bravery and blessed them and said that with the grace of God they would be the future rulers of two important states of Punjab. The prophecy was fulfilled. Ram Singh later became the ruler and founder of the state of Patiala and Tilok Singh the founder and ruler of the states of Nabha and Jind.

SAKHI 11.2

While still at Damdama the Guru baptised a Sikh called Dalla. One day, while walking with Dalla on the latter's fields, the Guru said that he had seen wheat and sugarcane growing on that land. Dalla looked at the Guru with surprise and replied that the whole land was barren and nothing would ever grow on it. The Guru smiled and said that God had accepted Dalla's requests and had made his land fertile and rich. This prophecy became true at the next harvest time.

SAKHI 12.1

When Guru Gobind Singh reached Nauhar village, he found the inhabitants proud of their wealth and very unfriendly. They refused to give any supplies or food to the Guru's retinue. The Guru said that all pride had very nasty falls and foretold that all the glory of that place, due to the hypocrisy and egotistic behaviour of the inhabitants would vanish. The prophecy was fulfilled, when in 1756 an expedition plundered and destroyed the whole village.

SAKHI 12.2

While the Guru was in Delhi, a goldsmith and his wife came to him and requested him to bless them with a son. The Guru was about to leave for a game of chase, he asked the couple to accompany him on that expedition. There in the forest, in a remote corner lay a child in a little basket crying . The Guru picked up the child and gave him to the goldsmith's wife and blessing them, said that they would have a very happy and prosperous life.

SAKHI 13.1

Guru Gobind Singh's amrit had infused fearless valour in all hearts. Once a group of Sikhs from Majha set out towards Anandpur. On their way some of the pilgrims halted for a rest besides a well. One young woman called Deep Kaur refused to rest and marched towards Anandpur all alone. On the way she countered four Mughal soldiers who blocked her way and wanted to molest her. She, in her heart prayed to Guru Gobind Singh and abruptly threw her golden bangles on the floor. The soldiers bent to pick them up, and in the spur of a moment she drew out her sword and cut two of them into pieces. The other two, shocked and scared, tried to flee but were obstructed by Deep Kaur. She challenged them to a fight, and in a brief encounter which followed she killed both of them. Then she knelt down and thanked Guru Gobind Singh for the courage and valour which had saved her honour and life. When she reached Anandpur with her companions and narrated that episode to Guru Gobind Singh, he smiled and said that whenever Sikhs would call out to him from their pure hearts he would always come to their rescue.

SAKHI 13.2

One day, when Guru Gobind Singh was sitting in his court, an old lady came weeping and crying bitterly. The Guru made her sit next to him and asked her the reason for her sorrow. She said that she was a very proud wife and an enviable mother, having sacrificed her husband and two sons for the cause of the Guru; but unfortunately her third son had fallen ill and was not able to serve in the Guru's army; she wanted the Guru to cure him so that he could also die a heroic death. She prayed to the Guru to grant her wish. The Guru patted her on her back and said that God would definitely listen to her prayers and her son would soon be cured. She went home to find her son miraculously cured and hale and hearty. Later, he joined the Guru's army and served him for a long time.

SAKHI 14.1

One day, Guru Gobind Singh asked a Sikh to fetch him a glass of water. A young boy who was sitting close by stood up and volunteered to bring the water for the Guru. The Guru noticed that the boy's hands were very tender and soft. On enquiry he told the Guru that he belonged to a rich family and had not done any work at home or outside. The Guru said that he would not accept water from him. The boy felt sad and fell at the Guru's feet and asked him the reason for such a denial. The Guru said that the service of mankind is the prime duty of a true Sikh and as the boy had not done any such service, he was not acceptable to the Guru. The boy took a vow in front of the congregation that he would lead his life in accordance with the teaching of the Guru and would serve in the Guru's langer and in the Guru's court. Guru Gobind Singh blessed him and made him his close disciple.

SAKHI 14.2

Once Guru Gobind Singh went to Kurukshetra on the occasion of a solar eclipse. Many local brahmins and yogis came to listen to him and became his followers. Most of the hill rajas were also in Kurukshetra attending the fair. They made a plan to ambush the Guru and kill him. They hurriedly employed two Mughal mercenary generals to engage the Guru in a fake battle and kill him. One of the generals, Saiyad Beg, later refused to attack the Guru when he came to know about his divinity. The other general named Alit Khan, with the support of the hill rajas, besieged the Guru when he left Kurukshetra on his way back to Anandpur. The Guru had only a handful of Sikhs with him. The situation was very desperate. General Alif Khan and the hill rajas were about two thousand in number. Then something dawned on General Saiyad Beg — he heard a voice from the skies directing him to go and help the Guru. He immediately ordered his men and jumped into the fray. He went directly to the Guru, fell at his feet and said that he should be allowed to fight for the Guru. The Guru patted him on his back and said that he was not fighting for the Guru but for the truth and for Allaha. Alif Khan and his combined forces were badly beaten by the joint forces of the Guru and Saiyad Khan and the Guru marched victoriously towards Anandpur.

SAKHI 15.1

Bhai Kanhaiya was a devout Sikh of Guru Gobind Singh. He belonged to villge Sodra in Gujjranwala district. He nursed the wounded in the battlefield. Once a group of Sikhs went to Guru Gobind Singh and complained that Bhai Kanhaiya was helping the enemy by offering them water and medicine. The Guru called Bhai Kanhaiya for an explanation. He said, with hand folded and eyes focussed on the feet of the Guru, "My Lord, I do not nurse Sikhs or Muslims, I nurse you and only you, for wherever I see a wounded soldier, in him I see you." "My Lord, you are present everywhere and in everyone." The Guru stood up from his throne and embraced Bhai Kanhaiya. It is worth noting that Bhai Kanhaiya was the true forerunner of the modern ambulance and first aid services.

SAKHI 15.2

Once when Guru Gobind Singh was staying at Paonta Sahib, he went for a ferry ride. The ferryman took him around and showed to him a number of villages habited on the shores of Yamuna. At the end of the voyage the Guru offered him the fare. The ferryman fell at the Guru's feet and said that he did not want any money but if the Guru was so kind then he should offer him a safe journey across the ocean of the world as he had offered him a safe journey across river Yamuna. Guru Gobind Singh smiled and said that God had granted the ferryman *mukti* and that he would be freed from further transmigration.

SAKHI 16.1

Guru Gobind Singh was a great admirer of learned people and scholars. A pandit known as Kesho used to read epic poems to the Guru. One day some Sikhs asked the pandits about the validity of the stories, about the might and power of Bhim and Arjun. Kesho actuated by greed misled the questioners by telling them that the epic stories were true and the real reason of the might, power and strength of the Pandava brothers was the result of their worship and offerings to Goddess Durga and her personal appearance to them. The misguided Sikhs then requested Kesho to show them the way, the procedures and the rituals to make Goddess Durga manifest and grant them the same boons as she had granted the Pandava brothers. Kesho, blinded in his ego and inwardly rejoicing that the Sikhs had fallen back into his trap, replied that though in this evil age of Kaliyug no gods make personal appearance, it could be made possible by organising a great 'havan' by him. The Sikhs told the Guru regarding their dialogue with Kesho and requested him to release unlimited funds to organise the 'havan'. The Guru agreed to their request and at the same time called a meeting of his close associates to warn them about the futility of Kesho's actions. He told them that Kesho had sown the corrupt seeds of suspicion in the minds of innocent Sikhs and the only way to make them realise their folly was to accept their request and go through the havan proceedings of Kesho.

Kesho started the 'havan' proceeding on Naina Devi, a scared resort of the Hindus. Many hundred thousand rupees were spent on the 'havan' material and many top Brahmins were summoned to assist Kesho in reciting the mantras. The days passed by, the mantras mingled with the air of Naina Devi but Goddess Durga did not manifest herself. One night all Brahmins including Kesho disappeared in the thick of night to avoid the wrath of the Sikhs for their unsolicited prophecy. The Sikhs ran back to the Guru and explained to him the new situation. The Guru at once sent out orders to the Sikhs to come and assemble at the site of the havan. When they had all come the Guru went near the 'havan fire' and ordered them to throw in the fire all the rest of the material. When many tons of oil, ghee and dry fruits were thrown into the fire, and the flames went up to touch the skies, Guru Gobind Singh drew his sword and shouted at the top of his voice that all powers and strengths are the blessing of the Almighty God and that it did not need any rituals or ceremonies. His sword was Durga and would perform the deeds of chivalry and heroism in the future.

SAKHI 17.1

In the historical account of the world prophets, Guru Gobind Singh is the only prophet who has written his autobiography and has told the world in his own words about his mission. He named his autobiography as *Bachitar Natak* and composed it in Braj Basha (language). It was complied in 1692 at Anandpur.

Describing the call of God and his ordained mission, Guru Gobind Singh says:

> I shall now tell my own history,
> How God brought me into the world . . . . . .

When I was performing austerities and meditating on Kali and Maha Kal on the lofty Hem Kunt in the high Himalayas, I became absorbed in the Immortal One and was one with the Lord because of the devotion of my mother and father. I did not wish it, but the order came for me to take birth in the Kali Yug (the Present Evil Age). The Immortal One told me how the demons were first created, but they trusted in their own arms and so were destroyed. Then the gods were created, but they became proud (worshipped their own strength) and called themselves Parameshwar (Supreme God). Maha Deva (Shiva) called himself The Imperishable; Vishnu appointed himself Parameshwar; Brahma stated that he was Par Brahm (Supreme Brahma); but none of them knew the True Lord. Then the Lord created the Eight Witnesses (Earth, Sun, Moon, Fire, Wind, etc.) but people began to worship them. Some people worshipped stones, some worshipped water, and became ensnared in egoism. The Siddhs and Sadhs likewise founded their own Panths (Sects), and went astray in quarrels and pride. When I created Dattatraiya, he only let his finger-nails grow long and matted his hair, but he failed to meditate on the love of Hari. Gorakh made disciples of great rajas, but only taught them to split their ears and put in earrings. Ramanand became a Bairagi and wore a wooden necklace, but forgot the Lord. All the Great Souls only founded their own Sects. Muhammad was ordained King of Arabia by the Lord, but he only taught circumcision to his devotees. He caused his own name to be repeated and did not proclaim the True Name. So the Immortal one said to me,

"I have glorified you as my son, I have created you to proclaim the Panth; go, spread the faith there, and restrain the people from folly." I stood up, made obeisance, and said, "This Panth will spread in the world when Thou gives assistance." For this reason the Lord sent me; then I took birth and came into the world. What He spoke, that I speak, and I bear no enmity to anyone. Those who call me Parameshwar shall all fall into the pit of Hell; know me as His slave only, — have not the least doubt of that. I am the slave of the Supreme Being, and have come to behold the spectacle of the world; what the Lord told me, that I tell the world, and I will not remain silent through fear of mortals.

(vs. 29-33)

We have come into the world for this purpose,
For the sake of the faith the divine Guru sent us:
"Wherever you extend the faith,
Seize and hurl down evil deceivers."
For this very purpose we have taken birth —
All you saints, understand this in your heart;
To spread the faith, to protect the saints,
And to extirpate all evildoers

(vs. 42, 43 *Bachitar Natak*)

SAKHI 18.1

The Sikhs under the command of Guru Gobind Singh fought eleven battles after the creation of the Khalsa in March, 1699. Of these, six battles were fought at Anandpur and one each at Nirmongarh, Bharsali, Sirsa, Chamkaur and Mukatsar. All these battles were fought for survival as the Mughal rulers and the hill rajas had sworn to crush the Guru and annihilate the Khalsa Brotherhood. The post-Khalsa period battles were fought as follows:

The first and second battles of Anandpur	1699
The battle of Nirmogarh	1700
The battle of Bharsali	1700
The battle of Chamkaur	1702
The third battle of Anandpur	1703
The fourth battle of Anandpur	1703
The fifth and sixth battles of Anandpur	1704
The battle of Sirsa	1704
The second battle of Chamkaur	1704
The battle of Mukatsar	1705

SAKHI 18.2

Guru Gobind Singh passed away on 7 October, 1708. Before his death he gave command of the Khalsa to Banda Bahadur alias Banda Singh Bahadur and sent him to Punjab to finish the task started by him. Banda Singh marched towards the direction of Sirhind and captured it on 12 May, 1710. He punished all the enemies of the Khalsa and established the first Sikh empire in the hilly areas of Punjab, now called Himachal Pradesh. He ruled up to 1715 when he was captured and tortured to death.

SAKHI 19.1

Once a Jain yogi named Hans came to see Guru Gobind Singh and brought with him a fine painting of a sunrise scene. He wanted to have an audience with the Guru. The Guru said that Hans's heart was dark and callous, so he would not give him an audience. Sainapat, one of the Guru's court poets pleaded that the painter's request be reconsidered. The Guru then sent Bhai Daya Singh, one of the Panj Piyaras, to a nearby cave to call a young ascetic, who was in a very poor state of health and shock, in order to explain to Hans the cause of the Guru's denial. The Guru asked the ascetic to relate to show Hans the tragedy of his life story. The ascetic said that about twelve years ago he had lived as a monk in a monastery supervised by Yogi Hans. One day he had seen a girl who had been his childhood friend and had entered the nunnery a few days ago. Yogi Hans had taken a very serious view of this innocent meeting and had ordered that the girl should be blinded and the monk should be placed in rigorous imprisonment for twelve years. Yogi Hans immediately realised the cause for Guru's refusal to grant him an interview. He fell down at the threshold of the Guru's court, cried like a child and begged for forgiveness. The Guru sent his Sikhs to find the blind girl. She was found after some effort and time, and was brought in the presence of the Guru. He blessed her and she regained her eyesight. The ascetic and the girl were married in the presence of the Guru and Yogi Hans was pardoned by the Guru.

SAKHI 19.2

Once Maharaja Ranjit Singh, marching on an expedition, halted at the gates of a gurdwara, near Shakar Ganj, and went in to say his prayers. He requested the Bhai-granthi to perform the Ardas and requested the Guru-God for his victory. The Bhai-granthi performed the Ardas, read the Vak from *Guru Granth Sahib* and put a saffron victory mark on the forehead of the Maharaja and said that Waheguru would definitely grant him the victory. The Maharaja went to the battle and inflicted a crushing defeat on the enemy and returned home with the victory colours. On the way home he again halted on the outskirts of the same gurdwara, went in with the triumphant-glory, summoned the Bhai-granthi and asked him for any gift from the Maharaja, as he had won the battle. The Bhai-granthi stood up in rage and asked that how the Maharaja had all of a sudden, become a donor, when until a few days ago he had been only a beggar? And how could he donate to the Guru what he actually got by His grace and blessings? The Maharaja realised his mistake, bowed to *Guru Granth Sahib* and begged forgiveness for his egotistic behaviour.

SAKHI 20.1

Guru Gobind Singh created Khalsa brotherhood on 30 March 1699 at Kesgarh in Anandpur. He created an ideal man who was perfect in all respects, he was a combination of both devotion (*Bhakti*) and strength (*Shakti*). The Guru also combined charity (*Deg*) with the sword (*Tegh*).

Guru Gobind Singh is the father of the Khalsa and Mata Sahib Devan is the mother of the Khalsa. Anandpur is the birthplace of the Khalsa. Khalsa is a combination of wisdom, morality, courage and discipline. Khalsa represents the army of God. The five beloved ones are the first group of Khalsa; they hailed from the North (Punjab,—Bhai Daya Singh, a Khatri; Delhi-Bhai Dharam Singh, a Jat), West (Gujarat — Bhai Mohkam Singh, a washerman from Dwarka), South (Andhra — Bhai Sahib Singh, barber from Bidar) and East (Orissa — Bhai Himmat Singh, a water-carrier from Jagannath). Three of the Punj Piyaras, Bhai Mohkam Singh, Bhai Himmat Singh and Bhai Sahib Singh died at the battle of Chamkaur in 1704 and the other two, Bhai Daya Singh and Bhai Dharam Singh, were with the Guru when he breathed his last at Nanded in 1708.

SAKHI 20.2

Guru Gobind Singh injected loyalty and devotion in the Sikhs. Once a Hindu, Bhai Dalla, came to the Guru and assured to him the loyalty and bravery of his well-trained soldiers. The Guru desired to test them. He sent for a musket and asked Dalla to summon one of his soldiers to try out the musket. None of Dalla's soldier's volunteered, then the Guru called two of his own Sikhs. He told them what he wanted to try on them. They both eagerly volunteered for the test, in fact they competed to be the target for the Guru's first shot. Dalla was astonished by the obedience and devotion of the Guru's Sikhs and felt sorry and ashamed for the conduct of his mercenaries.

SAKHI 21.1

Guru Gobind Singh was a true karam yogi. He is called 'Sarbans Dani' (one who sacrificed his whole family for the cause of justice and for the religious freedom). He was only nine years old when his father, Guru Tegh Bahadur, offered his life to save the religion of the Hindus; when he was thirty-eight years old he sacrificed all his children, his mother, and many thousands of his disciples on the altar of justice. He conferred the Guruship on Guru Granth Sahib and declared that after him all Sikhs must take their spiritual guidance from the Granth. He himself had written a large number of hymns but he did not include any one of them in Guru Granth Sahib. He was a symbol of humility. After having baptised the 'Panj Piyaras' he knelt down before them and requested them to baptise him as well. Bhai Gurdas II, a contemporary of Guru Gobind Gingh, has sketched this scene very beautifully in his var. The Guru was a great protagonist of democracy and freedom. He had declared that the future disputes amongst the Sikhs would not be settled by any one authority but would be settled by a group of five baptised Sikhs. To follow these principles the Sikhs later developed the tradition of Sarbat Khalsa and Gurmata.

SAKHI 21.2

Guru Gobind Singh was a messenger of God. He was the tenth Nanak. He was ordained by Almighty God to create the Khalsa Brotherhood. His message was to worship One Abstract God, to believe in freedom and democracy, to believe in the teachings of the Sikh Gurus, to be honest, truthful and loyal, to love children and to serve the poor and the needy. His compositions are contained in *Dasam Granth* which was arranged by Bhai Mani Singh after the Guru's death. In *Shabad Hazare*, a collection of ten hymns, the Guru has dealt with the duties of the householder and has explained the meaning of 'Jeewan-mukt'; in *Swayas* he has explained the balance between secular and spiritual tasks, the significance of human life and the importance of meditation and recitation of God's glories; in *Akal Ustat*, he has sung the greatness and glories of God. In other hymns and compositions he has also dealt with the social and family problems, the description of the war weapons and the reasons of wielding the sword. He has also translated the stories of twenty-four incarnations of Vishnu and Brahma and has written his own autobiography. The Guru was a linguist, a scholar and a great general. He was master of Punjabi, Sanskrit, Braj, Persian and Arabic languages; he was an exponent of both Hindu and Muslim scriptures; he fought a number of battles with the mighty Mughals with a handful of his own Sikhs and won most of them. In this sense he was a great solider and a great general.

SAKHI 22.1

Raja Medni Prakash, chief of the Himalayan state of Nahan, invited Guru Gobind Singh to come and stay in his state. The Guru reached Nahan on April 14, 1685, and made his residence at a place which he named as Paonta, later known as Paonta Sahib. Most of Guru Gobind Singh's bani were composed at this place. He engaged fifty-two poets to translate the stories of the *Ramayanya*, the *Puranas* and the *Mahabharata* into simple language. About twenty-five miles from Paonta, at a place called Sadhaura, there lived a Muslim saint named Pir Budh Shah. He came to see the Guru and the Guru received him warmly and kindly. He offered him a seat beside him. The Pir begged to the Guru to make him his follower and to show him the way to salvation and mukti. The Guru said that God was all merciful and benevolent. He loved all of us as a gentle father. Those who repent for their sins and bad karmas and resolve never to do them again are forgiven by God. Meditation of God and good actions are the two fundamental duties of human beings. Those who render their prayers and live a truthful life are acceptable to God to live in heavens forever; the others are condemned to hell and sufferings.

SAKHI 22.2

Guru Gobind Singh's letter to Aurangzeb, known as Zafarnama, was delivered to the emperor by Bhai Daya Singh and Bhai Dharam Singh at Ahmednagar in the south. The two dressed themselves as hajis and made their way to the emperor's camp. Aurangzeb was moved by the Guru's letter and issued instructions to all his Governors not to trouble the Guru any more. He also issued orders that the Guru should be provided safe conduct, all utilities and expert guides on his way to Ahmednagar. He invited the Guru to come and forgive him for all his sins, injustice and cruelty. He also wanted the Guru to bless him and become his friend. On return to the Guru, Bhai Daya Singh and Bhai Dharam Singh conveyed personally to the Guru, the emperor's keen and honest desire to see him. The Guru was deeply moved and made preparations to meet the emperor. He started towards Ahmednagar. When he reached near Baghaur, he heard the news of the death of Aurangzeb. Aurangzeb died on 20 February, 1707.

INTRODUCTION

In the 'Banis' of daily recitation, the Swayas are read as the third Bani. This bani is composed by Guru Gobind Singh and is a part of his long hymn 'Akal Ustat'. This bani has ten stanzas called 'Swayas'. From the recitation of this bani one understands the myth of superstitions, rituals and delusions. According to Guru Gobind Singh, the realisation of God is a straight route, only the priests have made this path difficult for the devotees, to highlight their own importance. God is ever manifest and merciful, he is easily approachable and realisable. The easiest route to reach God's house is the recitation of his bani, good actions and service to humanity.

PART - II

SWAYAS

ੴ ਵਾਹਿਗੁਰੂ ਜੀ ਕੀ ਫਤਹ ॥ ਪਾ: ੧੦ ॥

ਤੁਪ੍ਰਸਾਦਿ ਸਵੱਯੇ

ਸ੍ਰਾਵਗ[1] ਸੁੱਧ[2] ਸਮੂਹ[3] ਸਿਧਾਨ[4] ਕੇ, ਦੇਖਿ[5] ਫਿਰਿਓ[6] ਘਰ[7] ਜੋਗ[8] ਜਤੀ[9] ਕੇ ॥

ਸੂਰ[10] ਸੁਰਾਰਦਨ[11] ਸੁੱਧ[12] ਸੁਧਾਦਿਕ,[13] ਸੰਤ[14] ਸਮੂਹ[15] ਅਨੇਕ[16] ਮਤੀ[17] ਕੇ ॥

ਸਾਰੇ[18] ਹੀ ਦੇਸ[19] ਕੋ ਦੇਖਿ[20] ਰਹਿਓ[21] ਮਤ,[22] ਕੋਊ[23] ਨ ਦੇਖੀਅਤ[24] ਪ੍ਰਾਨਪਤੀ[25] ਕੇ ॥

ਸ੍ਰੀ[26] ਭਗਵਾਨ[27] ਕੀ ਭਾਇ[28] ਕ੍ਰਿਪਾ[29] ਹੂ ਤੇ, ਏਕ ਰਤੀ[30] ਬਿਨ[31] ਏਕ ਰਤੀ[32] ਕੇ[33] ॥੧॥

Ik Onkar Waheguru ji ki Fatah. Patsahi 10 (Dasvin)

TAV PRASAD(I) SAVAIYE

Sravag[1] sudh[2] samuh[3] sidhan[4] ke, dekh(i)[5] phirio[6] ghar[7] jog[8] jati[9] ke.

Sur[10] surardan[11] sudh[12] sudhadik[13], sant[14] samuh[15] anek[16] mati[17] ke.

Sare[18] hi des[19] ko dekh(i)[20] rahio[21] mat[22], kou[23] na dekhiat[24] Pranpati[25] ke.

Sri[26] Bhagvan[27] ki bhae[28] kripa[29] hu te, ek rati[30] bin(u)[31] ek rati[32] ke[33].

TAV PRASAD SWAYA
BY YOUR GRACE SWAYA

Notes

[1]the monks belonging to the Jain and Buddhist faiths; [2]the truthful; [3]groups; [4]holy men; [5]to look; [6]wandering; [7]house, camps; [8]wanderers; [9]unmarried; [10]brave; [11]demons; [12]holy; [13]gods, those who drink nectar; [14]saints; [15]groups; [16]many; [17]belonging to different faiths; [18]all; [19]countries; [20-21]have-looked; [22]no one; [24]watch; [25]Lord; [26]great; [27]God; [28]love; [29]blessing; [30]a little bit; [31]without; [32-33]of little value.

SWAYA 1

Theme

The greatest faith of a person is his love for God.

Literal Meaning

I have seen the camps of Jain and Buddhist monks and of the holy men of other faiths,
I have also visited the bivouac of brave and courageous men, gods, demons and saints of other denominations,
I have also studied the religions of other countries,
but none have so far explained to me the secrets of my beloved God.
The people and abodes on whom God has not showered His blessings are of no value.

Summary

There are numerous religions and faiths in the world. There are monks and nuns who have taken the oath of celibacy but only those who are blessed by Him get His audience. The labels of religions and beliefs make no differences. God is above all religions and faiths.

ਮਾਤੇ[1] ਮਤੰਗ[2] ਜਰੇ[3] ਜਰ[4] ਸੰਗ,[5] ਅਨੂਪ[6] ਉਤੰਗ[7] ਏਰੰਗ[8] ਸਵਾਰੇ[9] ||
ਕੋਟ[10] ਤੁਰੰਗ[11] ਕੁਰੰਗ[12] ਸੇ ਕੁਦਤ,[13] ਪਊਨ[14] ਕੇ ਗਊਨ[15] ਕੋ ਜਾਤ[16] ਨਿਵਾਰੇ[17] ||
ਭਾਰੀ[18] ਭੁਜਾਨ[19] ਕੇ ਭੂਪ[20] ਭਲੀ[21] ਬਿਧਿ[22] ਨਿਆਵਤ[23] ਸੀਸ[24] ਨ ਜਾਤ[25] ਬਿਚਾਰੇ[26] ||
ਏਤੇ[27] ਭਏ[28] ਤੁ ਕਹਾ[29] ਭਏ[30] ਭੂਪਤਿ,[31] ਅੰਤ[32] ਕੋ ਨਾਂਗੇ[33] ਹੀ ਪਾਇ[34] ਪਧਾਰੇ[35] ||੨||

Mate[1] matang[2] jare[3] jar[4] sang[5] ,anup[6] utang[7] surang[8] savare[9].
Kot[10] turang[11] kurang[12] se kudat[13], paun[14] ke gaun[15] ko jat[16] nivare[17].
Bhari[18] bhujan[19] ke bhup[20] bhali[21] bidh(i)[22] niavat[23] sis[24] na jat[25] bichare[26].
Ete[27] bhae[28] tu kaha[29] bhae[30] bhupat(i)[31] , ant[32] ko nange[33] hii pane[34] padhare[35].

SWAYA 2

Notes

[1]intoxicated; [2]elephants; [3]beaded, decorated; [4]gold; [5]with; [6]incomparable; [7]tall; [8]with different colours; [9]decorated; [10]numerous; [11]horses; [12]deer; [13]galloping; [14]wind, breeze; [15]gait, the way to walk; [16-17]to excel; [18]strong, powerful; [19]arms; [20]kings; [21-22]neatly, the right way; [23]bow; [24]heads; [25-26]cannot be estimated; [27-28]many have; [29]where have; [30]kings; [31]at the end; [33]naked; [34-35]leave the world.

Theme

Everyone, despite his power, position and wealth, has to go back, bare-handed from this world.

Literal Meaning

All those who are wealthy and possess intoxicated, tall and proud elephants, decorated with golden trappings and colours;

and have in their possession strong and beautiful horses, who gallop like deers and run faster than the wind;

and have powerful kingdoms, and people pay them obeisance and homage in countless modes;

their greatness and status cannot make them different from all others; for when the end comes all leave this world naked and bare-handed.

Summary

The entry and exit from this world is controlled by Almighty God. Everyone comes into this world and leaves this world naked and bare-handed. The wealth and power which one earns in this world remain behind.

ਜੀਤ[1] ਫਿਰੈ[2] ਸਭ[3] ਦੇਸ[4] ਦਿਸਾਨ[5] ਕੇ, ਬਾਜਤ[6] ਢੋਲ[7] ਮ੍ਰਿਦੰਗ[8] ਨਗਾਰੇ[9] ||
ਗੁੰਜਤ[10] ਗੁੜ[11] ਗਜਾਨ[12] ਕੇ ਸੁੰਦਰ,[13] ਹਿਂਸਤ[14] ਹੀ ਹਜਰਾਜ[15] ਹਜਾਰੇ[16] ||
ਭੂਤ[17] ਭਵਿੱਖ[18] ਭਵਾਨ[19] ਕੇ ਭੂਪਤ,[20] ਕਉਨੁ[21] ਗਨੈ[22] ਨਹੀ ਜਾਤ[23] ਬਿਚਾਰੇ[24] ||
ਸ੍ਰੀ[25] ਪਤਿ[26] ਸ੍ਰੀ ਭਗਵਾਨ[27] ਭਜੇ[28] ਬਿਨੁ,[29] ਅੰਤ[30] ਕਉ[31] ਅੰਤ[32] ਕੇ ਧਾਮ[33] ਸਿਧਾਰੇ[34] ||੩||

Jit[1] phirai[2] sabh[3] des[4] disan[5] ko, bajat[6] dhol[7] mridang[8] nagare[9].

Gunjat[10] gur[11] gajan[12] ke sundar[13], hinsat[14] hi hayraj[15] hajare[16].

Bhut[17] bhavikh[18] bhavan[19] ke bhupat[20], kaun(u)[21] ganai[22] nahin jat[23] bichare[24].

Sri[25] -pat(i)[26] Sri Bhagwan[27] bhaje[28] bin(u),[29] ant[30] kau[31] ant[32] ke dham[33] sidhare[34].

Notes

[1]victorious; [2]went; [3]all; [4]countries; [5]directions; [6]beat; [7]drum; [8]trumpet; [9]Indian type of drum; [10]resound; [11]crowd, group; [12]elephants; [13]beautiful; [14]sound of the animals, neigh; [15]noble breed horses; [16]thousand; [17]past; [18]future; [19]present; [20]kings; [21]who; [22]cannot count; [23-24]cannot guess; [25]supreme; [26]head; [27]Lord; [28]worship; [29]without; [30]at the end; [31]at; [32]at the end; [33]home; [34]to go.

Theme

All worldly glories and honours are of no avail if they are not acceptable to God.

Literal Meaning

All those who have conquered many countries and regions and have returned home beating drums and playing trumpets;

whose gorgeous elephants also trumpeted loud, and whose countless steeds of first class breed neighed in victory;

such kings filled with the lust of victory were there in the past, are there in the present and would be there in the future. But if they did not remember God in their hearts, they all came and would come to an inglorious end.

Summary

The real honour of a person is the honour conferred on him by God. All the worldly honours and positions are temporary and would not remain forever. Meditate on His name to have His blessings and the divine honour.

ਤੀਰਥ[1] ਨਾਨ[2] ਦਇਆ[3] ਦਮ[4] ਦਾਨ[5], ਸੁ[6] ਸੰਜਮ[7] ਨੇਮ[8] ਅਨੇਕ[9] ਬਿਸੇਖੈ[10] ||

ਬੇਦ[11] ਪੁਰਾਨ[12] ਕਤੇਬ[13] ਕੁਰਾਨ[14], ਜਮੀਨ[15] ਜਮਾਨ[16] ਸਬਾਨ[17] ਕੇ ਪੇਖੈ[18] ||

ਪਉਨ[19] ਅਹਾਰ[20] ਜਤੀ[21] ਜਤ[22] ਧਾਰ[23], ਸਬੈ[24] ਸੁ ਬਿਚਾਰ[25] ਹਜਾਰਕ[26] ਦੇਖੈ[27] ||

ਸ੍ਰੀ[28] ਭਗਵਾਨ[29] ਭਜੇ[30] ਬਿਨੁ[31] ਭੁਪਤਿ[32], ਏਕ[33] ਰਤੀ[34] ਬਿਨੁ[35] ਏਕ ਨ ਲੇਖੈ[36] ||੪||

Tirath[1] nan[2] daya[3] dam[4] dan[5] ,su[6] sanjam[7] nem[8] anek[9] bisekhai[10].
Bed[11] Puran[12] Kateb[13] Kuran[14] jamin[15] jaman[16] saban[17] ke pekhai[18].
Paun[19] ahar[20] jati[21] jat[22] dhar[23], sabai[24] su bichar[25] hajar-k[26] dekhai[27].
Sri[28] Bhagwan[29] bhaje[30] bin(u)[31] bhupat(i)[32] ek[33] rati[34] bin(u)[35] ek na lekhe[36].

Notes

[1]holy places, pilgrimage; [2]bath; [3]compassion; [4]to prevent mind from bad thoughts; [5]charity; [6]those; [7]the methods to control mind; [8]daily; [9]many; [10]special; [11]*Vedas*; [12]*Puranas*; [13]Semitic scriptures; [14]*Quran*; [15]earth; [16]time period; [17]all; [18]to watch, to read; [19]air; [20]food; [19-20]also meaning fasting and other penances; [21]people who control their organs with yogic exercises, nuns, monks etc.; [22-23]spiritual comfort; [24]all; [25]thoughts; [26]many thousands; [27]test; [28]supreme; [29]Lord; [30]worship; [31]without; [32]kings; [33]one; [34]little bit; [35]without; [34-36]are not counted.

SWAYA 4

Theme

The main objective of life to be one with God is to fall in love with Lord. The cleansing of mind is of paramount importance.

Literal Meaning

I have seen people who regularly bathe at holy places, give away money in charity and practise special exercise and disciplines; they read and master the *Vedas,* the *Puranas,* the *Quran* and other Semitic holy books and search the earth and skies for spiritual knowledge; they observe fasts, do yogic exercises, and comment on divine texts;
but without the true dedication to God all such princely or holy people are of no avail or acceptance.

Summary

The realisation of God has no prerequisites, such as a visit or bath at the holy places, charity, reading of holy texts, fasting and yogas. The basic qualifications of God-realisation are meditation and noble deeds performed from within.

ਸੁੱਧ[1] ਸਿਪਾਹ[2] ਦੁਰੰਤ[3] ਦੁਬਾਹ,[4] ਸੁ[5] ਸਾਜ[6] ਸਨਾਹ[7] ਦੁਰਜਾਨ[8] ਦਲੈਂਗੇ[9] ।।
ਭਾਰੀ[10] ਗੁਮਾਨ[11] ਭਰੇ[12] ਮਨ[13] ਮੈਂ[14], ਕਰ[15] ਪਰਬਤ[16] ਪੰਖ[17] ਹਲੇ[18] ਨ[19] ਹਲੈਂਗੇ[20] ।।
ਤੋਰਿ[21] ਅਰੀਨ[22] ਮਰੋਰਿ[23] ਮਵਾਸਨ[24], ਮਾਤੇ[25] ਮਤੰਗਨਿ[26] ਮਾਨ[27] ਮਲੈਂਗੇ[28] ।।
ਸ੍ਰੀ[29] ਪਤਿ[30] ਸ੍ਰੀ[31] ਭਗਵਾਨ[32] ਕ੍ਰਿਪਾ[33] ਬਿਨੁ[34], ਤਿਆਗਿ[35] ਜਹਾਨ[36] ਨਿਦਾਨ[37] ਚਲੈਂਗੇ[38] ।।4।।

Sudh[1] sipah[2] durant[3] dubah[4], su[5] saj[6] sanah[7] durjan[8] dalainge[9].

Bhari[10] guman[11] bhare[12] man[13] main[14], kar[15] parbat[16] pankh[17] hale[18] na[19] halainge[20].

Tor(i)[21] arin[22] maror(i)[23] mavasan[24], mate[25] matangan(i)[26] man[27] malainge[28].

Sri[29]-pat(i)[30] sri[31] Bhagwan[32] kripa[33] bin(u)[34], tiag(i)[35] jahan[36] nidan[37] chalainge[38].

SWAYA 5

Notes

[1]trained, experienced; [2]soldiers; [3]invincible; [4]incomparable; [5]those; [6] to put on, to set; [7]. bullet-proof dress; [8]enemies; [9]destroy, defeat; [10]heavy, to much, extreme; [11]pride; [12]fill; [13]mind; [14]in; [15]do; [16]mountains; [17] wings; [18]too move; [19]not; [20]move; [21]break; [22]enemies; [23]twist, submission; [24]those who revolt; [25]intoxicated, drunk; [26]elephants; [27]honour; [28]to break, to defeat; [29]supreme; [30]highest; [31]supreme; [32]Lord; [33]blessings, grace; [34]without; [35]to sacrifice, to leave; [36]world; [37]at the end, ignorance; [38] would go.

Theme

The human power and worldly status has no meaning if a person does not have God's blessings.

Literal Meaning

The trained and experienced soldiers, who are invincible in the warfare and look splendid in their bullet-proof garbs and destroy their enemies with ease;

they are filled with pride in their mind, for their strength and skill, for they can put the mountains to flight keeping themselves untouched and un-shaken;

they can destroy and twist the enemies and traitors, and can control and kill the drunk and strong elephants;

but without the Supreme God's grace they too would leave this world in contempt and shame.

Summary

The human power, skill, courage and bravery are acceptable to God if they are used for human protection and service. The Supreme Lord can crush and destroy even the mightiest soldiers like an insect, in a moment. The greatest human power is God's grace and blessings.

ਬੀਰ[1] ਅਪਾਰ[2] ਬਡੇ[3] ਬਰਿਆਰ,[4] ਅਬਿਚਾਰਹਿ[5] ਸਾਰ[6] ਕੀ[7] ਧਾਰ[8] ਭਛੱਯਾ[9] ॥

ਤੋਰਤ[10] ਦੇਸ[11] ਮਲਿੰਦ[12] ਮਵਾਸਨ,[13] ਮਾਤੇ[14] ਗਜਾਨ[15] ਕੇ ਮਾਨ[16] ਮਲੱਯਾ[17] ॥

ਗਾੜੇ[18] ਗੜ੍ਹਾਨ[19] ਕੋ ਤੋੜਨ-ਹਾਰ,[20] ਸੁ ਬਾਤਨ[21] ਹੀ ਚਕ[22] ਚਾਰ[23] ਲਵੱਯਾ[24] ॥

ਸਾਹਿਬੁ[25] ਸ੍ਰੀ ਸਭ[26] ਕੋ ਸਿਰਨਾਇਕ,[27] ਜਾਚਕ[28] ਅਨੇਕ ਸੁ ਏਕ[29] ਦਿਵੱਯਾ[30] ॥੬॥

Bir[1] apar[2] bade[3] bariar[4], abichareh[5] sar[6] ki[7] dhar[8] bhachhaya[9].
Torat[10] des[11] malind[12] mavasan[13], mate[14] gajan[15] ke man[16] malaya[17].
Gare[18] garan[19] ko toran-har[20], su batan[21] hin chak[22] char[23] lavaya[24].
Sahib(u)[25] sri sabh[26] ko sir-naik,[27] jachak[28] anek su ek[29] divaya[30].

Notes

[1]brave, hero; [2]numerous; [3]big, great; [4]strong; [5]careless, without thought; [6]steel; [7]sharpness; [8]to take; [9]to win, to inflict defeat; [10]to break; [11]countries; [12]to make one's subject, to conquer; [13]enemies; [14]furious, drunk; [15]elephants; [16]pride; [17]destroy; [18]thick, strong; [19]forts; [20]to demolish; [21]with dialogues; [22]earth; [23]four corners; [24]to win, to take over; [25]Lord; [26]all, [27]master; [28]beggars; [29]many; [30]donor.

Theme

The kings and conquerors are all called strong and winners in this world but they all are beggars in the court of Almighty God.

Literal Meaning

There are countless powerful and irresistible heroes who are ever ready to face the sharp blades of the sword.

they conquer many lands, crush their enemies and are acclaimed as world conquerors; they also humble the pride of many furious and drunk elephants;

they destroy the resistance of strong and well fortified forts, and whose firm resolution is enough to scare the enemy all around the globe;

but they all are beggars in the court of God, for they too seek blessings from the Lord before they embark upon their expedition.

Summary

Your only master is the Lord God. Do not spread your fringe in front of men for however much strong or wealthy they are, they too are beggars in the court of God. The real giver is only God, beg from Him and not from man who is both selfish and greedy.

ਦਾਨਵ[1] ਦੇਵ[2] ਫਨਿੰਦ[3] ਨਿਸਾਚਰ,[4] ਭੂਤ[5] ਭਵਿਖ[6] ਭਵਾਨ[7] ਜਪੈਗੇ[8] ||
ਜੀਵ[9] ਜਿਤੇ[10] ਜਲ[11] ਮੈਂ, ਥਲ[12] ਮੈ, ਪਲ[13] ਹੀ ਪਲ ਮੈ ਸਭ[14] ਥਾਪ[15] ਥਪੈਗੇ[16] ||
ਪੁੰਨ[17] ਪ੍ਰਤਾਪਨ[18] ਬਾਢ[19] ਜੈਤ[20] ਧੁਨ,[21] ਪਾਪਨ[22] ਕੇ ਬਹੁ[23] ਪੁੰਜ[24] ਖਪੈਗੇ[25] ||
ਸਾਧ[26] ਸਮੂਹ[27] ਪ੍ਰਸੰਨ[28] ਫਿਰੈ[29] ਜਗ,[30] ਸਤ੍ਰੁ[31] ਸਭੈ[32] ਅਵਲੋਕ[33] ਚਪੈਗੇ[34] ||੧||

Danav[1] dev[2] fhanind[3] nisachar[4], bhut[5] bhavikh[6] bhavan[7] japaige[8].
Jiv[9] jite[10] jal[11] mai thal[12] mai, pal[13] hi pal mai sabh[14] thap[15] thapaige[16].
Punn[17] pratapan[18] badh[19] jait[20] dhum[21], papan[22] ke bau[23] punj[24] khapaige[25].
Sadh[26] samuh[27] prasann[28] phirai[29] jag[30], satr[31] sabhai[32] avlok[33] chapainge[34].

SWAYA 7

Notes

[1]demons; [2]gods; [3]cobras; [4]ghosts; [5]past; [6]furture; [7]present; [8]to pray; [9]the living objects; [10]as many; [11]water, oceans, seas; [12]land; [13]moment; [14]all; [15]creation; [16]to create; [17]noble deeds; [18]glow; [19]increase; [20-21]the sound of victory; [22]sins; [23]many; [24]heaps; [25]destroyed; [26]saints; [27]group; [28]happiness, glad; [29]wander; [30]world; [31]enemy; [32]all; [33]to look at; [34]are pressed hard.

SWAYA 7

Theme

All those people who meditate on the name of God, they are honoured both in this world and the next world; their sins are pardoned and they live a happy life.

Literal Meaning

In all the times, past, present and future, God is worshipped by the nobles and the sinners. The demons, gods, villains (poisonous creatures like cobras), the living people and the dead (ghosts) all worship God;

all the living beings whether in the water or at land are created by Him in the split of a second;

the noble people are glorified and the atmosphere resounds with their victory slogans, whereas all the sinners are destroyed;

the saints of God live in eternal happiness whereas the enemies of God are annihilated.

Summary

The men of God do their meditation and perform the noble deeds. It is both worship and actions which make a man a man of God. Worship without action and actions without worship are not acceptable in Sikh religion. A man of God is high in character and honest in deeds. He is protected by God at all times and is glorified and honoured in both the worlds.

ਮਾਨਵ¹ ਇੰਦ੍ਰ² ਗਜਿੰਦ੍ਰ³ ਨਾਰਧਪ,⁴ ਜੌਨ⁵ ਤ੍ਰਿਲੋਕ⁶ ਕੋ⁷ ਰਾਜ⁸ ਕਰੈਂਗੇ⁹ ॥

ਕੋਟਿ¹⁰ ਇਸਨਾਨ¹¹ ਗਜਾਦਿਕ¹² ਦਾਨ,¹³ ਅਨੇਕ¹⁴ ਸੁਅੰਬਰ¹⁵ ਸਾਜ¹⁶ ਬਰੈਂਗੇ¹⁷ ॥

ਬ੍ਰਹਮ¹⁸ ਮਹੇਸਰ¹⁹ ਬਿਸਨ²⁰ ਸਚੀਪਤਿ,²¹ ਅੰਤ²² ਫਸੇ²³ ਜਮ²⁴ ਫਾਸ²⁵ ਪਰੈਂਗੇ²⁶ ॥

ਜੇ²⁷ ਨਰ²⁸ ਸ੍ਰੀਪਤਿ²⁹ ਕੇ ਪ੍ਰਸ³⁰ ਹੈ ਪਗ,³¹ ਤੇ ਨਰ³² ਫੇਰ³³ ਨ ਦੇਹ³⁴ ਧਰੈਂਗੇ³⁵ ॥੮॥

Manav[1] Indr[2] Gajindr[3] naradhap[4], jaun[5] trilok[6] ko[7] raj[8] karanige[9].

Kot(i)[10] isnan[11] gajadik[12] dan[13], anek[14] suanbar[15] saj[16] barainge[17].

Brahm[18] Mahesar[19] Bisan[20] sachipat(i)[21] ant[22] phase[23] jam[24] phas[25] parainge[26].

Je[27] nar[28] Sripat(i)[29] ke pras[30] hain pag[31], te nar[32] pher[33] na deh[34] dharainge[35].

Notes

[1]humans; [2]Indra — king of heaven; [3]large elephants; [4]kings; [5]who; [6]the universe, the three level of worlds; [7]of; [8] rule; [9]would; [10]many, numerous; [11]baths, holy bath; [12]elephants; [13]donations; [14]many; [15]the tradition of selection of a husband by the bride; [16]pomp and show; [17]to get married; [18]Brahma; [19]Shiva; [20]Vishnu; [21]Indra (Indra is the husband of 'Sachchi'), the husband of Sachi; [22]at the end; [23]entangled; [24]the messengers of death; [25]to get entangled; [26]to fall in; [27]those; [28]people; [29]the great Lord; [30]to touch; [31]feet; [32]people; [33]again; [34]human body; [35]transmigration.

Theme

The luxuries of life, the baths at the holy places and the status of the holy men are not the qualifications to realise God. The real test is prayers and meditation.

Literal meaning

The humans, the gods, the rich (masters of the stock of elephants) and the kings who rule and command numerous territories;

the people who take baths at the holy places, give away donations of large magnitudes (even of elephants), and make arrangements of religious get-togethers like glorified swayambars (marriages by choice and action) of Sita; and even the gods like Brahma, Shiva, Vishnu and Indra are all subject to predestined time of death;

but only those who take shelter at God's feet would be spared from the rules of transmigration.

Summary

God's rules apply to all, whether human or god. The man-made rules like holy baths, donations or swayambars are not divine laws and thus have no spiritual support. The axioms of God are universal and must apply. Those who take shelter at God's lotus feet are spared from divine punishments and fines.

ਕਹਾ¹ ਭਯੋ² ਜੋ³ ਦੋਉ⁴ ਲੋਚਨ⁵ ਮੂੰਦ⁶ ਕੈ⁷ ਬੈਠਿ⁸ ਰਹਿਓ⁹ ਬਕ¹⁰ ਧਿਆਨ¹¹ ਲਗਾਇਓ¹² ॥

ਨ੍ਹਾਤ¹³ ਫਿਰਿਓ¹⁴ ਲੀਏ¹⁵ ਸਾਤ¹⁶ ਸਮੁਦ੍ਰਿਨ,¹⁷ ਲੋਕ¹⁸ ਗਯੋ¹⁹ ਪਰਲੋਕ²⁰ ਗਵਾਇਓ²¹ ॥

ਬਾਸ²² ਕੀਓ²³ ਬਿਖਿਆਨ²⁴ ਸੋਂ²⁵ ਬੈਠ²⁶ ਕੈ,²⁷ ਐਸੇ²⁷ ਹੀ²⁸ ਐਸੇ²⁹ ਸੁ³⁰ ਬੈਸ³¹ ਬਿਤਾਇਓ³² ॥

ਸਾਚੁ³³ ਕਹੋਂ³⁴ ਸੁਨ³⁵ ਲੇਹੁ³⁶ ਸਭੈ,³⁷ ਜਿਨ³⁸ ਪ੍ਰੇਮ³⁹ ਕੀਓ⁴⁰ ਤਿਨ⁴¹ ਹੀ⁴² ਪ੍ਰਭ⁴³ ਪਾਇਓ⁴⁴ ॥੯॥

Kaha¹ bhayo² jo³ dou⁴ lochan⁵ mund⁶ kai⁷, baith(i)⁸ rahio⁹ bak¹⁰ dhian¹¹ lagaeo¹².

Nhat¹³ phirio¹⁴ lie¹⁵ sat¹⁶ samudran(i)¹⁷ lok¹⁸ gayo¹⁹ Parlok²⁰ gavaio²¹.

Bas²² kio²³ bikhian²⁴ son²⁵ baith²⁶ kai, aise²⁷ hi²⁸ aise²⁹ su³⁰ bais³¹ bitaio³².

Sach(u)³³ kahon³⁴ sun³⁵ leh(u)³⁶ sabhai³⁷, jin³⁸ prem³⁹ kio⁴⁰ tin⁴¹ hi⁴² Prabh⁴³ paio⁴⁴.

Notes

[1]what; [2]happened; [3]if; [4]both; [5]eyes; [6-7]to close; [8]sit; [9]keep (sitting); [10]gander; [11]concentration; [12]to be in; [13]bath; [14] wander; [15]taken; [16]seven; [17]oceans [18]this world; [19]to lose; [20]next world; [21]lost; [22-23]have lived; [24]life of lust;[25] greed and sin; [26]this way; [27]this; [28]and; [29]this; [30]one's [31] life; [32]to pass over, have lived; [33]truth; [34]saying; [35]listen; [36-37]everyone listen; [38]those; [39]love; [40]have (loved); [41]they; [42]only; [43]God; [44]realised;

Theme

God is love and you have to fall in love with Him and with his world to realise Him.

Literal Meaning

What if people close their eyes and like a crane, sit in samadhi (meditation); and bathe in the seven seas (all the holy places) but if their minds are corrupt and filled with sin), they would not only lose this world but also the next world.

Those who indulge in wine, wealth and women (sins), they too waste their lives.

I tell you all the real truth — if you want to realise God then love truly and honestly. Falling in love is the right path of God-realisation.

Summary

True and pure love is the only way to reach and realise God. The samadhis, penances, charities and prayers without purity of mind are useless. God has created this world as a symbol of love and loyalty; fall in love and serve humanity with honesty and purity, God Himself will come to you and embrace you.

ਕਾਹੂ[1] ਲੈ[2] ਪਾਹਨ[3] ਪੂਜ[4] ਧਰਯੋ[5] ਸਿਰ,[6] ਕਾਹੂ[7] ਲੈ[8] ਲਿੰਗ[9] ਗਰੇ[10] ਲਟਕਾਇਓ[11] ॥
ਕਾਹੂ[12] ਲਿਖਿਓ[13] ਹਰਿ[14] ਅਵਾਚੀ[15] ਦਿਸਾ[16] ਮਹਿ,[17] ਕਾਹੂ[18] ਪਛਾਹ[19] ਕੋ[20] ਸੀਸੁ[21] ਨਿਵਾਇਓ[22] ॥
ਕੋਊ[23] ਬੁਤਾਨ[24] ਕੋ ਪੂਜਤ[25] ਹੈ ਪਸੁ,[26] ਕੋਊ ਮ੍ਰਿਤਾਨ[27] ਕੋ ਪੂਜਨ[28] ਧਾਇਓ[29] ॥
ਕੂਰ[30] ਕ੍ਰਿਆ[31] ਉਰਝਿਓ[32] ਸਭ[33] ਹੀ[34] ਜਗ,[35] ਸ੍ਰੀ[36] ਭਗਵਾਨ[37] ਕੋ[38] ਭੇਦੁ[39] ਨ ਪਾਇਓ[40] ॥੧੦॥

Kahuu[1] lai[2] pahan[3] puj[4] dhario[5] sir[6], kahu[7] lai[8] ling[9] gare[10] latkaio[11].

Kahu[12] lakhio[13] har(i)[14] avachi[15] disa[16] mah(i)[17], Kahu[18] Pachhah[19] ko[20] sis[21](u) nivaio[22].

Kou[23] butan[24] ko pujat[25] hai pas(u)[26], kou mritan[27] ko pujan[28] dhaio[29].

Kur[30] kriya[31] urjhio[32] sabh[33] hi[34] jag[35], Sri[36] Bhagwan[37] ko[38] bhed(u)[39] na paio[40].

SWAYA 10

Notes

[1]why; [2]have; [3]stones; [4]worship; [5]to put; [6]head, forehead; [7]why; [8]have; [9]a stone representing Shiva; [10]around the neck; [11]to hang; [12]why; [13]to watch, to know; [14]every; [15]East, the direction of Dwarka; [16]direction; [17]towards; [18]why; [19]West; [20]to; [21]head; [22]to bow; [23]some; [24]idols; [25]worship; [26]animal, stupid; [27]dead people, tombs; [28-29]to do worship; [30]false, useless; [31]actions, deeds; [32]entangled; [33-34]all of them; [35]supreme; [36]God; [37]of; [38]secret; [39]could not find.

Theme

God is omnipresent and beyond images and names.

Literal Meaning

Many people worship stones, and wear an idol of Shiva around their necks; many bow their head toward East to salute Krishna's temple of Dwarka, yet many bow towards West to salute Mecca the birthplace of Prophet Mohammed;

many ignorant fools worship various stones and many worship their dead and their tombs;

most of us are engrossed in futile and useless activities, rituals and superstitions;

This is the reason that none of them could unfold the secrets of Almighty God.

Summary

God is manifest in His creation, He is the Father of all and lives in everyone's heart. He is not bound to either East of West; He is not a captive of temples, mosques or churches. He is beyond images, garbs and names. Those who worship images and tombs waste their lives in useless rituals. God is love and can be realised only with true love and honest living. Sun, fire, air, water and vegetation are God's witnesses, one must not excel them above God, it would be a blasphemous act. Worship only God and no one else.

SAKHIS

SAKHI 1.1

The first battle fought by Guru Gobind Singh was the battle of Bhangani and was fought on 16 April, 1689. After the battle Saiyyad Budhu Shah, a disciple and ally of the Guru, went to him to bid him goodbye. His surviving sons and disciples were with him. He requested the Guru to give him some relics to preserve in the memory of the Guru. The Guru at that time was combing his hair and a Sikh was standing nearby, holding his turban. The Guru asked Saiyyad to demand any gift. Saiyyad immediately asked for the Guru's comb with his loose hair in it. The Guru was amazed at Saiyyad's request. He gave him his comb and the loose hair and many more gifts of great value. He also gave to him an Order of Merit. These relics remained in Saiyyad's family for many hundred years and later they were acquired by Raja Bharpur Singh of Nabha and were preserved as sacred relics in that state.

SAKHI 1.2

Once Harji, a minister of Raja Medni Prakash of Nahan, came to him and told him about the engagement of the daughter of Fateh Shah, Raja of Bilaspur, with the son of Bhim Chand, the Raja of Kahlur. Fateh Chand had already occupied some land of Raja Medni Prakash. This new relationship of Fateh Chand alerted the Raja of Nahan, and made him more scared of Fateh Chand. Raja Medni Prakash consulted his ministers. They all suggested to him to accept the supremacy of Fateh Chand and to become his subordinate raja. Raja Medni Chand rejected all the suggestions. He believed in a life of grace and honour. Then he called his priest and asked for his advice. He counselled him to go and meet an old Sadhu who lived in the thick of the forest. Next day, the Raja along with his minister, Harji, left for the forest. With great difficulty they found the mud hut of the saint. He received them with honour and asked them the reason for their visit. The Raja told him about his fears and the growing power of Fateh Chand. The old Sadhu closed his eyes, remained silent for a few minutes and then spoke to the Raja. He said that in Kaliyug a prophet was born to restore justice, that he was young, handsome, tall, with long unshorn hair and a flowing beard, that he wore weapons and kept a small army; only that prophet could save the state of Nahan from falling under the rule of Fateh Shah. Raja Medni Chand asked the whereabouts of the prophet; the Sadhu directed him to go towards Anandpur to find him.

Next day the Raja sent his ambasador to Anandpur Sahib and invited the Guru to come and stay with him at Nahan. The Guru accepted his invitation and marched towards Nahan. The Guru lived there for about four years and during that period Fateh Shah did not even dream of attacking Nahan.

SAKHI 2.1

During the times of Guru Gobind Singh, in the City of Multan, the local police arrested a Sikh named Roopa mistaking him for the robber Roopa belonging to a different caste and religion. All the police witnesses went against Roopa and before he could be sentenced, the Qazi asked him who he was and why he had committed the crime, Roopa said that he was not a robber but a Sikh of Guru Gobind Singh and that he had not committed any crime. The Qazi was stunned to hear that Roopa was a Sikh, for according to the belief of those times a Sikh could not be robber and a Sikh would not utter lies. The Qazi turned to the police officer and asked him if he was sure about Roopa's identity. The Police Kotwal said that he was very sure and that the witnesses had already proved the charges against Roopa. The Qazi was confused, for from his experience he knew that the Sikhs were brave and truthful and despite all the odds would not speak a lie. Before the sentence could be passed a messenger from a neighbouring village arrived and gave to the Qazi a letter from the other police officer. The letter stated that the other police officer had arrested the much wanted dacoit Roopa in a police raid while this Roopa was a true Sikh of Guru Nanak and was a very honourable and respected citizen. The Qazi immediately issued the orders for the release of Roopa and reprimanded the city Kotwal for his lapses and irresponsible arrest. Both apologised to Roopa. Roopa knelt down and bowed in the direction of Anandpur and thanked God for justice.

SAKHI 2.2

Roopa wanted to go to Anandpur to have an audience of Guru Gobind Singh and thank him for his release. But his wife fell ill and he could not start his journey. He went to the local Masand named Dulcha and gave him a large number of gifts for the Guru which included hundred pearls, 50 gold coins, two beaded bracelets, one golden dagger, one silken suit for the Guru and two silken suits for the Guru's Mother. On the way to Anandpur, Dulcha became greedy and hid the two bracelets in his turban and when he reached Anandpur he presented the other gifts to the Guru, on behalf of Roopa. The Guru looked at the gifts and admired them. Then he asked Dulcha if there was anything else which he had forgotton. Dulcha said that he had presented to the Guru everything he had brought from Roopa. The Guru then called Dulcha near him, and in front of the congregation asked him to untie his turban. Dulcha resisted. Guru then asked one of his followers to do the needful. When the turban was opened the two bracelets fell down. Dulcha was filled with shame, he fell at the Guru's feet and asked forgiveness.

SAKHI 3.1

In one of his journeys Guru Tegh Bahadur went to Assam, where he blessed Raja Ram Rai, the king of the state, who later became a Sikh of the Guru. Raja Ram Rai did not have any children, he begged the Guru to bless him with a son so that he could have an heir to his throne. Guru Tegh Bahadur at the time had a ring in his hand, he struck the forehead of the Raja with his ring and said that the Raja would soon have a son who would have a mark on his forehead like the mark which the Guru had made on the Raja's forehead. Raja Ram Rai made his son also a Sikh of Guru Nanak and named him Rattan Rai. When Rattan Rai grew up he came to see Guru Gobind Singh at Anandpur with his mother; Raja Ram Rai had since died. Young Rattan Rai brought with him lots of gifts which also included a white elephant, a huge marquee, a five-in-one gun and many other valuable articles. The elephant was named Parsadi and was trained to serve the Guru to wash and wipe his feet, bring his clothes, clean his shoes, and to fan him.

SAKHI 3.2

Guru Gobind Singh erected forts all around Anandpur for its protection from future conflicts and invasions. On a Baisakhi day he also installed a big drum which was played at the time of arrival and departure of the Guru from the court. He also formalised the installation of the Sikh flag outside all the gurdwaras and started educational and musical classes at Anandpur for the benefit of his followers and their children. He himself was an expert with a number of musical instruments and also a scholar of Hindu, Muslim, Buddhist and Jain scriptures.

SAKHI 4.1

Bhai Nand Lal was a court poet and a close confidante of Guru Gobind Singh. He came to the Guru in 1682 and presented to him his book called *Bandgi Nama*. Later he went and joined the service of Prince Muazzam who became the emperor after Aurangzeb's death. Aurangzeb wanted to convert Nand Lal into Islam, so Nand Lal resigned and came back to Guru Gobind Singh in Anandpur. In 1688, Aurangzeb arrested his son Prince Muazzam and his grandsons. While in prison Prince Mauzzam called for Bhai Nand Lal and asked him to work for his release. Bhai Nand Lal mentioned to him the divinity and spirituality of Guru Gobind Singh and said that with his prayers he could be released unharmed. Prince Mauzzam sent his request to the Guru through Bhai Nand Lal. When Bhai Nand Lal mentioned this to the Guru, he closed his eyes and said that one day the prince would be an emperor of India. The prophecy was fulfilled and the prince became emperor Bahadur Shah. He sent many gifts to the Guru and issued strict instructions to his Governors not to harass and trouble the Sikhs.

SAKHI 4.2

After the victory in one of the Sikh battles with the Mughals and hill Rajas, the Sikhs also brought a young girl along with the ammunition and horses of the enemy. When Guru Gobind Singh came to know of this act he became very angry and summoned the Sikhs and the girl to his court. He reprimanded the Sikhs and ordered that the girl be sent back to her parents with dignity and honour. Some of the Sikhs argued that such actions were essential to teach the Mughals a lesson. The Guru said that he wanted to create such Sikhs who could keep their high character even during the battle. The revenge and imperialism were not part of the Sikh war code. No Sikh was allowed to plunder and harm the innocent. The womenfolk of the enemy were to be treated with utmost honour.

SAKHI 5.1

The Sikh missionary posts and centres were first established by Guru Amardas and later rationalised by Guru Ramdas. The head of the post was called a Masand. The Masands played an important part in the build-up of the Sikh history. The word masand is a Persian word and it means 'one belonging to a high place'. The masands were God-fearing and true Sikhs, they were honest and of high character. But with the lapse of time they became dishonest and corrupt. They burnt alive Ram Rai, the older son of Guru Harrai, when he was in a 'samadhi' (trance). Many other complaints of their cruelty and compulsory extortion of money from the poor Sikhs were also lodged with Guru Gobind Singh. The Guru called an emergent meeting of all the masands on Baisakhi of 1698, reprimanded them for their wrongs and shameful acts, dismissed them all and declared that the tradition of the masands was finished for good. Many masands revolted against the Guru's orders but the Sikhs in general rejected them and all the future offerings were directly routed to Anandpur. In one of the Guru's Hukamnama (order) issued in February 1698 the Guru said that all the future offerings should be directly sent to Anandpur and that all the masands had been dismissed and no further approach be made to them.

SAKHI 5.2

Once Guru Gobind Singh ordered his Sikhs to throw all the personal treasures of the Guru in the river Sutlej. On enquiry from the Sikhs he told them that a Sikh must not become a slave of his possessions. The real wealth of a Sikh is God's name. Those who say their daily prayers and live a truthful life are the richest Sikhs. Some Sikhs asked why the Guru had accepted offerings from others. The Guru smiled and answered that all the offerings were the pledges. The money was being given to the Guru to be spent on the well being of the Sikhs, on the construction of schools and clinics and for the construction of prayer rooms. Thus the offerings made to the Guru were a deposit with the Guru as a banker and in utmost trust.

SAKHI 6.1

Once the Sikhs in Guru Gobind Singh's court appreciated the kirtan of certain musicians and asked the Guru about his opinion. The Guru said that the musicians had sung the 'God's word' for they had the spade in their possession. The Sikhs asked the Guru to explain this. The Guru said that once in a village a person had lost his spade. He had called a drummer-announcer and had paid him a rupee to go around the village to announce the loss of the spade. Everyone had searched in his house but the spade could not be found. Someone in the village said that the house of the announcer should also be searched. The search had been duly made and the spade had been found. So they sang God's praises and told people that greed was a sin but they themselves were in the grip of greed. Those musicians who sing for divinity were the acceptable musicians and were worth the praise.

SAKHI 6.2

Once a Sikh came and started serving in the Guru's langar. He was very honest and humble. He had a keen desire to have an audience with the Guru. He approached a Sikh who was very near the Guru to fix an appointment with the Guru, but that Sikh behaved in an arrogant way and refused to comply. It happened two or three times. In the end the Sikh himself approached the Guru and got his audience. At the end of the meeting the Sikh told the Guru of his displeasure and disappointment with the people who were close to the Guru and were responsible for fixing the Guru's daily meetings. The Guru summoned the concerned Sikhs and asked them to bring a bowl of water. He asked them to put some stones in it and also a few sugar cubes. Then he asked them to stir the water. At the end he called them all and asked them to sort out the stones from the cubes. They could not take do this as the sugar had merged with the water. The Guru said that the Sikhs who behaved arrogantly were like the stones and the those who behaved honestly and with humility were like the sugar cubes. He loved only those who were like the sugar cubes and these would eventually get his blessings.

SAKHI 7.1

Once Guru Gobind Singh called two Sikhs to his court, one was his caretaker and the other one was a puppeteer plyer. He told the congregation that it was their concentration of mind which took them nearer to God. He pointed towards his caretaker and said that though he was watching the Guru's camp yet his mind was in the puppet show, whereas the puppeteer while performing his tricks had his mind in the Guru's court. Thus the puppeteer was nearer to the Guru and was acceptable to God.

SAKHI 7.2

The Khalsa was created on the Baisakhi day. It was the Baisakhi of 1699 and fell on 30 March. The importance of the day of Baisakhi had started since Guru Nanak Dev's times. It was the first of Baisakh when Guru Nanak Dev had started his missionary journeys. Guru Amardas had started the construction of Baoli Sahib on the morning of that day; Guru Harkrishen had nominated Guru Tegh Bahadur as the ninth Guru of the Sikhs on the rise of the first ray of the sun on the first day of Baisakh. The month of Baisakh represented awakening.

SAKHI 8.1

When Guru Gobind Singh evacuated the fort of Anandpur, his younger sons, Baba Zorawar Singh and Baba Fateh Singh and his mother, Mata Gujri, were separated from him. The three of them were lost in the thick of the forest. Some way off they met a Brahmin called Gangu, who had once been a cook at the Guru's house. He took them to his house, promising shelter and protection, but he proved to be a cheat and fraud. At night time he stole Mata Gujri's saddle bag which contained valuables and money and tipped the Governor of Sirhind about their whereabouts in exchange for a large reward. The Mughal soldiers arrested all three of them, confined them in a tower of the fort and produced them in the court of Wazir Khan next morning. The Governor offered the young lads money, comfort and riches if they would embrace Islam, otherwise a tortuous death. The lions of Guru Gobind Singh replied that they would not change their religion and would prefer to die. The Governor ordered them to be buried alive and the order was soon executed. The young sons of Guru Gobind Singh who were only six years and eight years old were entombed by bricks near the fort of Sirhind.

SAKHI 8.2

When Guru Gobind Singh ordered Banda Bahadur to take the command of the Sikh nation he asked him to close his eyes and see the streams of blood flowing through the streets of Hindustan. Banda Bahadur who was a Bairagi Sadhu, had shown his reluctance to take up the weapons and declare a war against the injustice. As Lord Krishna had shown to Arjun the battlefield of Kurukshetra and his duties theirin; similarly Guru Gobind Singh showed Banda Bahadur the pain and plight of the innocent people, the walls of Sirhind which had buried the young sons of the Guru, the battlefield of Chamkaur which had absorbed the blood of the older sons of the Guru and many more cremation grounds and graves of the innocent people which were inviting a saint-soldier to rise and crush the tyrant. Banda Bahadur closed his eyes and saw the unbearable scenes of corpses and blood, and fell at the Guru's feet. Next day he was baptised as a Khalsa and took over the command of the Sikh nation. Later, after the death of Guru Gobind Singh, he marched on Sirhind and killed all the tyrants and cruel rulers.

SAKHI 9.1

Before Anandpur was besieged by the Mughals, a man called Duni Chand came to Anandpur with five hundred soldiers and offered his services to the Guru. The Guru accepted Duni Chand's offer of services and gave him a plot of land to camp his soldiers. A few days after the siege began, Duni Chand conferred with his men and decided to run away from Anandpur to save their lives. One dark night they put a long ladder on the fort of Anandpur, climbed it and left Anandpur for their homes in Amritsar. Duni Chand broke his leg while jumping the wall. When Guru Gobind Singh was told about this betrayal, he smiled and said that Duni Chand had fled for fear of death but death did come even in Amritsar or Anandpur. A few days after they had fled, Duni Chand was bitten by a snake and died instant.

SAKHI 9.2

During the siege of Anandpur, the total artillery of the Mughals was pointing its cannon balls towards the Guru. Their main objective was to kill Guru Gobind Singh. The cannon balls would fall around him but not near enough to harm him. Many Sikhs, out of awe, had requested the Guru to sit in hiding but the Guru had refused their request. He said that he would always lead his Sikhs and die a heroic death. The Mughal General, Wazir Khan, brought in the most skilled markers and shooters to throw the cannon balls at the Guru but they all failed. None of them could break the divine net of safety which God had webbed around Guru Gobind Singh.

SAKHI 10.1

When Guru Gobind Singh was besieged in the fortress of Chamkaur it was a hopeless situation. On one side was the entire Mughal army and on the other side were only the Guru, his two older sons and about forty faithful Sikhs. Despite the number of Mughal forces and their organised attack the enemy could not break the defence of the Guru. Then Nahar Khan, one of the Mughal officers, shouted that why were they wasting their time and they should attack the fortress with the combined might of the Mughals and the hill Rajas. They all marched towards the fortress in a military order. Guru Gobind Singh ordered his men to stop using their ammunition and arrows and himself went to the top of the fortress and challenged the enemy forces with his own arrows. His arrows went like hail-stones, piercing the chest of the advancing army and creating confusion amongst them. They started running in all directions. There was bedlam and stampede. The commander blew the trumpet of retreat and the soldiers of the combined armies ran back to their bases.

PART III

ARDAS
THE SIKH PRAYER

INTRODUCTION

The Ardas of a Sikh is an expression of his heart and not of his words. Its sound emerges from the depth of one's emotions and reaches beyond the skies. The Ardas is a lyric of the spirit and is not a poem of words. The modes of salutations and the posture of bowing are only outer actions and if they are not done with the involvement of heart and feelings then they are useless and are not acceptable to God.

The literal meaning of the word Ardas is to present one's request, to thank and to beg. The words Ardas can also be analysed as follows:

A means 'antaryami' - one who can read our inner-thoughts,
R means 'rakhwala' - i.e., caretaker,
DA means 'datar' - i.e, one who gives to all of us,
S means 'sahara ' - i.e., one who gives support, helper,

meaning that Ardas is a request to have the support of 'antaryami', caretaker and 'datar' God.

For discussion and research purposes, the Sikh Ardas can be divided into three sections: the first; section composed by Guru Gobind Singh is a part of his composition, 'Var Bhagauti'; the second section traces the important events during the history of the Sikhs; and the third section is the thanksgiving narration of a devotee. The format and the wordings of the complete Ardas, i.e., the three parts mentioned above, have been set by the *Sikh Rehat Maryada* (Code of Conduct) published by the Shrimoni Gurdwara Parbandhak Committee, and individuals are not allowed to change either its wordings or its format.

ਅਰਦਾਸ

ੴ^{1}੨^2 ਵਾਹਿਗੁਰੂ^{3} ਜੀ^{4} ਕੀ^{5} ਫਤਹ^6 ॥

ਸ੍ਰੀ^{7} ਭਗੌਤੀ^{8} ਜੀ ਸਹਾਇ^9 ॥

ਵਾਰ^{10} ਸ੍ਰੀ^{11} ਭਗੌਤੀ^{12} ਜੀ^{13} ਕੀ^{14} ਪਾਤਸ਼ਾਹੀ^{15} ੧੦॥

ਪ੍ਰਿਥਮ^{16} ਭਗੌਤੀ^{17} ਸਿਮਰਿ^{18} ਕੈ,^{19} ਗੁਰ^{20} ਨਾਨਕ^{21} ਲਈਂ^{22} ਧਿਆਇ^{23} ॥

ਫਿਰ^{24} ਅੰਗਦ^{25} ਗੁਰ^{26} ਤੇ^{27} ਅਮਰਦਾਸੁ,^{28} ਰਾਮਦਾਸੈ^{29} ਹੋਈ^{30} ਸਹਾਇ^{31} ॥

ਅਰਜਨ^{32} ਹਰਗੋਬਿੰਦ^{33} ਨੋ, ਸਿਮਰੈ^{34} ਸ੍ਰੀ^{35} ਹਰਿਰਾਇ^{36} ॥

ਸ੍ਰੀ^{37} ਹਰਿਕਿਸ਼ਨ^{38} ਧਿਆਈਐ,^{39} ਜਿਸ^{40} ਡਿਠੇ^{41} ਸਭਿ^{42} ਦੁਖਿ^{43} ਜਾਏ^{44} ॥

ਤੇਗ^{45} ਬਹਾਦਰ^{46} ਸਿਮਰਿਐ,^{47} ਘਰ^{48} ਨਉ^{49} ਨਿਧਿ^{50} ਆਵੈ^{51} ਧਾਇ^{52} ॥

ਸਭ^{53} ਥਾਈਂ^{54} ਹੋਇ^{55} ਸਹਾਇ^{56} ॥

ਦਸਵਾਂ^{57} ਪਾਤਸ਼ਾਹ^{58} ਸ੍ਰੀ^{59} ਗੁਰੂ^{60} ਗੋਬਿੰਦ^{61} ਸਿੰਘ ਸਾਹਿਬ^{62} ਜੀ, ਸਭ^{63} ਥਾਈਂ^{64} ਹੋਇ^{65} ਸਹਾਇ^{66} ॥

ਦਸਾਂ^{67} ਪਾਤਸ਼ਾਹੀਆਂ^{68} ਦੀ^{69} ਜੋਤ,^{70} ਸ੍ਰੀ^{71} ਗੁਰੂ^{72} ਗ੍ਰੰਥ^{73} ਸਾਹਿਬ ਜੀ ਦੇ ਪਾਠ^{74} ਦੀਦਾਰ^{75} ਦਾ^{76} ਧਿਆਨ^{77} ਧਰ^{78} ਕੇ ਬਲੋ^{79} ਜੀ ਵਾਹਿਗੁਰੂ^{80}!

ARDAS

Ik^1 onkar^2 vaheguru^3 ji^4 ki^5 fatah^6.

Sri^7 bhagauti^8 ji sahae^9.

Var^{10} Sri^{11} bhagauti^{12} ji^{13} ki^{14} patshahi^{15}

Pritham^{16} bhagauti^{17} simar(i)^{18} kai^{19}, Gur^{20} Nanak^{21} lain^{22} hiae^{23}.

Phir^{24} Angad^{25} Gur^{26} te^{27} Amar Das(u)^{28}, Ram Dasai^{29} hoin^{30} sahae.^{31}

Arjan^{32} Hargobind^{33} no, simrau^{34} Sri^{35} Har(i) Rae.^{36}

Sri^{37} Harikishan^{38} diaiai^{39}, jis^{40} dithe^{41} sabh(i)^{42} dukh(i)^{43} jae^{44}.

Teg^{45} Bahadar^{46} simriai^{47}, ghar^{48} nau^{49} nidh(i)^{50} avai^{51} thae^{52}.

Sabh^{53} thain^{54} hoe^{55} sahae^{56}.

Dasvan^{57} Patshan^{58} Sri^{59} Guru^{60} Gobind^{61} Singh Sahib^{62} ji, sabh^{63} thain^{64} hoe^{65} sahae^{66}.

Dasan^{67} Patshaiah^{68} di^{69} jot^{70}, Sri^{71} Guru^{72} Granth^{73} Sahib ji de path^{74} didar^{75} da^{76} dhian^{77} dhar ke bolo^{79} ji Vaheguru^{80}!

Notes

[1]prayer; [2]one universal God; [3-4]God; [5]of; [6]victory; [7]supreme; [8]God, Supreme power; [9]protector, supporter; [10]var (a type of lyrical composition); [11]supreme; [12-13]Lord, All Powerful; [14]of; [15]composed by the tenth Master-Guru Gobind Singh; [16]the only, firstly; [17]All powerful God; [18]worship; [19]after; [20]guru; [21]Nanak; [22-23]whom Guru Nanak worshipped; [24]then; [25]Guru Angad; [26]guru; [27]and; [28]Guru Amardas; [29]Guru Ramdas; [30-31]had been a protector; [32]Guru Arjan; [33]Guru Hargobind; [34]who was worshipped by ; [35-36]Guru Harrai; [37]supreme; [38]Guru Harkrishen; [39]was worshipped by; [40]who; [41]witnessed, suffered; [42]all; [43]sufferings, miseries ; [44]have; [45-46]Guru Tegh Bahadur; [47]was worshipped by; [48]home; [49-50]the nine treasures, the treasure of all the worldly ambitions; [51]come; [52]on one's own; [53]all; [54]places; [55-56]are protector; [57]tenth; [58]king; [59-62]Guru Gobind Singh; [63]all; [64]places; [65-66]are protectors; [67-70]the *Granth Sahib*; [74]hymns, path; [75]audience; [76]of; [77]attention, concentration; [78]to concentrate on; [79]say, speak out; [80]God is wonderful.

Theme

All must worship only one God who was worshipped by all the prophets including the Sikh Gurus.

Literal Meaning

God is one and He is always victorious.
The Supreme power always protects.
The hymn is composed in Var Bhagauti by Guru Gobind Singh.
Worship only one Almighty God,
Who was worshipped by Guru Nanak,
Who protected Guru Angad, Amardas and Ramdas,
Who was worshipped by Arjan, Hargobind and Harrai,
Who was also meditated by Sri Harkrishen who sacrificed his life for the sufferings of the others,
Who was also worshipped by Teg Bahadur, who was bestowed the nine treasures of this world,
Who is the protector at all the places,
Who was worshipped by the tenth Master, whom He protected at all the places,
Whose Word is contained in *Guru Granth Sahib* — the light and spirit of the ten Gurus.
With the name and prayers of *Guru Granth Sahib* in your mind, say Waheguru.

Summary

Worship only one Almighty God in His abstract form. No one is allowed to worship any images and idols. The all-powerful God was worshipped by all the world prophets of all the faiths. The Sikh Gurus also worshipped Him. His word as spoken by the Sikh Gurus is contained in the *Guru Granth Sahib*. All Sikhs are commanded to bow to and respect the *Guru Granth Sahib* — the light and spirit of the Sikh Gurus.

ਪੰਜਾਂ-ਪਿਆਰਿਆਂ,[1] ਚੌਹਾਂ-ਸਾਹਿਬਜ਼ਾਦਿਆਂ,[2] ਚਾਲ੍ਹੀਆਂ-ਮੁਕਤਿਆਂ,[3] ਪੰਜਾਂ-ਤਖ਼ਤਾਂ,[4] ਸਰਬੱਤ-ਗੁਰਦੁਆਰਿਆਂ[5] ਦਾ[6] ਧਿਆਨ[7] ਧਰ[8] ਕੇ ਬੋਲੋ[9] ਜੀ[10] ਵਾਹਿਗੁਰੂ[11]!

[1]*Panjan-piarain*, [2]*chauhan Sahibzadian*, [3]*chalhian-muktian*, [4]*Panjan* *Takhatan*, *sarbat*[5] *gurduarian da*[6] *dhian*[7] *dhar*[8] *ke bolo*[9] *ji*[10] *Vaheguru*[11]!

Notes

[1]five beloved ones; [2]four princes; [3]forty liberators; [4]five thrones; [5] all gurdwaras; [6] of; [7] thought; [8] think [9-11]say Waheguru.

Theme

Always remember the first five baptised ones, the four sons of Guru Gobind Singh and the forty librartors of the war of Mukatsar who sacrificed their lives for freedom and justice.

Literal Meaning

Always remember the sacrifice of the five beloved ones,
four princes,
forty liberators.
Always show reverence to the five thrones,
all gurdwaras, and at the end say Waheguru.

Summary

Remember the sacrifices of the kith and kin and the followers of the Sikh Gurus for the cause of restoring justice and breaking the chains of slavery.

ਜਿਨ੍ਹਾਂ[1] ਸਿੰਘਾਂ[2] ਸਿੰਘਣੀਆਂ[3] ਨੇ[4] ਧਰਮ[5] ਹੇਤ[6] ਸੀਸ[7] ਦਿੱਤੇ,[8] ਬੰਦ[9] ਬੰਦ[10] ਕਟਾਏ,[11] ਖੋਪਰੀਆ[12] ਲੁਹਾਈਆਂ,[13] ਚਰਖੀਆਂ[14] ਤੇ[15] ਚੜ੍ਹੇ,[16] ਆਰਿਆਂ[17] ਨਾਲ[18] ਚਿਰਾਏ[19] ਗਏ,[20] ਪੁੱਠੀਆਂ[21] ਖਲਾ[22] ਲੁਹਾਈਆਂ,[23] ਗੁਰਦਆਰਿਆਂ[24] ਦੀ[25] ਸੇਵਾ[26] ਲਈ[27] ਕੁਰਬਾਨੀਆਂ[28] ਕੀਤੀਆਂ,[29] ਧਰਮ[30] ਨਹੀ[31] ਹਾਰਿਆ,[32] ਸਿੱਖੀ[33] ਕੇਸਾਂ[34] ਸੁਆਸਾਂ[35] ਨਾਲ[36] ਨਿਬਾਹੀ,[37] ਤਿਨ੍ਹਾਂ[38] ਦੀ[39] ਕਮਾਈ[40] ਦਾ[41] ਧਿਆਨ[42] ਧਰ[43] ਕੇ, ਖਾਲਸਾ[44] ਜੀ![45] ਬੋਲੋ[46] ਜੀ[47] ਵਾਹਿਗੁਰੂ[48]!

ਹਥੀਆਂ,[49] ਜਪੀਆਂ,[50] ਤਪੀਆਂ,[51] ਜਿਨ੍ਹਾਂ[52] ਨਾਮ[53] ਜਪਿਆ,[54] ਵੰਡ[55] ਛਕਿਆ,[56] ਦੇਗ[57] ਚਲਾਈ,[58] ਤੇਗ[59] ਵਾਹੀ,[60] ਦੇਖ[61] ਕੇ ਅਣਡਿੱਠ[62] ਕੀਤਾ, ਤਿਨ੍ਹਾਂ[63] ਪਿਆਰਿਆਂ[64] ਸਚਿਆਰਿਆਂ[65] ਦੀ ਕਮਾਈ[66] ਦਾ ਧਿਆਨ[67] ਧਰ[68] ਕੇ, ਖਾਲਸਾ[69] ਜੀ! ਬੋਲੋ[70] ਜੀ ਵਾਹਿਗੁਰੂ[71]!

Jinhan[1] Singhan[2] Singhanian[3] ne[4] Dharam[5] het[6] sis[7] dite[8], [16]band[9] band[10] katae[11], khoparian[12] luhaian[13], charkhain[14] te[15] charhe[16], arian[17] nal[18] chirae[19] gae[20] , puthain[21] khalan[22] luhaian[23], Gurduarian[24] di[25] seva[26] lai[27] kurbanian[28] kitian[29], Dharam[30] nahin[31] haria[32], Sikhi[33] kesan[34] suasan[35] nal[36] nibahi[37], tinahan[38] di[39] kamai[40] da[41] dhian[42] dhar[43] ke, Khalsa[44] ji![45] Bolo[46] ji[47] Vaheguru![48]

hathian[49], japian[50], tapian[51], jiinhan[52], Nam[53], japia[54], vand[55], chhakia[56], deg[57], chalaai[58], teg[59], vahi[60], dekh[61], ke andith[62], kita, tinhan[63], piarian[64], sachiarian[65], di kamai[66], da dhian[67], dhar[68], ke, khalsa[69], ji! Bolo[70], ji Vaheguru[71]!

Notes

[1]those; [2]male Sikhs; [3]female Sikhs; [4]have; [5]religion; [6]for; [7]heads [8]sacrifice; [9-10]limb by limb; [11]chopped; [12]skulls; [13]broken, cut; [14]wheels; [15-16]sacrificed on; [17]saws; [18.] with; [19-20]were sawed; [21]reverse; [22]skins; [23]skinned; [24]gurdwaras; [25]of; [26]service; [27]for; [28]sacrifices; [29]done; offered; [30]religion, faith; [31]not; [32]defeat; [33]the Sikh faith; [34]uncut hair; [35]breaths; [36]with; [37]lived up to the last; [38]those; [39]of [40]earnings; [41]of; [42]thought; [43]with concentration; [44-45]all-Khalsa; [46-48]say Waheguru.

Theme

Always remember the sacrifices of the countless Sikhs on the altar of their faith.

Literal Meaning

Those Sikhs who sacrificed their heads for their faith;
who were chopped limb by limb,
whose skulls were scraped and cut,
who were crushed on the wheels,
who were cut into pieces by saws,
who were skinned alive,
who sacrificed their lives for the service of gurdwaras,
but who did not give in their faith,
who lived with their uncut hair up to their last breath,
remember the sacrifices of all of them and say Waheguru.

Summary

Only those religions which remember their history remain alive. It is the blood of the followers which lays the foundation of a strong religious tradition.

ਪ੍ਰਿਥਮੇ[1] ਸਰਬੱਤ[2] ਖਾਲਸਾ[3] ਜੀ[4] ਕੀ[5] ਅਰਦਾਸ[6] ਹੈ[7] ਜੀ, ਸਰਬੱਤ[8] ਖ਼ਾਲਸਾ[9] ਜੀ ਕੇ ਵਾਹਿਗੁਰੂ,[10] ਵਾਹਿਗੁਰੂ, ਵਾਹਿਗੁਰੂ ਚਿਤ[11] ਆਵੈ,[12] ਚਿਤ ਆਵਨ[13] ਕਾ[14] ਸਦਕਾ[15] ਸਰਬ[16] ਸੁਖ[17] ਹੋਵੈ[18]!

ਜਹਾਂ[19] ਜਹਾਂ ਖ਼ਾਲਸਾ[20] ਜੀ ਸਾਹਿਬ, ਤਹਾਂ[21] ਤਹਾਂ ਰਛਿਆ[22] ਰਿਆਇਤ,[23] ਦੇਗ[24] ਤੇਗ[25] ਫ਼ਤਹ,[26] ਬਿਰਦ[27] ਕੀ[28] ਪੈਜ[29] ਪੰਥ[30] ਕੀ ਜੀਤ,[31] ਸ੍ਰੀ ਸਾਹਿਬ[32] ਜੀ ਸਹਾਇ,[33] ਖ਼ਾਲਸੇ[34] ਜੀ ਕੇ ਬੋਲ[35] ਬਾਲੇ,[36] ਬੋਲੋ[37] ਜੀ ਵਾਹਿਗੁਰੂ[38] ॥

Prithme[1] sarbat[2] Khalsa[3] ji[4] ki[5] ardas[6] hai[7] ji, sarbat[8] Khalsa[9] ji ko Vaheguru[10], Vaheguru chit[11] avai[12], chit avan[13] ka[14] sadka[15] sarab[16] sukh[17] hove[18].

Jahan[19] jahan Khalsa[20] ji sahib, tahan[21] tahan rachhia[22] riait[23], deg[24] teg[25] fatah[26], birad[27] ki[28] paij[29], panth[30] ki jit[31], Sri Sahib[32] ji sahae[33], Khalse[34] ji ke bol[35] bale[36], Bolo[37] ji Vaheguru![38]

Notes

[1]first; [2]all; [3-4]the Khalsa; [5]of; [6]prayer; [7]is; [8]all; [9]the Khalsa; [10]God; [11-12]remember him; [13-15]for the sacrifice of the remembrance; [16]all; [17-18]be happy, be comfortable; [19]wherever; [20]the Khalsa; [21]there; [22]protection; [23]grace, concessions; [24]kitchen; [25]sword; [26]victory; [27]devotees; [28]of; [29]honour; [30]the Sikh religion; [31]victory; [32]the supreme God; [33]be protector; [34]the Khalsa; [35-36]to get honour; [37]say; [38]God.

Theme

The only prayer of the Sikh nation is that Khalsa be victorious all over the world, the gurdwaras run the langar and the Sikhs protect the innocent.

Literal Meaning

The first prayer of the Sikh nation is that the Khalsa all over the world should always remember God, and may God shower on them the comforts and happiness of life.
Wherever the Khalsa is settled, may Waheguru give them grace and protection,
may the Guru's free kitchen run and may the Khalsa protect the innocent everywhere,;
may the devotees be saved and the Sikh nation always remain victorious,
may God always protect all of us;
may the Khalsa be always honoured and respected;
say Waheguru

Summary

As long as the Khalsa remains pure and perfect God would shower the bounties on him. The safety of the innocent, the free kitchen, the singing of the hymns of the Sikh Gurus are the essential parts of the Sikh way of life and it must be maintained at all costs everywhere in the world. If the Khalsa remains perfect God would always protect and support him.

ਸਿਖਾਂ[1] ਦਾ[2] ਮਨ[3] ਨੀਵਾਂ,[4] ਮਤ[5] ਉੱਚੀ,[6] ਮਤ[7] ਦਾ[8] ਰਾਖਾ[9] ਆਪਿ[10] ਵਾਹਿਗੁਰੂ[11] ॥

ਸਿੱਖਾਂ[12] ਨੂੰ[13] ਸਿੱਖੀ-ਦਾਨ,[14] ਕੇਸ-ਦਾਨ,[15] ਰਹਿਤ-ਦਾਨ,[16] ਬਿਬੇਕ-ਦਾਨ,[17] ਵਿਸਾਹ-ਦਾਨ,[18] ਭਰੋਸਾ-ਦਾਨ,[19] ਦਾਨਾਂ-ਸਿਰ-ਦਾਨ[20] ਨਾਮ-ਦਾਨ,[21] ਸ੍ਰੀ[22] ਅੰਮ੍ਰਿਤਸਰ[23] ਜੀ ਦੇ[24] ਇਸ਼ਨਾਨ[25] ।

ਚੌਕੀਆਂ[26] ਝੰਡੇ[27] ਬੁੰਗੇ[28] ਜੁਗੋ-ਜੁਗ[29] ਅਟੱਲ,[30] ਧਰਮ[31] ਕਾ[32] ਜੈਕਾਰ,[33] ਬੋਲੋ[34] ਜੀ ਵਾਹਿਗੁਰੂ[35]!!!

ਹੇ[36] ਨਿਮਾਣਿਆਂ[37] ਦੇ ਮਾਣ,[38] ਨਿਤਾਣਿਆਂ[39] ਦੇ ਤਾਣ,[40] ਨਿਓਟਿਆਂ[41] ਦੀ ਓਟ,[42] ਸਚੇ[43] ਪਿਤਾ,[44] ਵਾਹਿਗੁਰੂ! ਆਪ[45] ਦੇ ਹਜ਼ੂਰ[46] ਸੋਦਰ[47] ਰਹਿਰਾਸਿ[48] ਦੀ ਅਰਦਾਸ[49] ਹੈ ਜੀ। ਅਖਰ[50] ਵਾਧਾ[51] ਘਾਟਾ[52] ਭੁਲ[53] ਚੁਕ[54] ਮਾਫ਼[55] ਕਰਨੀ[56] ਜੀ।

ਗੁਰੂ[57] ਨਾਨਕ[58] ਨਾਮ[59] ਚੜ੍ਹਦੀ[60] ਕਲਾ[61] ॥

ਤੇਰੇ[62] ਭਾਣੇ[63] ਸਰਬੱਤ[64] ਦਾ ਭਲਾ[65] ॥

ਵਾਹਿਗੁਰੂ[66] ਜੀ[67] ਕਾ[68] ਖਾਲਸਾ[69] ! ਸ੍ਰੀ[70] ਵਾਹਿਗੁਰੂ[71] ਜੀ ਕੀ[72] ਫਤਹ[73]!

Sikhan[1] da[2] man[3] nivan[4], mat[5] uchi[6], mat[7] da[8] rakha[9] ap(i)[10] Vaheguru[11].

Sikhan[12] nun[13] Sikhi[14] dan, kes[15] dan, rahit[16] dan, bibek[17] dan, visah[18] dan, bharosa[19] dan, danaan[20] sir dan nam[21] dan, Sri[22] Anmritsar[23] ji de[24] ish-nan[25].

Chukian[26] jhande[27] bunge[28] jugo[29] jug atal[30], Dharam[31] ka[32] jaikar[33], Bolo[34] ji Vaheguru[35]!

He[36] nimanian[37] de man[38], nitanian[39] de tan[40], niotian[41] di ot[42], sache[43] Pita[44], Vaheguru! ap[45] de Hazur[46] Sodar[47] Rahras(i)[48] ji di ardas[49] hai ji. Akhar[50] vadha[51] ghata[52] bhul[53] chuk[54] maf[55] karni[56] ji.

Nanak[57] Nam[58] charhdi[59] kala[60], tere[61] bhane[62] sarbat[63] da bhala[64].

Vaheguru[65] ji[66] ka[67] Khalsa[68]. Vaheguru[71] ji ki[72] Fateh[73].

Notes

[1]Sikhs; [2]of; [3]mind; [4]low; [5]knowledge; [6]high; [7]knowledge; [8]honour; [9]protector; [10]himself; [11]God; [12]Sikhs; [13]to; [14]gift of Sikh traditions; [15]gift of uncut hair; [16]gift of obedience to the Sikh Code of Conduct; [17]gift of wisdom; [18]gift of firm faith; [19]gift of strong belief; [20-21]gift of the supreme gift of God's world; [22-25]the gift of the holy bath at the Golden Temple; [26]the choirs; [27]the flags; [28]the rest houses; [29-30]remain forever; [31]religion; [32-33]the victory; [34-35]say Waheguru; [36]O!; [37]meek; [38]honour; [39]helpless; [40]help, support, power; [41]homeless; [42]shelter; [43]true; [44]father; [45]himself; [46]in front; [47-48]evening prayers; [49]ardas; [50]word; [51]excess; [52]less, short; [53-54]errors, omissions; [55]apology; [56]do pardon; [57-58]Guru Nanak; [59]Word of God; [60-61]be exalted; [62]your; [63]will; [64]all; [65]prosper, be well; [66-69]Khalsa belongs to Waheguru; [70-73]Khalsa is always victorious.

Theme

All the necessities and comforts of life are granted by Almighty God. He is the compassionate donor of all the gifts.

Literal Meaning

May all the Sikhs be humble,
may all the Sikhs be wise,
may Waheguru protect our honour;
may Waheguru give us the gifts of the:

observance of the Sikh traditions,
observance of the Sikh rules,
firm faith and strong belief,
greatest boon of the Word of God,
holy bath at Golden Temple Amritsar,
company of choirs,
hoisting of flags,
the construction of guest houses.

May Waheguru make us ever victorious,
may religion always prosper,
may Sikh belief survive with uncut hair until the last breath,
O! Waheguru, you are the—

Honour of the meek,
Support of the helpless,
Shelter for the homeless.

O! True Father Waheguru, we have recited in Your presence the hymns of Sodar and Reharas, pardon us for any omissions and errors; O! God, Your name be exalted and may the whole universe prosper. The Khalsa belongs to God and God is always victorious.

Summary

God is the Supermost Power. He is the Greatest Donor. If you want any gift pray to God. He is the Father of the universe. He is most merciful, compassionate and gracious. Hail Him, Salute to Him and bow to Him.

EXPLANATIONS

In this section explanations on each section and sub-section of the Ardas are given.

1.VAR SRI BHAGAUTI JI KI PATSHAHI DAS . . .

ੴ ਵਾਹਿਗੁਰੂ ਜੀ ਕੀ ਫ਼ਤਹ।

ਸ੍ਰੀ ਭਗਉਤੀ ਜੀ ਸਹਾਇ।

ਵਾਰ ਸ੍ਰੀ ਭਗਉਤੀ ਜੀ ਕੀ। ਪਾਤਸ਼ਾਹੀ ੧੦।

ਪ੍ਰਿਥਮ ਭਗਉਤੀ ਸਿਮਰ ਕੈ ਗੁਰ ਨਾਨਕ ਲਈਂ ਧਿਆਇ।

ਫਿਰ ਅੰਗਦ ਗੁਰ ਤੇ ਅਮਰਦਾਸੁ ਰਾਮਦਾਸੈ ਹੋਈ ਸਹਾਇ।

ਅਰਜਨ ਹਰਿਗੋਬਿੰਦ ਨੋ ਸਿਮਰੌ ਸ੍ਰੀ ਹਰਿ ਰਾਇ।

ਸ੍ਰੀ ਹਰਿਕ੍ਰਿਸਨ ਧਿਆਈਐ ਜਿਸੁ ਡਿਠੇ ਸਭ ਦੁਖ ਜਾਇ।

ਤੇਗ ਬਹਾਦਰ ਸਿਮਰੀਐ ਘਰਿ ਨਉ ਨਿਧਿ ਆਵੈ ਧਾਇ।

ਸਭ ਥਾਈਂ ਹੋਇ ਸਹਾਇ ॥੧॥

_ਚੰਡੀ ਦੀ ਵਾਰ, ੧.

The first hymn of the Ardas is the first 'Pauri' of Guru Gobind Singh's composition titled Bhagauti ki Var/ Chandi Var. It is recorded after the Chandi Charitar. Here Bhagauti refers to God, the Ultimate Power.

1.1 Pratham Bahaugati simar kay -

A Sikh must worship only the abstract form of one Almighty God. He is not allowed to worship any images and idols.

1.2 Guru Nanak lae dhaye - - -

God was also worshipped by Guru Nanak Dev, the founder of Sikhism. The important dates in the life period of Guru Nanak Dev are as follows:

GURU NANAK - THE FIRST GURU OF THE SIKHS

1469	Born at Talwandi
1474-1482	Education at Talwandi
1487	Marriage with Mata Sulakhni
1494	Birth — Sri Chand
1485-1504	Work at home with father
1504	Employment at Sultanpur (where sister Nanaki and brother-in-law Jai Ram Uppal lived)
1507	Resigned from the job
23 Aug, 1507	Angels took Nanak to the house of God from river Bein
26 Aug 1507	Came back from God — First commandment at Sultanpur
1507-1521	Travels (for 14 years)
1507-1510	First Journey — accompanied by Bhai Mardana
	Multan — conversion of Sheikh Sajjan
	Panipat — discourse with Shah Sharif
	Delhi — revived a dead elephant; meeting with Sultan Ibrahim
	Banares — discourse with Pundit Chatur Das
	Nanakmata — discourse with Yogis
	Assam (Kamrup) — conversion of Nur Shah
	Orissa — Puri — hymn of Aarti
	Talwandi — meeting with parents
	Goindwal — healing of a leper
	Saidpur — Emanibad, Babur's attack, Guru Nanak's arrest; Mallick Bhago and Lalo
	Lahore — Duni Chand
	Talwandi — meeting with parents
1510-1515	Second journey (5 years) — South of India and Ceylon
	Madhya Pradesh — conversion of Kauda
	Ceylon — enlightenment of Raja Shivnabn
1515-1517	Third journey (two years) — North of India
	Kashmir — discourse with Pandit Brahma Das. Mount Sumer — discourse with Siddhs Achal Batala — festival of Shivratri; discourse with yogis.
1517-1521	Fourth journey — West of Asia
	Mecca — discourse with Qazi Rukundin
	Baghdad — discourse with Pir Datgir
	Hasan Abdal — discourse with Wali Qandhari
1521	End of missionary journeys — settlement at Kartarpur, on the banks of Ravi
1532	Meeting with Bhai Lehna
1539	Anointment of Lehna as the second Guru of the Sikhs, 14th July
22nd Sept. 1539	Death of Guru Nanak (2 months and 8 days after the anointment of Guru Angad)

1.3 Phir Angad Guru........

Guru Angad Dev, the second Guru of the Sikhs also meditated on Waheguru. He was born in district Ferozepur and breathed his last at the age of forty-eight at Khadur Sahib.

GURU ANGAD — SECOND GURU OF THE SIKHS

1504	Born at Mata ki Serai — District Ferozepur
1519	Marriage with Mata Khivi
1524	Birth — Dasu (son)
1532	Meeting with Guru Nanak
1537	Birth — Dattu (son)
1539	Anointment as the second Guru of the Sikhs
1540	Visit of Emperor Humayun on his way to Iran
1552	Death

1.4 Tey Amardas ....

Guru Amardas, the third Guru of the Sikhs, also worshipped God. Guru Amardas became Guru at the age of seventy-three and served the Sikh religion for twenty-two years.

GURU AMARDAS — THIRD GURU OF THE SIKHS

1479	Birth at Baserke
1502	Marriage with Mata Sulakhni
1540	Meeting with Guru Angad
1549	Founded Goindwal
1552	Anointment as the third Guru of the Sikhs
1553	Travels — Kurukshetra
1554	Organised first Sikh Baisakhi Mela
1559 — 1564	Construction of Baoli at Goindwal
1565	Visit by Emperor Akbar
1574	Death

1.5 Ramdas hoi sahai . . . .

Bhai Jetha, who later became the fourth Guru of the Sikhs, also preached the name of one Waheguru, who is the Ultimate Support of all. Guru Ramdas remained Guru for seven years. He died at the age of forty-seven.

GURU RAMDAS — THE FOURTH GURU OF THE SIKHS

1534	Born at Choona Mandi, Lahore
1553	Marriage with Bibi Bhani at Goindwal
1558	Birth of Prithi Chand
1560	Birth of Mahadev
1563	Birth of Arjan Dev
1570	Digging of Santokhsar
1574	Anointment as the fourth Guru of the Sikhs, founded Amritsar
1577	Started Sarovar at Amritsar
1581	Death

1.6 Arjan. . . . .

Guru Arjan, the fifth Guru of the Sikhs contributed a lot for the development of Sikhism. He constructed the Golden Temple and compiled *Guru Granth Sahib*. He always remembered and glorified God.

GURU ARJAN DEV — THE FIFTH GURU OF THE SIKHS

1563	Born at Goindwal
1579	Marriage with Mata Ganga
1581	Anointed as the fifth Guru of the Sikhs
(28 Dec) 1588	Foundation stone of Harimandir by Mian Mir
1595	Birth — Guru Hargobind
1598	Emperor Akbar's visit at Goindwal
1601	Started compilation of *Guru Granth Sahib*
1603	Visited Baba Mohan for the collection of Mohan Pothis
1604	Completion and installation of *Guru Granth Sahib* at Harimandir
1605	Emperor Akbar's stay at Batala, inspection of *Guru Granth Sahib* and gift of estates and gold coins for the spread of Word of God as contained in *Granth Sahib*
1605 (October)	Prince Khusrau's (Akbar's son) visit
1606	Martyrdom at Lahore

Construction of Gurdwaras

1586	Harimandir sarovar surfaced
1588	Completed Santokhsar
1588	Founded Harimandir
1590	Taran Taran — Sarovar started
1593	Kartarpur (Jallandar) founded
1596	Taran Taran — Harimandir founded
1597	Chherta Sahib Gurdwara founded
1597	Gobindpur founded
1599	Baoli Sahib at Lahore founded
1602-3	Ramsar (Amritsar) founded and completed

1.7 Hargobind noo. . . . .

Guru Hargobind, the sixth Guru of the Sikhs, served the Sikh religion for thirty-eight years, the longest pontificate amongst the Sikh Gurus. He meditated on the Only One, the most Powerful God.

GURU HARGOBIND — THE SIXTH GURU OF THE SIKHS

1595	Born at Wadali, Chherta
1604	Marriage with Mata Damodri (who died in 1631)
1606	Anointed as the sixth Guru of the Sikhs, Construction of Akal Takhat
1612	Imprisoned in the fort of Gwalior
1613	Birth of Baba Gurditta (son of Damodri) (died in 1638 — at the age of 25) (Dhirmal and Guru Har Rai were the sons of Baba Gurditta)
1614	Released from prison
1614	Marriage with Mata Nanki (who died in 1678)
1615	Birth of Bibi Viro (daughter of Damodri)
1615	Marriage with Mata Mahadevi (who died in 1645)
1617	Birth of Suraj Mal (son of Mahadevi)
1618	Birth of Ani Rai (son of Nanki) (died in 1644 — at the age of 26)

1619	Birth of Baba Atal (son of Nanki) (died in 1628 — at the age of 9)
1621	Birth of Tegh Bahadur (son of Nanki)
1628-35	Battles with the Mughals when Shah Jahan was the emperor of India
1635	Moved to Kiratpur from Amritsar
1644	Died at Kiratpur

1.8 Simro Sri Harrai . . . .

Guru Harrai, the seventh Guru of the Sikhs, was the younger grandson of Guru Hargobind. He died at the young age of thirty one. He worshipped only one Almighty God.

GURU HARRAI — SEVENTH GURU OF THE SIKHS

1630	Born at Kiratpur, younger, son of Baba Gurditta
1640	Marriage with Mata Kishen Kaur
1644	Anointed as the seventh Guru of the Sikhs
1645	Moved to Nahan to avoid confrontation with elder brother, Dhirmal
1646	Birth of Harkrishen
1657	Moved back to Kiratpur
1658	Dara Shikoh (eldest son of Shah Jahan) visited Guru Harrai
1658	Aurangzeb became the Emperor of India, after killing all his brothers and capturing his ailing father, Shah Jehan
1661	Aurangzeb invited Guru Harrai — Ramrai sent to meet Emperor Aurangzeb; Guru's declaration of disowning Ramrai
1661	Died at Kiratpur

1.9 Sri Harkrishen dhiayeea......

God was also worshipped by Guru Harkrishen, the child Guru of the Sikhs. He took upon himself the pain and the sufferings of the others and died for them.

GURU HARKRISHEN — THE EIGHTH GURU OF THE SIKHS

1656	Born at Kiratpur
1661	Anointed as the eighth Guru of the Sikhs
1663	Guru's dialogue with Brahmins at Parigkhara, near Ambala, en route to Delhi.
1664	Guru's visit to Delhi at the invitation of Raja Jai Singh, at the instigation of Emperor Aurangzeb; Bangla Sahib Gurdwara where the Guru stayed in Delhi. Bala Sahib Gurdwara, where the Guru died
1664	Death of the Guru

1.10 Teg Bahadur simreea......

Guru Tegh Bahadur, the ninth Guru of the Sikhs always remembered and meditated on God, served the Sikh religion for eleven years and laid down his life for the protection of the Hindu religion.

GURU TEGH BAHADUR — THE NINTH GURU OF THE SIKHS

1621	Born at Amritsar
1632	Marriage with Mata Gujri
1664 (30 March)	Guruship declared at Bakala — death of Guru Harkrishen
(October) 1664	Makhan Shah found the Guru in a bhora (cellar) at Bakala
(November) 1664	Visit to Amritsar (Harji, grandson of Prithi Chand who had declared himself the 8th Guru of the Sikhs, shut the doors of the gurdwara and did not allow the Guru to enter Harimandir Sahib)
1665 (May)	Visited Kiratpur and Bilaspur
1665	Visited Malwa
1665 (November)	Visited Kurukshetra, Mathura, Bindraban, Agra, Allahabad
1666	Birth Guru Gobind Singh at Patna
1666	Founded city of Anandpur
1666-1670	Visited Bengal and Assam
1670	Return to Punjab

1673-1674	Second tour of Malwa
1675 (May)	Visit of Kashmir Pundits
1675 (July)	The Guru's challenge to Emperor Aurangzeb, and the Guru's arrest; July-Oct kept at Sirhind; November-moved to Delhi
1675	Martyrdom, November 11 at 11. a.m. Guru's dead body cremated by Lakhi site — Rakabganj time 8 p.m. Guru's severed head smuggled to Anandpur by Jaita; distance 320 km covered in 5 days; Jaita reached Anandpur on 16 November.

1.11 Sub Thaee......

God protects you at all the places and at all the times.

2. DASVEY PATHSHAH GURU GOBIND SINGH JI......

Guru Gobind Singh, the tenth Guru of the Sikhs, created Khalsa and called him a saint soldier. He commanded that a Sikh must always remember and worship God who is Omnipresent and is the Protector of humanity.

GURU GOBIND SINGH — THE TENTH GURU OF THE SIKHS

1666	Born at Patna, Godfather-Raja Maini
1670	Moved to Anandpur
1675	Martyrdom of Guru Tegh Bahadur Anointment of Gobind Rai as the tenth Guru of the Sikhs
1677	Marriage with Mata Jito who died in 1700
1685	Marriage with Mata Sundri,, who died in 1747
1686	Birth of Ajit Singh (at Paonta from Mata Sundri) who died 1704 (age 18)
1687	Went to Dehra Dun to help Punjab Kaur and to punish the masands
1690	Birth of Jujar Singh (from Mata Jito) died 1704 (age 14)
1696	Birth of Zorawar Singh (from Mata Jito) who died 1704 (age 8)

1699	Marriage with Mata Sahib Devan who died in 1745
	Birth of Fateh Singh (from Mata Jito) who died 1704 (age 5)
	Birth of Khalsa at Takhat Kesgarh, Anandpur
1706	Compilation of second version of the *Guru Granth Sahib* at Damdama Sahib
1707-20th Feb	Death of Aurangzeb
1707 — June	Bahadur Shah coronated as the emperor of India
1707 2nd August	Visited Bahadur Shah at Agra
1708- Sept 15	Reached Nanded
1708-2nd October	Sent Banda Bahadur to Punjab; Mata Sahib Devan was also asked to go with Banda
1708	Death at Nanded

3. DASAN PATHSHIAN KI ATMIC JYOT.....

Guru Granth Sahib is the spiritual light for a Sikh. It contains the Word of God revealed to the world by the Sikh Gurus and other saints. It was given the status of a living Guru by Guru Gobind Singh

Guru Granth Sahib — The Spiritual Guru of the Sikhs

1539	Death of Guru Nanak Dev. The first Pothi of hymns handed by Guru Nanak to Guru Angad.
1552	Death of Guru Angad. The Pothi of hymns (first pothi plus the hymns of Guru Angad) handed by Guru Angad to Guru Amardas.
1574	Death of Guru Amardas. The updated Pothi of hymns handed by Guru Amardas to Guru Ramdas.
1581	Death of Guru Ramdas. The updated Pothi (including hymns of Guru Nanak Dev, Guru Angad, Guru Amardas and Guru Ramdas and some bhagats) was taken over by Baba Mohan, son of Guru Amardas.
1601	Guru Arjan Dev started the compilation of *Granth Sahib*.
1602	Pothi, now known as Mohan Pothi, recovered by Guru Arjan from Baba Mohan.
1604	Completion of *Granth Sahib* and installation of the *Granth* at Harimandir. Guru Arjan called the *Granth*, *Pothi Sahib*. The scribe of the *Granth* was Bhai Gurdas, a maternal uncle of Guru Arjan.
1605	Emperor Akbar paid homage to the *Granth* at Batala. He also offered 51 gold moharas as offering.
1604-1635	*Granth Sahib* remained at Amritsar.
1635	*Granth Sahib* moved to Kiratpur Sahib by Guru Hargobind.
1644	Original Bir (copy) stolen by Dhirmal, a

grandson of Guru Hargobind from the Guru's palace.

1661   Emperor Aurangzeb summoned Guru Harrai to Delhi to defend some of the hymns of the *Granth Sahib*.

1661   Guru Harrai sent his older son Ramrai to Aurangzeb. Ramrai dared to change a hymn of the *Granth*. Guru Harrai disowned Ramrai. Death of Guru Harrai.

1674   Original Bir recovered by the Sikhs from Dhirmal, but returned to him again by the orders of Guru Tegh Bahadur.

1706   Second version of the *Granth* compiled by Guru Gobind Singh at Damdama Sahib. The scribe was Bhai Mani Singh.

1706   Four copies of the *Granth* made by Baba Deep Singh.

1708   The *Granth Sahib* was declared as the spiritual Guru of the Sikhs, by Guru Gobind Singh, at Nanded.

1762   Original Bir (second version) taken by Ahmed Shah Abdali to Kabul.

1849   Original Bir (first version) discovered by the Britishers at the Lahore Court with its golden stand.

1849-1850   Court case for the possession of the original Bir.

1850   Court gave its custody to the descendants of Dhirmal.

1850   A copy of the *Granth* presented to Queen Victoria by the Sodhis (Dhirmal clan).

1900-1990   Attack on *Guru Granth Sahib* by the leaders of Arya Samaj and the Nirankaris.

4. FIVE BELOVED ONES

4.1 The word 'Punj Piyarey' refers to those five Sikhs who were baptised as the first Khalsa. They were:

i. Bhai Daya Singh, a Khatri from Lahore, was aged 30 years when baptised. He was with Guru Gobind Singh at Nanded when the Guru breathed his last.

ii. Bhai Dharma Singh, a Jat from Delhi, aged about 33 years when baptised. He too was with Guru Gobind Singh at Nanded.

iii. Bhai Muhkam Singh, a washerman from Dwarka, aged about 36 years at the time of baptism. He died in the battle of Chamkaur in 1704.

iv. Bhai Sahib Singh, a barber from Bidar, aged about 37 years when baptised at Kesgarh. He too died in the battle of Chamkaur.

v. Bhai Himmat Singh, a water-carrier from Jagannath Puri, was aged 39 when baptised by Guru Gobind Singh. He also died in the battle of Chamkaur.

4.2 Sometimes the world 'Punj Piyarey' also refers to five Sikhs who were left with Guru Gobind Singh on the eve of the battle of Chamkaur and who passed a gurmata and requested Guru Gobind Singh to leave the fortress.

4.3 At other times the word 'Panj Piyarey' refers to a group of five baptised Sikhs.

5. CHAR SAHIBZADEY Four sons of Guru Gobind Singh

The word 'char sahibzadey' refers to the four sons of Guru Gobind Singh. They were:

i. Baba Ajit Singh born in 1687 and died in the battle of Chamkaur in 1704.

ii. Baba Jujhar Singh born in 1690 and died in the battle of Chamkaur in 1704.

iii. Baba Zorawar Singh born in 1696 and buried alive in Sirhind in 1704.

iv. Baba Fateh Singh born in 1699 and buried alive in Sirhind along with his brother.

6. CHALI MUKTEY — The Forty Liberators

6.1 The forty liberators refer to those Sikhs who deserted Guru Gobind Singh at the time of the siege of Anandpur and later apologised and laid down their lives at the battle of Mukatsar. Their names as listed in the Mahan Kosh are: Sahj Singh, Sardul Singh, Saroop Singh, Sahib Singh, Sujan Singh, Ber Singh, Sewa Singh, Sango Singh, Sant Singh, Hardas Singh, Himmat Singh, Karam Singh, Kirpal Singh, Kharag Singh, Gurdas Singh, Gurdit Singh, Gulab Singh, Ganga Singh, Ganda Singh, Charat Singh, Jawahar Singh, Jaimal Singh, Jwala Singh, Jhanda Singh, Tek Singh, Thakur Singh, Trilok Singh, Dayal Singh, Damodar Singh, Narayan Singh, Nihal Singh, Punjab Singh, Prem Singh, Basawa Singh, Bisan Singh, Bhagwan Singh, Mehtab Singh, Mohkam Singh, Ranjit Singh, Ratan Singh and Mahan Singh.

6.2 The forty liberators also refer to those forty Sikhs who went in with Guru Gobind Singh to the fortress of Chamkaur and laid down their lives for their right of freedom and for protecting the life of their prophet.

7. JAPI, TAPI, HATHI

Japi means a person who renders his/her daily prayers. Tapi means those people who submit themselves to the Guru and who perform relentless service to mankind. Hathi refers to those people who give their lives but not their faith.

8. JINA NAM JAPAYA . . . .

This phrase refers to those people who meditate on the Name of God and worship only the abstract form of God. The humming of the world 'Ek Ong Kar' opens the gateway of God's kingdom.

9. WAND KEY CHAKAYA . . . . . (sharing one's wealth and food)

Guru Nanak Dev laid down three pillars for the Sikh society. They were : Nam Japna (meditation), Kirt Karna (honest work) and Wand Key Chhakna (sharing of one's wealth and belongings).

At the time of Farukhsiar, there were four Sikhs imprisoned in a common cell. They were not given anything to eat for many days. One day the prison officer gave them two chapatis to eat. For a few moments no one touched any of the chapatis. Later the oldest one took the chapatis and put them in front of the youngest Sikh and said that he was the future of the community, so he should eat them. He refused and gave them back to the oldest of them and said that they all could still live without food for many days but the oldest one needed the food now. They all in their turn refused to eat and passed the chapatis back to the oldest of them. At the end they all shared the chapatis, said their prayers and thanked God for the enlightenment.

10. DEG CHALAYEE — (Arrangement of Langar)

The best way to thank God is to help the needy, feed the hungry and give shelter to the homeless. The tradition of langer, i.e., free kitchen, is the blood and soul of Sikhism. This tradition was started by Guru Nanak Dev and has become an integral part of the Sikh religion.

11. TEG WAHI (Wielding the Sword)

Guru Gobind Singh referred to God as Steel, All Powerful, the Sword and by many other names which represent weapons. According to the Sikhs thought the weapons are essential for the destruction of evil and tyranny. The expression 'Teg Wahi' represents those Sikhs who raised arms for the protection of the innocent and the weak.

12. VEKH KEY ANDITH KEETA (To Forgive)

There is an English saying that to err is human and to forgive is divine. A Sikh must not hate others and must not believe in revenge. He must develop a personality of forgiving others and loving others.

13. DHARAM HEYT SEES DITEY (To be a Martyr)

All those who sacrifice their lives for a cause are called martyrs. All death is inevitable but a heroic death makes one immortal. He is remembered in all the prayers and lives forever thereafter.

14. BUND BUND KATWAEY: (Chopped to Death)

All those Sikhs who were chopped to death but remained firm in their faith. Bhai Mani Singh, a contemporary of Guru Gobind Singh and the scribe of the second version of *Guru Granth Sahib* compiled by Guru Gobind Singh at Damdama Sahib, was cut limb by limb by the Mughals for refusing conversion to Islam. He died in 1735 in Lahore.

15. KHOPRIAN UTARVAEEAN (Crushing of Skull)

Bhai Taru was the first martyr who was tortured and killed by this method. His skull was crushed by a sharp steel hoe. Later many Sikhs were killed similarly. He died in 1747 at Lahore during the period of Governor Zakria Khan.

16. CHAKHARIAN CHAREY (Crushed on the Wheel)

The first Sikhs to die on the wheels were Subheg Singh and his son Shahbaz Singh. This tragedy also happened during the time of Governor Zakria Khan and in Lahore in 1747.

17. AREYA NAL CHIRAEY GAYE (Cut into Pieces by a Saw)

Bhai Mati Das was the first Sikh who was cut into two pieces by a saw at Chandni Chowk, Delhi. He was a companion of Guru Teg Bahadur. He died in 1675 during Aurangzeb's time.

18. BHANEY NU MITHA KAR KEY MUNNAEYA: (Acceptance of God's Will)

The Sikhs believe in the unconditional acceptance of God's will. They worship Him in both adversity and happiness. They exalted Him when they were being cut into pieces by a butcher's knife, pierced into halves by sharp saws, and crushed to death on the wheels. According to the Sikh faith, a Sikh must never complain to God. God's orders, laws and judgment must be accepted in full and without conditions.

19. SIKHI SIDAK KESAN SUASSAN NAL NIBANA (Living with Uncut Hair until the Last Breath)

The world 'Sidak' refers to a promise with God to love Him, to be faithful to Him and to serve Him forever. It is also an unbreakable oath that the Sikhs would live with their unshorn hair until their last breath.

20. PANJ TAKHAT (Five Throne Designated Historical Gurdwaras)

The word takhat means a throne of a king. In the Ardas it refers to those places from where the Sikh Gurus regulated the Sikh affairs. From there the orders were issued, in there the disputes were settled and the plans made. Today there are five such takhats. For a long time there were only four takhats, the fifth one viz., Damdama Sahib, was added in the seventies. The five takhats are as follows:

  i. Gurdwara Akal Takhat—Designed and constructed under the supervision of Guru Hargobind in 1665.

 ii. Gurdwara Pantnao Sahib—the birthplace of Guru Gobind Singh. The first building was constructed by Maharaja Ranjit Singh.

iii. Gurdwara Kesgarh Sahib—the birthplace of Khalsa.

 iv. Gurdwara Damdama Sahib—the place where Guru Gobind prepared the latest version of *Guru Granth Sahib*. The service of this place was entrusted to Baba Deep Singh and his descendants.

  v. Gurdwara Hazur Sahib Nanded—the place where Guru Gobind Singh breathed his last. The first gurdwara was contructed here under the supervision of Maharaja Ranjit Singh.

The head priests of these takhats form the Sikh parliament and the resolutions passed by them are binding on the Sikh nation for the religious laws.

21. SARBAT GURDWARE (All Gurdwaras)

A Sikh always remembers in his/her prayers all the places; where there is the *Guru Granth Sahib*; the Sikh congregation assembles, kirtan is recited and Sikh ardas are rendered. There are about 174 historical Sikh gurdwaras in and outside India and numerous other gurdwaras in almost all the countries of the world where the Sikhs have settled. An approximate count of the historical gurdwaras related to the Sikh Gurus is as follows:

GURUS	NUMBER OF GURDWARAS
Guru Nanak	41
Guru Angad	1
Guru Amardas	4
Guru Ramdas	3
Guru Arjan	12
Guru Hargobind	16
Guru Harrai	13
Guru Harkrishen	4
Guru Tegh Bahadur	16
Guru Gobind Singh	64
Total	174

22. PRITHME SARBAT KHALSA JI KI ARDAS (The Ardas is by the Whole Sikh Nation)

The invocation of God, in the Sikh ardas, is made by the whole nation and not by an individual. An ardas represents a request, or a thanks from the whole Sikh community. Sikhism does not recognise a formal priesthood, thus any Sikh can lead the congregation, in a gurdwara, in a Sikh ardas. This phrase in the Ardas represents the unity of the Sikh nation.

23. WAHEGURU NAM CHIT AVE (One must Always Remember God)

The memory of God and the Sikh ardas are very closely related. A Sikh is reminded that he/she must not forget God even for a second. In both conscious and subconscious minds, a Sikh must hum the name of God. The relationship of a Sikh and God is very deep rooted.

24. JAHAN JAHAN KHALSA JI SAHIB TAHAN TAHAN RACHIA RIAIT (Wherever Khalsa Resides, God should be his Protector)

This saying represents the love and respect of Sikhs for each other. 'Jahan Jahan' means residences all over the globe, wherever the Sikhs are and the words 'rachia riait' means 'may God protect them'. This line was added in the Sikh ardas during the Sikh holocausts. This phrase also represents the harmony and closeness of the Sikhs for each other.

25. DEG TEG FATEH (Victory for the Sikhs in Arranging Langars and Fighting Battles)

In the Sikh ardas, the Sikhs request God to grant them the means and strength to run free kitchens and to be victorious in the righteous wars. A Sikh believes in freedom and justice and in love and peace and does not tolerate any injustice and threat to captivity.

26. BIRDH KI PAIJ (Honour of the Devotees)

A Sikh always requests God that the honour of His devotees be saved. One root-language of the world 'Bird' is Sanskrit, here it refers to the long adjectives which were read by the door attendants at the time of the arrival of a king. In this context a Sikh requests God to protect the honour of all His devotees. The other meaning of the world 'Bird' is a promise. In this sense the phrase means that a Sikh must always fulfil his/her promise. God is requested to give him/her strength to do that.

27. PANTH KI JIT (Victory for the Sikh Nation in the Path to Realise God)

The literal meaning of the world 'Panth' is a passage, a nationality or a group. In the context of the Sikh ardas it refers to the way to realise God.

28. KHALSA JI KE BOL BALE (Honour to the Khalsa)

The word 'bol-bale' means getting honours. A Sikh requests in his ardas that the Khalsa should always be respected and honoured.

29. SIKHI DAN (Gift of Sikhism)

The word Sikhi or Sikhism represents:
a. The application of the Sikh rules and the Sikh traditions,
b. the worship of one God,
c. the honest living,

d. the life of a household and
e. sharing one's wealth and belongings with others.

30. KES DAN (Gift of Uncut Hair)

The premise of the Sikh glory rests on the tradition of keeping long and uncut hair. In the dark period of the Sikh history, from 1715 to 1762, the Sikhs were hunted for their long hair and the cruellest punishment for a Sikh was when his hair were cut. A Sikh requests God to give him/her the gift of long and uncut hair.

31. RAHET DAN (Gift of Code of Conduct)

The word 'rahet' refers to the rules of living. The Sikh 'Rahet Namas' (Books of Code of Conduct) were written during the life time of Guru Gobind Singh; they are four in number and were written by Bhai Daya Singh, Bhai Desa Singh, Bhai Chaupa Singh and Bhai Nand Lal. Shiromani Gurdwara Prabandhak has published a book of *Rahet Maryada* incorporating the rules given in the four books of *Rehat Maryada*. A Sikh prays to God that he/she should always live within these rules.

32. VISA DAN (Gift of Firm Faith)

The words 'visa' means faith. To fall in love with God represents the true meaning of the word. A Sikh longs to love his Master for ever, he requests God to grant him a gift of true love for Him.

33. BAROSA DAN (Gift of Belief)

A Sikh in his prayers requests God to give him/her a gift of firm belief in His laws and existence. The literal meanings of the word are: hope, base, support, refuge, pillow and protection etc.

34. DANA SIR DAN, NAM DAN (The Supreme Gift of the Name of God)

The greatest gift of God is His manifestation in humanity. A Sikh longs to remember God for ever. In Sikhism, kirtan, i.e., singing God's name, is the surest way of God-realisation. In Sikh ardas a Sikh requests God to be with him/her for ever. He asks Him for a gift of His Name and Word.

35. SRI AMRITSAR JI DE DARSHAN ISHNAN (Gift of a Dip in the Holy Pool and a Visit of the Holy Shrine)

The foundation stone of Amritsar was laid in 1577 by Guru Ramdas and in the same year he started the construction of the holy pool. Guru Arjan later built, in the midst of the pool, the holiest of the holy Sikh shrine now known as Golden Temple. The construction of the temple was started in 1588 and Guru Granth was placed in there, for the first time, in 1604. A dip in the holy pool and a visit in the holy shrine is an earnest desire of every Sikh.

36. CHAUKIAN (Choirs)

A Sikh requests that he should participate in choirs all his life. There are three types of choirs:

    i. Choirs for daily prayers,
    ii. Choirs for historical events,
    iii. Choirs for pilgrimage tours.

The choirs of daily prayers are held at five different timings of the day:

a. The choir of Asa Di-Var, held early in the morning,

b. The choir of rag Bilawal, held at sunrise.

c. The choir of service, held at about 11 a.m when a hymn called 'Charan kanwal prab ke nit . . . . . ' is sung.

d. The choir of Sodar, held at the time of dusk, just before the recitation of 'Rehras'.

e. The choir of Kalyan, held at night time, after the passage of four 'garis'. The hymns of Rag Kalyan are sung at this time of the night.

The choirs of historical events were started during the times of Guru Hargobind. The first choir was held when Guru Hargobind had gone to village Dreli to bless Bhai Sai Das and his wife from Amritsar, the congregation , under the leadership of Bhai Budha started choirs. The choirs were lead by the Sikhs holding the Sikh flag and going around the 'parikrama'. Similarly, when Guru Hargobind was arrested and imprisoned in the fort of Gwalior, Baba Budha arranged choirs which would leave Harimandir and march towards Gwalior. The choirs were led by the Sikh flag, followed by the men representing the desire of freedom, the lanterns represented the longing of light and righteous deeds and hymns represented the power of Almighty God.

The pilgrimage choirs are arranged by the groups of people who plan to visit a holy place. The groups march towards the holy shrine/place singing hymns with the beat of drums.

37. JHANDE (Flags)

The flag of a nation or country represents its power of existence. The first Sikh flag was of white colour with the words 'Ek Ong Kar' printed in the middle of it. It was unfurled for the first time during the times of Guru Amardas. It was hoisted in front of holy tank called 'Boali Sahib'. After the martyrdom of Guru Arjan, Guru Hargobind changed the colour of the Sikh flag to orange (*kesri*) and put in the middle of it the drawing of the Sikh emblem. The new flag was hoisted in front of a Akal Takhat by Guru Hargobind. The flag which stands in front of Harimandir was first hoisted by the Chief of the Bhangi misl. The tradition of two flags at the side of the Akal Takhat at a place known as 'Jande Bunge' was started in 1775 by an Udasi Sadhu named Baba Santokh Das. The flags represent 'Miri' (royalty) and 'Piri' (spirituality). In 1881, as a result of a very strong hurricane, the flags fell down. They were later re-erected by Maharaja Sher Singh. These days, both these flags are fixed in one big structure and are tied with each other. A Sikh flag is found outside every Sikh temple all over the world. A Sikh, in his ardas requests God to protect his flag.

38. BUNGE (Rest-houses)

The Sikhs built rest-houses adjoining the important and historical gurdwaras. These houses were built by the Sikh leaders and the Sikh knights. In Amritsar there were six different types of bunges:

i. The bunge of the teachers: Here classes were held to teach Sikh religion and Punjabi language.

ii. The bunge of musicians: Here the classes were held to teach kirtan and musical instruments.

iii. The bunge of Akalis: In these houses classes were held to teach the use of weaponry.

iv. The bunge of associations: These rest-houses were owned by different organisations which held their own assemblies therein.

v. The bunge of the knights: These inns were built and owned by rich Sikh Sardars. They themselves along with the Sikhs from their areas came and stayed there during Sikh festivals and assemblies.

vi. The religious bunge: These were used for religious assemblies.

39. DHARAM KA JAIKAR (The Religious Banners)

It is a declaration that the religion will never yield; it will not tolerate any injustice and persecution. Any conversion under threat would not be tolerated and would be resisted at all costs.

40. MAN NIVAN (Humility)

A true Sikh longs for humility and requests God to grant him/her such a boon. The greatest enemy of a person is his ego. All prayers and meditations go in vain if a person indulges in pride or ego. To realise God a person must be humble and meek.

41. MAT UCHI (High Knowledge)

A true Sikh requests God to grant him/her knowledge of religion and morality. A Sikh must live in humility but with wisdom. Knowledge of righteous acts and nobility is a pre-requisite of true Sikhism.

42. MAT PAT KA RAKHA AAP WAHEGUR (God is the Protector of Knowledge and Honour)

The Sikh, while praying, requests God to protect him/her at all times and at all the places. God is the Ultimate Protecter of all of us. The Sikh longs for an honourable and simple life.

43. NANAK NAM CHARDI KALA (God's Name be Exalted)

'Chardi kala' represents a state where there is no fear, no enmity and no ego. It is a state of exaltation and optimism. It points to a firm belief in God and His rules.

44. TERE BHANE SARBAT DA BHALLA (Prosperity of All with Your Command)

The words 'Bhana' represents God's will, 'Sarbat' means all and 'Bhalla' states prosperity. A Sikh respects all religions and faiths. It believes in the unity of man and fatherhood of God. It rejects the theories of chosen people and high and low castes. According to the Sikh thought all people have one common father, called by different names, viz., Waheguru, Allaha, Parameshwar and Jehova. At the end of the Sikh prayer a Sikh requests God to give propserity to all human beings.

Code of Conduct of an Ardas

According to the Sikh traditions, a Sikh ardas can be said anywhere, at all the times, and by anyone. In the presence of *Guru Granth Sahib,* the ardas must be while facing the *Guru Granth Sahib* otherwise it can be recited facing any direction. Unlike Hinduism and Islam, there are no holy western or eastern directions in Sikhism. During congregational, individual and general Ardas, all must stand with folded hands and concentrate on God; in private and special Ardas, i.e., ardas at the time of a marriage, engagement, naming a child, etc., only the related parties stand and all others keep sitting.

Dictionary of Jap Sahib

Word		Reference: Number of Compositions
ਅ		
ਅਰੁ	Or, And	1, 86
ਅਚਲ	Immovable	1
ਅਨਭਉ	Fearless	1
ਅਮਿਤੋਜਿ	Immeasurable Power	1
ਅਸੁਰ	Demons	11
ਅਕਾਲੇ	Beyond death, Immortal	2
ਅਰੂਪੇ	Incorporates all the beauty, Sum total of beauty	2
ਅਨੂਪੇ	Sum total of all the praises, beyond peerage	2
ਅਭੇਖੇ	Beyond uniforms, Garbless	3
ਅਲੇਖੇ	Beyond description	3
ਅਕਾਏ	Has no body, made of five elements, i.e., Air, Water, Fire, Earth & Sky	3
ਅਜਾਏ	Beyond Births, Unborn	3
ਅਗੰਜੇ	Imperishable, Beyond destruction	2, 4, 8
ਅਭੰਜੇ	Unbreakable	2, 4, 8
ਅਨਾਮੇ	Beyond names, Nameless	4
ਅਠਾਮੇ	Beyond specific home, Omnipresent	4
ਅਕਰੰਮ	Not subject to 'Karma' Theory	5
ਅਧਰੰਮ	Beyond religion, Belongs to all religions	5
ਅਨਾਮੰ	Beyond specific names	5,147
ਅਧਾਮੰ	Has no specific abode, Omnipresent	5
ਅਜੀਤੇ	Invincible	6
ਅਭੀਤੇ	Unshakable	6
ਅਬਾਹੇ	Immovable	6
ਅਧਾਹੇ	Undefeatable	6
ਅਨੀਲੇ	Spotless	7

Word		Reference: Number of Compositions
ਅਨਾਦੇ	Beyond beginning	7
ਅਛੇਦੇ, ਅਛੇਦੀ	Impenetrable	7, 61
ਅਗਾਧੇ	Unfathomable	7, 64
ਅਪਾਰੇ	Limitless,	8,
ਅਨੇਕੈ	Innumerable	9,
ਅਭੂਤੇ	Incorporal, not made of five elements i.e., Water, Air, Fire, Ether, Earth	9,84
ਅਜੂਪੇ	Unchainable, Free from entanglements	9
ਅਲੇਖੇ	Invisible	12,
ਅਸੋਕੇ	Beyond distress,	12,
ਅਥਾਪੇ	Cannot be installed	13,
ਅਗਾਹੇ	Unfathomable	14, 64
ਅਸਰਗੋ	Unborn, Uncreated	14,
ਅਰੰਗੇ	Incorporates all colours	15
ਅਭੰਗੋ	Unbreakable	15,85,87
ਅਗੰਮੇ	Incomprehensible	16
ਅਜਾਤੇ	Beyond castes	17
ਅਪਾਤੇ	Beyond lineage	17
ਅਮਜਬੇ	Belonging to no creed	17
ਅਜਬੇ	Marvellous	17
ਅਦੇਸੰ	Beyond the limit of regions	
ਅਦੇਸੇ	Abodeless,	18, 63, 84
ਅਭੇਸੇ	Garbless	18, 63, 84
ਅਭੇਵੈ	Ever mysterious	21,44
ਅਜਨਮੇ	Unborn	21
ਅਬਰਨੇ	Beyond caste or creed	23
ਅਮਰਨੇ	Immortal	23

Word		Reference : Number of Compositions	Word		Reference : Number of Compositions
ਅਬੰਧੇ	Unbonded, Free from bondage	24, 136	ਅਮੀਕ	Unfathomable	36
ਅਨੰਤੇ	Infinite	26	ਅਧੰਧ	Free from worldly bondages	36
ਅਰੂਪ	Formless	29, 58	ਅਬੰਧ	Free from attachment	36
ਅਨੂਪ	Unparallel	29, 58	ਅਸੁਝ	Beyond comprehension	37
ਅਜੁ	Immutable	29, 63	ਅਕਾਲ	Beyond time, beyond death	37, 66, 84, 167
ਅਭੁ, ਅਭੂ	Beyond birth	29	ਅਜਾਲ	Beyond attachment	37
ਅਲੇਖ	Beyond description	29	ਅਲਾਹ	Lord God, Allaha	38
ਅਭੇਖ	Garbless	30, 44, 53	ਅਜਾਹ	Omnipresent	38
ਅਨਾਮ	No-name	30, 49, 61, 128	ਅਨੰਤ	Infinite	38
ਅਕਾਮ	Desireless	30, 61	ਅਲੀਕ	Unblemished, beyond boundaries	39
ਅਧੇ	Inconceivable, beyond thought	31	ਅਸੰਭ	Self-created	39
ਅਭੇ, ਅਭੇਦੀ	Mysterious	31, 61, 62	ਅਰੀਮ	Inaccessible	40
ਅਜੀਤ	Invincible	31, 42	ਅਜੀਮ	Unborn, uncausable	40
ਅਭੀਤ	Fearless	31, 42, 62	ਅਛੂਤ	Intangible, Beyond sense of Perceptions	40
ਅਸਰਗ	Unborn, self-created	32	ਅਲੇਕ	Invisible, Beyond sight	41
ਅਨੀਲ	Without colour or hue	33	ਅਸੋਕ	Beyond sorrows	41
ਅਨਾਦਿ	Without beginning	33, 79, 83, 128, 167, 187	ਅਕਰਮ, ਅਕਰਮੰ	Beyond rituals/karmas	41
ਅਜੇ	Invincible	33	ਅਭਰਮ, ਅਭਰਮੰ	Beyond delusions	41, 53
ਅਜਾਦਿ	Bondage of birth	33	ਅਬਾਹ, ਅਬਾਧੇ	Unshakable, uncontrollable	42, 64
ਅਜਨਮ	Unborn	34	ਅਗਾਹ	Unfathomable	42
ਅਬਰਨ	Indescribable	34	ਅਮਾਨ	Immeasurable	43
ਅਭੂਤ	Beyond physical elements, spirit	34, 40	ਅਨੇਕ	Many, Innumerable	43, 81
ਅਭਰਨ	Without ornaments	34	ਅਭੇਖੀ	Garbless	44, 53
ਅਰੀਜ, ਅਰੀਂਜੇ	Imperishable, Immortal	35, 65	ਅਨੰਗੀ	Formless	46, 49
ਅਭੰਜ, ਅਭੰਜੇ	Indestructible	35, 65	ਅਨਾਥੇ	One's own master	46
ਅਭੂਤ	Invincible	35	ਅਸਤ੍ਰ-ਮਾਣੇ	Wielder of weapons	52
ਅਝੰਝ	Detached, Beyond fretful affairs of the world	35	ਅਭਰਮੀ	Beyond delusions	53, 41

Word		Reference : Number of Compositions
ਅਜਨਮੰ	Birthless	100
ਅਜਾਏ	Not born from mother's womb	100
ਅਦੀਸੈ	Primal-being	102
ਅਦ੍ਰਿਸੈ	Invisible	102
ਅਕ੍ਰਿਸੈ	Ever Almighty, All Powerful	102,
ਆਛਿੱਜ	Imperishable	103, 168
ਆਭਿੱਜ	Impregnated	103
ਆਗੰਜ	Indestructible	103, 129
ਆਭੰਜ, ਆਭਿੰਜ	Impenetrable, Immortal	103
ਆਦਿਤ	The energy of sun	104
ਅਵਧੂਤ	Unattached	104
ਆਸੋਕ	Happy, Blissful	105
ਅਭਰਨੈ	To fulfil, sustain, to adorn with ornaments	105
ਅਨੂਪੈ	Unparallel	106, 126, 127, 147
ਅਨਭਉ	Experience, inner-thoughts	106
ਅਦੇਵ	Supreme, Greatest	107
ਆਪਿ	Self	107
ਅਧੀਨੈ	Under, Governed by some one else,	107
ਅਫ਼ਵੂਲ	Chief-justice, One who has the authority	
	To forgive or pardon	109
ਅਕਾਮੇ	Selfless	127
ਆਕਲ	Supreme	120
ਅਲਾਮੇ	Scholar, Enlightened	120
ਅਜੀਮੇ	Great	123
ਅਨੇਕੁਲ	Many	124
ਅਭੇਦ	Mysterious	124
ਅਡੰਗ	Immutable	124

Word		Reference : Number of Compositions
ਅਗਾਧ	Unfathomable, Unlimited	127, 129, 146
ਅਜ਼ੀਜਲ	Devotees	124
ਅਨੁਰਾਗੋ	Beyond beginning	128
ਅਨਾਦਿ		
ਅਛਿੱਜ	Inviolable	130
ਅਨਉਕਤਿ	Indescribable, undescribed	132
ਅਜੈ	Invincible	135, 149
ਅਭੈ	Imperishable	135
ਅਭੂਤ	Uncompoundable	135
ਅਧੂਤ	Unshakable	135
ਅਭਗਤ	Beyond worldly affairs	136
ਅਵਧਿ		
ਅਲਿੱਖ	Beyond description	138
ਅਦਿੱਖ	Beyond sight	138
ਅਢਾਹ	Undefeatable, Invincible	139
ਅਗਾਹ	Unfathomable	139
ਅਗੋਂਭ	Beyond the reach of comprehension	140
ਅਸੰਭ	Inconceivable	140
ਅਨਿੱਤ	Remarkable	141
ਅਨੀਲ	Stainless	140
ਅਨਾਦਿ	Without any beginning	140
ਅਜਾਤ	Without caste, Unborn	141
ਅਜਾਦਿ	Free of bonds	141
ਅਨੰਗੰ	Incorporeal	145, 147, 188
ਅਭੰਗੰ	Immutable	145, 188
ਅਮਿਤੋ	Immeasurable	149, 159, 160
ਅਮੀਕ	Unfathomable	149

Word		Reference: Number of Compositions	Word		Reference: Number of Compositions
ਅਜਾ	Unborn	149	ਅਜਪਾ	Self-innovated	177
ਅਗੰਜੁਲ	Invincible	154	ਆਥਪਾ	Self-installed	177
ਅਜ਼ੀਜ਼	Dependent, Juniors	156	ਅਕ੍ਰਿਤਾ	Self-created	177
ਅਦੀਸ	Invisible, One who existed from the beginning	157	ਐਮ੍ਰਿਤਾ	Immortal	177,178
ਅਦੇਸੁਲ	Abode	157	ਅਮ੍ਰਿਤਾ	Immortal	177,178
ਅਮੀਕੁਲ	Immeasurable	158	ਅਮ੍ਰਿਤੇਸੁਰ	Immeasurable power	179
ਅਚਲੰ	Perpetual	159	ਅਜਬਾ	Peerless	180
ਅਜਬ	Wonderful	159	ਅਮ੍ਰਿਤ	Mortality	180
ਆਤਮ	Spirit	160	ਅਕਲੰ	Perfection	183
ਅਭੰਗ	Indestructible	160	ਅੰਧਕਾਰੇ	Utter darkness	185
ਅਰਿ	Enemies	161	ਅਤੱਤੰ	Incorporeal	186
ਅਗੰਜ	Unconquerable	161	ਅਨਾਦੰ	Eternal, No beginning	187
ਅਮੰਡ	Self-created	162, 165	ਅਭੰਗੀ	Imperishable	188
ਅਨਗਣ	Countless	162	ਆਸ	Hope	188
ਅਨੁਭਵ	Self-realisation	163, 166	ਆਸੇ	Hopeful	188
ਅਨਿਛੱਜ	Inviolate	164	ਅਲੰਕਾਰ	Charm, Arts	188
ਅੰਗ	Part, Limb	164	ਅਲੰਕੇ	Charming, Adornment	188
ਅਭੰਡ	Manifest	165	ਏਕ ਅਛਰੀ	One word (name of the composition)	—
ਆਜਾਨ	Transmigration	166	ਅਲੈ	Imperishable	189
ਆਜਿਜ	Helplessness	168	ਅਜੈ	Invincible	189
ਅਨਝੰਝ	Beyond quarrels	169	ਅਭੈ	Beyond fear	189
ਅਨਰੰਜ	Beyond annoyance	169	ਅਬੈ	Beyond death	189
ਅਨਟੁਟ	Unbreakable	169	ਅਕਾਸ	Omnipresent, all pervading	190
ਅਨਠਟ	Un-Installable	169	ਅਭੁ	Uncaused, Unborn	190
ਆਡੀਠ	Invisible	170	ਅਭੱਖ	One who does not require sustenance	191
ਅਤਿਦੀਠ	Determined	170	ਅਜੁ	Unshakable	190
ਅਟਬੂਣ	Unharmed	170	ਅਜੋਨੀ	Beyond birth	194

Word		Reference: Number of Compositions
ਅਨਾਸ	Imperishable	190
ਅਸੋਨੀ	God's voice is never silent	194
ਅਜਾਇਬ	Beyond nobility	198

ਬ

Word		Reference: Number of Compositions
ਬਰਨ	Colour,	1
ਬਨ	Woods, Forests	1
ਬਰਨਤ	Describe, Recount	1
ਬਾਦ	Opera	48
ਬਾਦੇ	Conduction of orders	48
ਬਿਭੂਤੇ	Prosperity, Glorifier	49, 197
ਬਿਨਾ	Without	50
ਬ੍ਰਿਧੇ	Sovereign	51
ਬੁਧਦਾ	Intelligence Powers	59
ਬ੍ਰਿਧ	Prosperity	59
ਬੀਜ	Seed	72, 185
ਬੀਜੇ	To grow	72, 185
ਬਿਰਾਜਹੀ	You are present, Exist	79
ਬਿਹੀਨ, ਬਹੀ	Without	81, 82
ਬੇਦ	Vedas	82
ਬਣੂ	A missile	82
ਬਿਖੇ	In	83
ਬਿਸ੍ਰ	Universe	83
ਬਾਹੁ	Might, Power	88, 166
ਬਾਲਾਨ	High, Great, Child	90
ਬਾਲ	Child	90
ਬਾਢਜ	Unfound	93

Word		Reference: Number of Compositions
ਬਰਨੈ	Detached	104, 105
ਬਿਭੂਤ	Bestower of all powers	104, 145
ਬ੍ਰਹਮੰ	God, Primal	106
ਬੇ-ਐਬ	Pure, Holy	108
ਬਿਹੀਨੈ	Whose photo cannot be taken, Spirit	107
ਬਿਐਬ	Pure, Holy	108
ਬਿਲੰਦੁਲ	High, Supreme	122
ਬਿਭੁਗਤਿ	Blissful	131, 132
ਬਿਰਕਤ	Detached	137
ਬਹਿਸ਼ਤੁਲ	Heaven	155
ਬਰ	Big	161, 162, 167
ਬਿਅੰਤ, ਬੇਅੰਤ	Infinite	163
ਬਾਦ	Opera	48
ਬਾਦੇ	Conduction of opera	48
ਬਾਤ	Conversation	168, 169
ਬਿਸ੍ਰੰਭਰ	Sustainer	175
ਬ੍ਰਹਮੰਡਸ	Commander of all the spheres	176
ਬਸ	In-control	184
ਬ੍ਰਿੰਦ	Vast	185
ਬ੍ਰਿੰਦੇ	Multitude, Vast Panorama	185
ਬਾਂਕ	Elegance	188
ਬੰਕੇ	Beauty of posture	188

ਭ

Word		Reference: Number of Compositions
ਭੇਖ	Costume, Uniform	1
ਭੂਪੇ	King, Sovereign	19, 55
ਭਉਨੇ	All pervading	22

Word		Reference: Number of Compositions	Word		Reference: Number of Compositions
ਭੰਗੀ	Destroyer	22	ਭਾਨੋ	Enlightenment	113
ਭੋਤਾ	Consumption	28	ਭੇਖੀ	Manifest in all forms	115
ਭੋਗ	Consume	28, 69, 74	ਭਾਨੈ	Belonging to sun	119
ਚਜੰਗ	Name of a chhand (Composition)	44	ਭਾਗੇ	Fate, Destiny	129
ਚਉੰਨੈ	Pervading	45	ਭੰਡਾਰ	Warehouse, Stocks	169
ਭਾਨ	Sun	46, 47	ਭਰ	Nourisher, source of nourishment	174
ਭਾਨੇ	The energy of suns	46, 47, 76	ਭਵ	Fear	182
ਭੂਪ	Ruler	55	ਭੋਜ	Food	187
ਭੇਸੇ, ਭੇਸੈ	All costumes	66, 112, 114	ਭੋਜੇ	Sustenance, Granter	187
ਭੀਤੰ	Awe, Terror	69	ਭੁਗਤੇ	Emperon, Ruler	199
ਭੁਗਤਾ	Reveller, Emperor	77			
ਭੇਵੰ	Mysteries of Universe	78	**ਚ**		
ਭੇਸ	Costume, Uniform	80	ਚਕੁ	A ring; Form, Figure	1, 82
ਭੇਵ	Secrets	82	ਚਿਹਨ	Features, Contours	1
ਭੰਜਨਹਾਰ	Destroyer	83	ਚਾਚਰੀ	Name of a musicial composition	
ਭਰਮ	Delusions	84	ਚੰਦੁ	Moonlight	47
ਭੰਜਨ	Destroyer	84, 182	ਚੰਦੇ	(of the) Moon	47, 119
ਭਾਖਤ	To describe	86	ਚਰਪਟ	Name of a musicial composition	
ਭਾਨਾਨ	Sun of all suns	87	ਚਤੁਰ	Four	82
ਭਰਨਾਦਯ	Adornment, Fulfilment	93	ਚੱਕ	Directions	82
ਭਰਤੀ	Sustainer	97	ਚਉਦਹ	Fourteen spheres	83
ਭਰਮੰ	Delusion	99	ਚਿੱਤ ਚਿਤ	Mind, Thoughts	86
ਭਿਤੈ	Double-minded, Fear	99	ਚਤੂ-ਚਕੁ	Four corners, all over, Four directions	96
ਭਗਵਤੀ	Name of a composition	103	ਚਿਤ੍ਰੈ	Picture, Portrait	101
ਭੇਸੈ	Garb, Form	103, 117	ਚਿਤਿ	Mind	168
ਭਰਮੈ	Web of illusion	103	ਚਿਤੁੰ ਚਰਨ	To meditate	168
ਭਉਨੈ	Manifest, Omnipresent	111	ਚੰਦੈ	Moonlight	185

Word		Reference : Number of Compositions

ਭ

Word		Reference
ਛੰਦ	A type of musical composition	
ਛੱਪੈ	Name of a musical composition	
ਛਤ੍ਰੰ	Strength of the brave	106
ਛਤ੍ਰੀ	Brave, soldier	106

ਦ

Word		Reference
ਦਿਆਲੇ	Kind, Merciful	19, 23, 28
ਦੇਵੈ	Giver	21
ਦੇਵ	Gods	44, 79, 82, 83
ਦੇਵੇ	God of gods	44, 54
ਦਾਨ	Donation	56
ਦਾਨੇ	Benefactor	56,96
ਦਾਤਾ	Giver, Bestower	60, 76, 170
ਦਿਆਲੰ	Merciful	60
ਦੇਸੇ	All countries	66, 112
ਦ੍ਰਿਸੰ	To see, to watch	71
ਦੇਵੰ	Angles	78
ਦੇਸ	Country, Region	80
ਦਿਸਾ	Direction	80
ਦਰਸਨ	Audience	81
ਦੁਸਟ	Tyrant	84
ਦਾਇਕ	Giver, Provider	84
ਦੇਵਾਨ-ਦੇਵ	God of gods	89
ਦਾਨਕੈ	Donar, Bestower of bounties	98
ਦੇਸੈ	Countries, Universe	103, 112, 114
ਦਿੰਹਦ	Giver, Provider	109

Word		Reference
ਦਲੀ	Destroyer	109
ਦਾਨਿਕੈ	Granter	109
ਦੀਨੈ	Bestower of gifts	113
ਦਿਮਾਗ	Brain, Intelligence	151
ਦਿਹਿੰਦ	Giver, granter	152
ਦਿਸ	Direction, Side	165
ਦਿਆਲ	Merciful	192
ਦੁਕਾਲੰ	Life & death	199

ਧ

Word		Reference
ਧੰਧੇ	Pursuits	24
ਧਾਮੰ	Omnipresent	60
ਧਰਮੇ	Pure-ones, divine rulers	54, 74
ਧਰਮੰ	Rules, constitution of the divine	74, 75, 105, 144
ਧਾਮ	Abode	81, 84
ਧਰਮ	Religion, code of divine laws	84, 93, 170
ਧੁਜਾ	Flag, banner, symbol	105
ਧ੍ਰਿਤ	Of the earth	166, 173
ਧਰ	Centre, Pillar	166
ਧੁਰਾਸ, ਧਰਨ	Support, Pivot	166
ਧੂਣ	Support	173
ਧਰਣੀ	All earth, Universe	178
ਧ੍ਰਿਤੀ	Support	178
ਧਿਆਨ	Meditation	186
ਧਿਆਨੇ	Depth, Concentration	186

ਫ

Word		Reference
ਫਿਰ	Again	81

Word		Reference : Number of Compositions
ਫੈਲਿਓ	Pervading, Spread all over	80
ਫਿਰੈ	Moving, Orbiting,	82
ਫ਼ਹੀਮੇ	Intelligence	120
ਫਿਕੰਨ	Fear, Scarce	153

ਗ

Word		Reference : Number of Compositions
ਗਣਿਜੈ	Accounted (verb), Counted (verb)	1
ਗਉਨੇ	Immanent Everywhere	22
ਗਉਨੇ	To reach	45
ਗੀਤ	Lyric	47, 68
ਗੀਤੇ	The words of a lyric	47, 68
ਗਿਆਤਾ	Omniscient	52, 76, 142
ਗਿਆਨੰ	Sum total of knowledge	70
ਗਾਰਨ	Absolute creator	83
ਗਾਰਬ	Pride, Ego	85
ਗੰਜਨ	Crusher	85, 182
ਗੰਤਾ	One who knows everything	86, 115, 142
ਗੁਨ	Virtues	87, 91
ਗਨ	Infinite	87, 91
ਗਤਿ-ਮਿਤਿ	Speed measure	91, 164
ਗੁਨ-ਗਨ	Fountain	91
ਗੋਬਿੰਦੇ	Lord of universe	94
ਗ਼ੈਬੁਲ	Invisible	108
ਗ਼ੈਬ	Mysterious	108
ਗੁਨਾਹ	Sin	109
ਗਉਨੈ	One who reaches everywhere	111
ਗ਼ਨੀਮੁਲ	Enemy	122

Word		Reference : Number of Compositions
ਗ਼ਰੀਬੁਲ	Poor, Oppressed	122
ਗਨੀਮ, ਗਨੀਮੇ	Enemy, Foes	154
ਗਵੰਨ	One who reaches everywhere	156
ਗੁਨਿ-ਗੁਨ	Virtues	161, 163
ਗੁਰਬਰ	Supremacy	167
ਗਾਤ	Spirit, Power, Existence	168, 169
ਗਿਆਨ	Knowledge	186, 187
ਗਿਆਨੇ	Books of learning	186, 187
ਗਜਾਇਬ	Tyrant, Terrorist	198

ਘ

Word		Reference : Number of Compositions
ਘਾਲਕ	Annihilator	79
ਘਾਇਕ	Destroyer	86, 180
ਘਰ	House	
ਘਰਿ	House	168
ਘਾਲਜ	Destroyer	171

ਹ

Word		Reference : Number of Compositions
ਹਰਤਾ	Destroyer	27, 55, 96, 143
ਹੁਇ, ਹੋਇ	Is, has	80
ਹੰਤਾ	Destroyer	86, 115, 142
ਹੂੰ	Is	81
ਹਰੀਅੰ	Destroyer	95
ਹੁਸਨਲ	Extremely beautiful	121, 151, 152
ਹਮੇਸੁਲ	Ever, Always	121, 150
ਹਰੀਫੁਲ	Enemy, Opressor	123
ਹਾਜ਼ਰ	Present	150

Word		Reference: Number of Compositions
ਹਜ਼ੂਰ	In-Person	150
ਹਿਰਾਸੁਲ	One who scare others	153
ਹਰਿ	God, Hari	161
ਹਰਿਬੋਲਮਨਾ	Name of a chhand (musical composition)	

ਏ

Word		Reference: Number of Compositions
ਇੰਦੂ	God of heaven	1
ਇੰਦ੍ਰਾਣ	God of gods	1
ਏਕੈ, ਏਕ	One, absolute one	43, 81, 85
ਇਸਨਾਨੰ	Pure, Healthy	56
ਇਸਟ	Divine	57
ਇਸਟੇ	Of Divine	57
ਏਕ	One	43, 81, 85
ਇੰਦ੍ਰਾਣ	Power of Indra (god)	90
ਇੰਦ੍ਰੈ	Of Indra	90
ਈਸ	Lord, Master	157
ਇਆ	Religion, Faith	158
ਇੰਦ੍ਰੇ	Of God Indra, all powerful	119

ਜ

Word		Reference: Number of Compositions
ਜਾਤਿ, ਜਾਤ	Caste	1, 80, 82
ਜਿਹ	Whose	82, 83, 86
ਜਲਾਸਰੇ	Master of oceans, Manifest In all the waters	16
ਜਗਰੰ	One who does not age	24
ਜੋਗ	Yogic education,	28, 51, 53, 186
ਜੋਗੇ	Of yogis, for the creation	28, 74, 186
ਜੋਗੇਸੁਰੰ	Greatest yogi	51, 53

Word		Reference: Number of Compositions
ਜੁਗਤੇ	Skills	53
ਜਲੇ	Present in all the water	62
ਜੰਤੂ, ਜੰਤੂੰ	Mystic charms	70
ਜੀਤੰ	All victory, Victorious	69
ਜੀਵੰ	Living	72
ਜੀਵ	Life	72
ਜੁਗਤਾ	Companion	77, 144
ਜਤ੍ਰ-ਤਤ੍ਰ	Everywhere	79, 80
ਜਾਕਰ	Whose	80, 82
ਜਾਹਿ	Whose	81
ਜਾਨਹੀ	Have knowledge of	82, 86
ਜਾਨਈ	Have knowledge of	82
ਜੇਬ	Praise	82
ਜਾਤ	Caste	82, 84
ਜਨਮ	Birth	82
ਜਗ	World	83, 173
ਜਾਪਹੀ	Looks like	83
ਜਿੰਹ	His	83
ਜਾਪ	Invocation, Prayers	83
ਜਾਕਹਿ	Whose	84
ਜਾਨੇ	One who knows all	96
ਜਗਤੰ	Of the Universe	106
ਜਾਹੋ	Glory, Radiance	113
ਜਾਪਿਜੈ	Invocation	118
ਜਮੀਨੁਲ	Belonging to earth	122, 158
ਜਮਾਨੈ	All times	122
ਜੁਗਾਦਿ	Beginning of the time, time-less	134

Word		Reference : Number of Compositions	Word		Reference : Number of Compositions
ਜਾਤੈ	Caste	148	ਕਰਮ	Actions, Functions	1, 93, 170
ਜ਼ਾਹਰ	Visible, Manifest	150	ਕ੍ਰਿਪਾਲੇ	Kind, gracious	2
ਜ਼ਹੂਰ	Splendour	150	ਕਾਲੇ	Cause of death	19, 20, 45, 78, 114
ਜਮਾਲ	Efulgence, Glow	152, 158	ਕਾਲ	Death	23, 45, 79
ਜ਼ੁਬਾਂ	Tongue, Speech	155	ਕ੍ਰਿਤਰਿ	Creator of all	24
ਜ਼ਮਾ	All times, World	158	ਕਰੀਮੇ	Compassionate	25
ਜੁਰਅਤਿ	Heroism, Valour	158	ਕਰ	Creator	27, 96, 143, 183, 187
ਜਲ	Waters (oceans)	163, 165	ਕਲੰਕੰ	Blot, Stain	50, 154
ਜਗਤੇਸੁਰ	Lord	172, 175	ਕਲੰਕੀ	Polluted	50
ਜਗ	World	173	ਕ੍ਰੂਰ	Brutal, Cruel	54
ਜਾਨਿਜ	To know	173	ਕਰਮੇ	Actions, Deeds	54, 74
ਜਪ, ਜਪੁ	Prayers Recitation of hymns	177	ਕ੍ਰਿਸੰ	To attract	71
ਜਾਪਨ	To recite	182	ਕ੍ਰਿਪਾਲ	Gracious	73
ਜਸ	Praise, Glory	184	ਕੁਕਰਮੰ	Evil	73
ਜੁਧ ਜੁਧ	War	187	ਕਰਮੰ, ਕਰਮੇ, ਕਰਸ	Actions	74, 75, 100, 109, 144, 170
ਜੁਯੇ	Victory	187			
ਜੁਗਤੇ	Unifying, Yoked, Unified	199	ਕਾਮ	Desire	81, 84
			ਕੀਨ	Infinite	81
ਕ			ਕਤੇਬ	*Quran*	82
ਕੋਉ	No one, none	1	ਕਾਲ-ਹੀਨ	Beyond death	84
ਕਹਿ	To say (verb)	1	ਕਲਾ	Skill	
ਕਿਹ	Those, Which	1, 82	ਕਾਲਾਨ	Supreme death	90
ਕਹਿੱਜੈ	Called (verb)	1	ਕਰੀਅੰ	Creator	95
ਕੋਟਿ	Million	1	ਕਰੀਮ	Forgiver, Merciful, gracious	110, 151
ਕਹਤ	Call, Say	1	ਕਾਏ	Form, figure	100
ਕਥੈ	Account, describe	1	ਕਰਮੈ	Performance	103
ਕਵਨ	Who	1	ਕਰਨੈ	Doing (verb)	104

Word		Reference : Number of Compositions
ਮਾਹ	Moon	67
ਮਾਹੇ	Moonlight	67
ਮਾਨਤ	Belief	81
ਮਾਤ	Mother	82
ਮਰਨ	Death	82
ਮਾਨਹੀ	Believe in	82
ਮੁਕਤਿ	Liberation	84
ਮਝਬਾਰ	Name of a composition	87
ਮਹਿਮਾ	Praise, Glory	87
ਮਹਾਨ	Great	89
ਮਿਤਿ-ਮਤਿ	Measure-speed	92
ਮੁਨਿ	Saints	92
ਮੁਕੰਦੇ	Liberator, Emancipator	94
ਮਾਨਯੈ	Worshipped	98
ਮਿਤ੍ਰੈ	Friends	99, 101, 148
ਮਾਨਿਯੈ	Worshipped	111, 118
ਮਾਨੈ	Acclaimed	118, 119
ਮੁਦਾਯੈ	Eternal, Everlasting	121
ਮਕਾਨੈ	Abode, Mansion	122
ਮੁਕਤਾ	Liberator	144
ਮਾਤੇ	Mother	148
ਮੁਦਾਮ	Treasure	161, 163
ਮੁਨਿਮਨ	Sages, Holymen	162, 163
ਮਹਿ	Earth	171
ਮੰਡਨ	Decorator	171
ਮਨ	Mind	173
ਮਾਨਿਜ	Worshipped	173

Word		Reference : Number of Compositions
ਮ੍ਰਿਤ ਮ੍ਰਿਤਿ	Death	177, 178, 179, 180
ਮੰਤ੍ਰ-ਮੰਤ੍ਰੇ	Spirit of sacred texts which are recited and meditated upon	186

ੳ

ਉਦਾਰੇ	To shower generosity	87
ਉਰਧ	Sky	59
ਓਘ	Evil, Sins	59
ਉਦਾਰ	Generosity, Generous	79, 80, 87, 91, 164
ਉਸਤਤਿ	Praise	
ਉਪਮਾ	Praise, Peerage	87, 89
ਓਅੰ	God, Primal being	128
ਉਦਾਸ	Sad, Detached	136
ਓਅੰਕਾਰ	Omnipresent Lord	167
ਉਬਾਰਨ	Saviour	172

ਨ

ਨਹਿਨ	Has none (v)	1
ਨ	Not	1
ਨਰ	Men	1
ਨੇਤ	Woods, Blade of grass	1
ਨਾਮ	Name	1, 80, 81
ਨਮਸਤ੍ਰੰ	Salutation, Hail, Bow	1
ਨਮਸਤੰ	Salutation, Hail, Bow	1
ਨਿਕਰਮੇ	Beyond karmas	10
ਨਿਭਰਮੇ	Beyond delusions	10
ਨਿਦੇਸੇ	Does not belong to a specific region	10

Word		Reference : Number of Compositions
ਨਿਭੇਸੇ	Beyond specific costumes	10
ਨਿਨਾਮੇ	Beyond specific name	11, 95
ਨਿਕਾਮੇ	Beyond desires	11, 95
ਨਿਧਾਤੇ	Not made of five (fire, air, water, earth, ether) elements	11
ਨਿਘਾਤੇ	One who does not hit others, Beyond assault	11
ਨਿਧੁਤੇ	Ever, Steady, Immovable	12
ਨਿਤਾਪੇ	Beyond fevers or illness	13
ਨਿਧਾਨੇ	Master of all treasures	13, 32, 64
ਨਮਸਤਸਤੁ	Salutation	16
ਨਿਗਸਰੇ	Needs no support	16
ਨਿਧਾਮੇ	Needs no abode	18
ਨਿਬਾਮੇ	Needs no consort	18
ਨਮੇ	Bow to (verb)	19
ਨਿਸਾਕੇ	Beyond rivalry	39
ਨਿਬਾਕੇ		
ਨਿਧਾਨ	All treasures	32, 43
ਨਿਬੁਝ	Mysterious	37
ਨਿਸੀਕ	Beyond rivalry	39
ਨਿਲੰਭ	Beyond support	39
ਨਿਸੰਗੀ	Needs no companion	
ਨ੍ਰਿਤ	Dance	48
ਨ੍ਰਿਤੇ	Movements of dances	48
ਨਾਦ	Music	48
ਨਾਦੇ	Melody	48
ਨਿਤ	Daily, Eternal	54
ਨਾਰਾਇਣੇ	Lord	54

Word		Reference : Number of Compositions
ਨਮਸਤੰ	Hail, Salutation	56
ਨਿਵਾਸੀ	Resident	58, 73
ਨਿਧਾਨੈ	Treasures	64, 123
ਨਮਸਤੂੰ	Hail, Salutation	56
ਨਿਨਾਥੇ	Without any master, Guardless	65
ਨਹਿ	No	81
ਨਿਸਦਿਨ	Day & night	87
ਨਿਰਭੇ	Fearless	92
ਨਿਕਾਮ	Selfless	92
ਨਿਵਾਜ	Protection	153
ਨਿਰੁਕਤ	Indescribable	131, 132
ਨਿਬਾਧ	Beyond obstruction	127
ਨਰਕੰ	Hell	130
ਨਿਰੁਕਤਿ	Indescribable	131, 132
ਨਿਚਿੰਤ	Free from worries, Bond-free	138
ਨਰਕ	Hell	145
ਨਾਸੇ	Destroyer	145
ਨਿਭੰਗੀ	Imperishable	147
ਨਿਸਾਕੰ	Has-no relations	149
ਨਿਵਾਜ	Protection	153
ਨਿਵਾਸ	Residence	154, 155
ਨਾਸਿਜ	Destroyer	174
ਨਰ	Mew	161, 162, 180, 181
ਨਾਇਕ	Hero, Prime	180
ਨਾਮ	God's word	168
ਨਮਸਤੁਲ	Adorable God	197
ਨਿਵਾਸੇ	Inhabitant, Existence	197

Word		Reference : Number of Compositions
ਨਿਕਾਮੰ	Selfless	197
ਨ	No	168
	ਪ	
ਪਾਤਿ, ਪਾਤ	Lineage, Race	1, 82, 84
ਪ੍ਰਕਾਸ	Light	88
ਪ੍ਰਭੋਗੇ	Prime-enjoyer	15
ਪਾਲੇ	Sustainer	20, 28, 45, 78, 97
ਪੇਖੰ	Sustainer	27
ਪ੍ਰਜਾਤ	Name of a composition	44
ਪ੍ਰਮਾਥੇ	Destroyer	46, 49, 65
ਪਾਨ	Drum	48
ਪਾਨੇ	The sound of drums	48
ਪ੍ਰਭੰਗੀ	Tyrants	49
ਪਰਮ	Supreme, Great, Holy	50, 51, 52, 60, 85 86, 157, 186
ਪਾਨੇ	Weilder	52
ਪ੍ਰੇਤ	Evil-spirits	54
ਪ੍ਰਣਾਸੀ	Annihilator	58, 73, 197, 198, 199
ਪਰੰ	Supreme	60
ਪਰਮੇਸੁਰੰ	Lord	60, 72
ਪ੍ਰਫਪਾਲੰ	Invisibly sustains	60
ਪਰਾਜੀ	Unconquerable	61
ਪ੍ਰਭੁ	Lord	63
ਪੀਤ	Love	68
ਪੀਤੇ	Throb	68
ਪ੍ਰਿਸੰਜੇ	Kind, Merciful	72
ਪ੍ਰਾਣੰ	Life, Soul	77, 143

Word		Reference : Number of Compositions
ਪੁਰਖ	Omnipresent, Manifest in all	79, 80, 83, 84, 85
ਪਾਲਕ	Sustainer	79
ਪ੍ਰਨਿ	Ultimate	79
ਪੇਖਤ	To watch	81
ਪੁਰ	Regions, Worlds	82
ਪਰਮ	Supreme	83
ਪੂਰਨ	Perfect	83
ਪੁਨੀਤ	Holy	83
ਪ੍ਰਤਿਪਾਰ	Sustainer	85
ਪੁਰਾਣ	Puranas	85
ਪੁਰਾਨ	Puranas	85,86
ਪ੍ਰਨਾਮ, ਪ੍ਰਣਾਮ	Salutation	92, 161, 162, 163, 168
ਪ੍ਰਚੰਡ	Light	92
ਪਾਸੇ	All over the globe	98
ਪਰੇ	Transcendent	101
ਪਵਿਤ੍ਰੈ	Ever pure	101
ਪ੍ਰਿਥੀਸੈ	Master of the universe	102
ਪ੍ਰਭਾ	Glory	105, 131, 132, 160
ਪਾਕ	Pure	108
ਪਾਲੈ	Sustainer, Provider	114
ਪੇਖੀ	Witness	115
ਪੋਖੈ	Provider, Sustainer	116
ਪ੍ਰਾਨੇ	Life-giver	117
ਪ੍ਰਧਾਨਿਯੈ	Supremacy	118
ਪਰੱਸਤੇ	Protector	122
ਪਰਮੰ	Destroyer	130, 154, 155
ਪ੍ਰਣਾਸ	Union	131, 132

Word	Reference: Number of Compositions	Word	Reference: Number of Compositions
ਪ੍ਰਜਗਤਿ	Divine light — 137, 145, 159, 163	ਸਰਬ	All — 1, 19, 22, 64, 85, 129, 199
ਪ੍ਰਕਾਸੇ, ਪ੍ਰਕਾਸ਼	Annihilator — 146	ਸੁਮਤ	In devotion — 1
ਪ੍ਰਮਾਥੇ	Annihilator of tyrants — 146, 194	ਸੁਏਕੈ	Absolute one — 9
ਪ੍ਰਮਾਥ	Grandson — 148	ਸੁਜੋਗੇ	Attached with the creation — 15
ਪੰਤੂ	Son — 148	ਸੁਬਨਮੇ	Eternal beauty — 21
ਪੁੰਤੂ	Supreme — 157	ਸੱਤ	Truth — 24
ਪਾਂਤੇ	Creed — 148	ਸੁਹਾਗੇ	Blessed One — 26
ਪਸਾ	Vastness — 160	ਸੇਖੰ	Destroyer — 27
ਪ੍ਰਚੇਜ	To destroy, to eliminate — 161	ਸਮਸਤੀ	All — 49, 64
ਪਾਸਿਜ	With all, on all sides — 174	ਸਰੂਪੇ	Spirit, Form — 49, 50, 64, 197, 199
ਪਰਮੇਸੁਰ	Lord — 172, 179	ਸ੍ਰੇਰ	Supreme — 50
ਪਾਇਕ	Protector — 181	ਸਿੱਧੇ	Yogic power — 51
ਪਰਮਾਤਮ	Greatest God — 184	ਸੁ. ਸਸਤ੍ਰ-ਪਾਨੇ	Alike — 54, 129
ਪ੍ਰਣਾਮੇ	Homage — 197	ਸੁਧਰਮੇ	Like pure ones — 54
ਪ੍ਰਣਾਸੇ	Destroyer — 197	ਸਾਹ	King — 55, 67, 109
ਪਰ ਤੇ ਪਰ	Supreme of the supreme — 176	ਸਾਹੰ	Of the kings — 55, 109
ਪਾਨੇ ਪਾਨੇ	Essence of quencher of thirst — 187	ਸਦਾ	Always — 58, 59, 60, 73, 131, 132, 146, 198, 199
ਪ੍ਰਭਾ	Glory — 105, 131	ਸੱਚਦਾਨੰਦ, ਸੱਚਿਦਾਨੰਦ	Consciousness Bliss, Eternal Truth — 58, 198
ਪ੍ਰਿਥੀਉਲ	Earthly — 130	ਸਰਬੰ	Of All — 58, 109, 142
ਪ੍ਰਵਾਸ	Temporary — 130	ਸਮਸਤੁਲ	Everywhere, of all — 58, 150, 197
ਪਰੰ	Supreme — 157	ਸਿਧਦਾ	Spiritual Power — 60, 73, 199
		ਸਰਬਦਾ	Bestower — 60, 73, 199
ਸ		ਸਿਧ	Divine Powers — 60
ਸਕਤ	Can (verb) — 1	ਸਮਸਤੇ	Of all — 61
ਸਾਹੁ	King — 1, 88	ਸਮਸਤਸਤ੍ਰ	Everywhere — 61
ਸਾਹਾਣਿ	Of sovereign — 1, 88	ਸਾਜ	Splendour — 67
ਸੁਰ	Gods, angels — 1		

Word		Reference : Number of Compositions
ਸਾਜੇ	To adorn	67, 75
ਸਾਹੇ	Of kings	67
ਸੋਖ	Destroyer	68
ਸੋਖੇ	All-destruction	68
ਸਿਧਿ	Divine Powers	73
ਸਰਬੱਤੁ	All	111
ਸਦੈਵ	Always	
ਸੁਯੰਭਵ	Self-illuminated	83, 199
ਸੰਜੁਗਤਿ	With-it	84
ਸੁ	Is (verb)	84
ਸਾਸਤ੍ਰ	Scriptures	86
ਸਿੰਮ੍ਰਿਤ	*Smritis*	86
ਸਾਹਾਨ	Sovereign	87
ਸਰਬਾ	All of all	93, 129
ਸੱਤ੍ਰੈ	Enemies	99, 148
ਸੋਕੈ	Drought	104
ਸਾਜੈ	To decorate, to creat	112
ਸੋਖੈ	Destroyer, One who has the power to dry up Oceans	116
ਸਦੈਵੂੰ	Eternal	131, 145
ਸਾਹਿਬ	Supreme	151
ਸਲਾਮੈ	Safe, Salutation	121
ਸਲੀਖਤ	Offspring	121
ਸੁਭੰਗ	Beautiful	129
ਸਰੂਪ	Creation, Manifestation	130
ਸੁਨਿੰਤ	Beyond time, Eternal	138, 141
ਸੁਜੁਗਤਿ	All	146

Word		Reference : Number of Compositions
ਸਰਬ		
ਸਲਾਮ	Safe, Eternal	150
ਸੁੰਭੰ	Glorious	199
ਸਾਥੇ	Companion	146
ਸਰਬੰਗੀ	Sovereign	147
ਸਰੀਕ	Rivals	149
ਸਰਬੁਲ	All	156
ਸੁਬਾਸ	Fragrance	159
ਸਦਾਹ	Ever, Always	166
ਸਰਬੇਸ੍ਰ	Lord of all	175
ਸੂਰਜ	Sun	185
ਸੂਰਜੇ	Energy of Sun	185
ਸਰੂਪੇ	Regarding a form or existence	185, 188
ਸੁਧਰਮੰ	Rigtheous one	197
ਸੱਤ੍ਰੂੰ	Enemies	198
ਸੰਗੇ	Companion	197

ਸ

ਸ਼ਾਹ	King	55, 67, 109
ਸ਼ਾਹੇ	Belonging to a king	67
ਸ਼ਾਹਨ	Sovereign	87
ਸ਼ਿਕਸਤੇ	Defeat	122
ਸ਼ਿਕੰਨ	To break	153
ਸ਼ਾਤ	Peace	186

ਰ

ਰੂਪ	Beauty	1, 79, 82

Word		Reference : Number of Compositions
ਰੰਗ, ਰੰਗੋ	Colour	1, 80, 82, 84, 195
ਰੇਖ	Figure, attire	1, 80
ਰੰਮੇ	Extremely beautiful	16
ਰੂਪੇ, ਰੂਪ	All beautiful	19, 50, 55, 80, 81, 85, 186, 187, 188, 195
ਰੰਗੇ	Sum total of all colours	22, 71, 195
ਰਹੀਮੇ	Merciful, kind	25
ਰਾਗੋ	Musical notation, Rag	26, 195
ਰਫ਼ੀਕ	A friend in need	36
ਰਾਜ	Rule	50, 67
ਰਾਜੇਸ਼੍ਰੰਰ	King of kings	50
ਰਾਜੇ	Of the king	51, 67, 75
ਰੇਗ	Diseases	55
ਰਾਗ	Song, Love	55, 80, 84
ਰੇਗੇ	Diseases	56, 69
ਰੌਖ	Wrath	68
ਰੇਖੇ	Master of wrath	68
ਰਿਧਿ	Powers to produce physical objects	73
ਰਿਸਾਲ, ਰਸਾਲ	House of nectar, fountain of bliss	79
ਰਚਿਓ	Created	83
ਰਹਿਤ	Without	84
ਰਾਜਾਨ ਰਾਜ	King of kings	87
ਰੰਗੁ	Colour	86
ਰਾਜਾਨ	King	89
ਰੰਕਾਨ	Poorest, Humility, Meekness	90
ਰੰਕ	Poor	90
ਰਾਜੰ	Of the kings	105
ਰੋਜ਼ੀ	Livelihood	108

Word		Reference : Number of Compositions
ਰਜਾਕੈ	Granter, Giver	108
ਰਹੀਮੇ	Merciful	108, 198
ਰਿਹਾਕੈ	Emancipator	108
ਰਾਜ਼ਕ	Provider	110
ਰਹੀਮ	Merciful	110, 154
ਰਾਜੈ	Ruler	112, 116
ਰੁਜੂ	Focus of attention	121
ਰੁਜੂਅਲ	Centre of attention	123
ਰਜ਼ਾਇਕ	Provider of sustenance	123, 154
ਰਵੰਨ	Ever happy	156
ਰਿਪੁ	Opposition, Enemy	156
ਰਾਜਸੰ	Ambitions, Desires	186
ਰੇਖੇ	Shape, Contours	195
ਰਾਜ-ਰਾਜੇ	King of Kings	185

ੲ

ਠਾਮ	Abode	80

ਤ

ਤ੍ਰਿਭਵਣ	Three worlds (sky, earth, netherland)	1
ਤ੍ਰਿਣ	Infinite	1
ਤਵ	Yours	1
ਤ੍ਰਿਮਾਨੇ	Worshipped in all times (three times) past, present & future	13
ਤ੍ਰਿਬਰਗੇ	Three modes of worship — Satogun, Rajogun, Tamogun, Three boons	
ਤ੍ਰਪ੍ਰਸਾਦਿ	God's Grace	

Word		Reference : Number of Compositions
ਤ੍ਰਿਮਾਨ	Three worlds (sky, earth, netherlands)	32, 79
ਤ੍ਰਿਬਰਗ	Three Modes of Activity	32
ਤਾਨ	Tune	47
ਤਾਨੇ	Rhythm	47
ਤੰਤੁ	Magic	57
ਤੰਤੂੰ	Master of Magic	57
ਤਾਨੰ	Divine melody	70
ਤ੍ਰਿਭੰਗੀ	Bestower of three boons (righteousness, prosperity, liberation)	128, 129, 147, 188
ਤ੍ਰਾਣੰ	Protector	77, 143
ਤਾਹਿ	In his presence, In front of Him	81
ਤਾਤ	Father	82
ਤੀਨ	Three	82
ਤੂਣੇ	Source of Energy	117
ਤਮਾਮੁਲ	Totality, Sum total	121, 156
ਤਮੀਜ਼ੁਲ	Etiquettes	123
ਤਮਾਮੈ	Total All	123
ਤਰੰਗ	Waves	124
ਤ੍ਰਿਮੁਕਤਿ	Transending the modes or 'gunas'	125
ਤ੍ਰਿਕਾਮੇ	Fulfiller of the desiers in the three worlds	128, 147
ਤ੍ਰਿਬਰਗੀ	Three boons (dharma, arth, kaam) rightheousness, prosperity, fulfilment of desiers)	129, 147
ਤ੍ਰਿਬਾਧੇ	Master of the three worlds	129
ਤ੍ਰਿਭੁਗਤ	Sustainer of the three worlds	130
ਤਾਤੇ	(Of) Father	148
ਤਮੀਜ਼	Manner, etiquettes	156
ਤਾਪਨ	To challange	182

Word		Reference : Number of Compositions
ਤੇਜ	Heat	185
ਤੇਜੇ	Of light	185
ਤਾਮੰਸ	Darkness	186
ਤੱਤੰ	Spirit	186
ਤ੍ਰਿਕਾਲੇ	Destroyer of the three worlds	188
ਥ		
ਥਾਪੇ	Creator	20
ਥਲੇ	On land	62
ਥਾਪਿਜੈ	Establish	118
ਥਾਪਿਓ	Installed	83
ਥਲ	Land, Earth	163, 165
ਥਾਪ	To install	83
ਥਪ	Installation	177
ਵ		
ਵਿਸਾ	Corners	80
ਵਰਤੀ	Everywhere, In all directions	97
ਵਾਸੇ	Living, to reside	98
ਵਜੂ	Personification	121
ਵਿਸ	Corners, Central (common) place of directions	165
ਯ		
ਯਕੀਨੈ	Sure, Surety	123